GREATER COMMUNITY *Spirituality*

A NEW REVELATION

———≈———

Marshall Vian Summers

———≈———

Knowledge

GREATER COMMUNITY
Spirituality

Book design by Alan Bernhard, Argent Associates, Boulder, CO

Edited by Darlene Mitchell

ISBN: 978-1-884238-55-0 *Greater Community Spirituality*
Library of Congress Catalog Card Number: 97-66797
NKL POD Version 4.05

PUBLISHER'S CATALOGING-IN-PUBLICATION
Summers, Marshall Vian.
Greater Community spirituality : a new revelation / M.V. Summers — 1st ed.
p. cm.
Preassigned LCCN: 97-66797
ISBN: 978-1-884238-55-0

1. Society for The Greater Community Way of Knowledge—Doctrines.
2. Spiritual life—Society for The Greater Community Way of Knowledge. I. Title.

BP605.S58S86 1997   299'.93
                                                                  QBI97-40812

The books of the New Knowledge Library are published by The Society for The Greater Community Way of Knowledge. The Society is a religious non-profit organization dedicated to presenting and teaching The Greater Community Way of Knowledge.

Greater Community Spirituality serves as an introduction to The Greater Community Way of Knowledge. Formal study of The Greater Community Way of Knowledge is presented in the sacred texts *Steps to Knowledge* and *Wisdom from the Greater Community: Volumes I & II* which can be ordered directly from New Knowledge Library or requested at your local bookstore.

NEW KNOWLEDGE LIBRARY
P.O. Box 1724 • Boulder, CO 80306-1724 • (303) 938-8401
E-Mail: nkl@greatercommunity.org
Internet: www.newmessage.org

—◦◦◦—

Dedicated

to the power of Spirit

within each individual,

which is called Knowledge

in the Greater Community.

—◦◦◦—

GREATER COMMUNITY
Spirituality

CONTENTS

GREATER COMMUNITY
Spirituality

PREFACE

———∽∿∽———

$\mathcal{A}$S THE RECIPIENT AND WRITER OF THIS BOOK and of the other books of The Greater Community Way, I feel that it is my responsibility to introduce this revealed Teaching and the Tradition that it represents as purely as possible, just as it has been revealed to me. In doing so, it is my sincere desire to represent the greater spiritual association that serves everyone in manifest life throughout the Greater Community.

I cannot say why I was chosen for this task. Initially, it was a mystery even to me. The task itself is certainly greater than anything that I had anticipated at the outset. What began fifteen years ago as a new and effective method for solving problems and gaining spiritual direction in everyday life has evolved to become a religious tradition of spiritual teaching, preparation and contribution that is new to our world and yet older than our human existence.

I am not merely the scribe in this great undertaking. This Teaching and all that it contains is the product of my relationship with the Unseen Ones and the allies of humanity. To represent and to fulfill these relationships, it was necessary for me to become the first student of this Teaching, traveling a journey that perhaps few in our world have ever taken before. Strangely, since childhood I have been endowed with a body of information about life in the Greater Community. It is not the result of my reading or personal interests. It is simply there. It has always been there, troubling me, inspiring me, pushing me and moving me forward where no road seemed to go, yet always with a sense of an abiding and gracious spiritual presence. *Greater Community Spirituality* is the result of this inexplicable journey.

For you who can read this book and comprehend its deeper meaning and the great strength that it speaks for and advocates, I offer my encouragement. You are at the beginning of a great and mysterious journey, a journey into a larger universe and a deeper experience of the Divine in your own life. This book will be a gateway for you and for others who know that they are part of a greater life.

It is a blessing for me to share with you *Greater Community Spirituality* and to invite you to step beyond the limits of human awareness and understanding into a greater physical and spiritual universe called the Greater Community. As you are about to witness, our education about our life, meaning and spirituality is at a new beginning.

Marshall Vian Summers, 1998

INTRODUCTION

———◦◦◦———

$\mathcal{I}$N THE GREATER COMMUNITY OF WORLDS the idea of God is presented differently than it is in this world. In the Greater Community, the idea of God must be translatable from one society to another where the customs and the rituals, the ideas and the areas of specific application will be unique to each world's spiritual awareness and devotional practices. All that can be translated is the pure experience of Knowledge—the experience of Universal Mind, profound awareness and total relationship. This is the experience which will be presented in this book—an experience of translatable spirituality that is shared between intelligent life everywhere. Its application is universal. Its experience is universal. Its communication is universal. The direction that it establishes for sentient beings everywhere is universal.

Greater Community Spirituality encompasses a larger panorama of life and includes all that has been created here and beyond, in all dimensions, in all frameworks. So complete is it that you cannot fathom its Mystery, exhaust its Wisdom or penetrate its Knowledge. But you can be the recipient of these things, and you can translate them into your own experience and apply them here at great benefit to yourself and to others.

The world is now emerging into a Greater Community of Worlds. Therefore, it is necessary for Greater Community Spirituality to be presented here to enable humanity to prepare mentally, emotionally and spiritually for the great change that is coming and the great opportunities that this change represents. To learn about the Greater Community, you must learn of its reality. This, then, is a blessing: that you may receive a Greater Reality, a Greater Religion and a Greater God.

---✦✦✦---

*H*ere you will be focusing

on a God not of your world

and of your time

but a God of all worlds

and all times.

---✦✦✦---

CHAPTER ONE

WHAT IS GOD?

———❦———

$\mathcal{I}$N THE GREATER COMMUNITY, GOD IS KNOWLEDGE. In the Greater Community, God is experience. In the Greater Community, God is the communication of profound insight and recognition from one to another, permeating all manifest life. This comes into being in the realm of your experience.

God seems like different things to different people and to different races of beings in the Greater Community, but the essential experience that ignites the desire for God, the awareness of God and the relationship with God is the same everywhere. This religious impulse, the impulse towards union with God, is universal. Though it seems remarkably absent in some cultures and aberrantly expressed in others, the impulse is the same. What God is must be expressed in terms of your range of experience and your capacity for experience. In the Greater Community, God is so total and complete that any definition would always falter and fail.

Therefore, let us say that God is the experience of total relationship. You can experience this for a moment here and there and for longer periods should you prepare in The Way of Knowledge. This is an experience which can both be translated from one world to another and shared and demonstrated from one being to another, bypassing and transcending all divergences of race, culture, temperament and environment. This is God. God for you is God in action. God for you is an experience that is unlike any other experience in life, yet this experience gives meaning to all of your other experiences.

In the Greater Community, God is complete. In your world, God is a God of your world, a God of your race, a God of your history, a God of your temperament, a God of your fears and aspirations, a God of your great heroes, a God of your great tragedies, a God that is related to your tribe and your time. But in the Greater Community, God is so much greater, so complete—beyond the definitions of any race, beyond the history of any race, beyond the temperament, fears and aspirations of any race, beyond the grasp of any individual or collective philosophy. And yet, you find God in a pure impulse, in a timeless moment of recognition, in the desire to act beyond the sphere of your own personal interests and motives, in the recognition of another, in the motive to give, in the inexplicable experience of affinity. These are translatable. This is God in action. For you, this is God.

You must think of God now in the Greater Community—not a human God, not a God of your written history, not a God of your trials and tribulations, but a God for all time, for all races, for all dimensions, for those who are primitive and for those who are advanced, for those who think like you and for those who think so differently, for those who believe and for those for whom belief is inexplicable. This is God in the Greater Community. And this is where you must begin.

To believe in the God of the Greater Community is too great an attempt because you will realize that your race is small and the universe is great. Here you will be focusing on a God not of your world and of your time but a God of all worlds and all times. What kind of theology or philosophy can embody a God of this magnitude? What kind of human speculation and human ethics can encompass a God so complete as this?

Yet your theology of God must be the theology of God's work in this world. And if it is true, accurate and beneficial, it must focus on the experience of Knowledge. Knowledge is the beginning of religion.

Knowledge is the completion of religion. Knowledge is the evidence of God and the evidence that you are a part of a greater life beyond the limits of your time, beyond the boundaries of your race and beyond the confines of your present intellectual ability. Here there is no creation story. There are no heroes. There is no end of time. There is only the total experience of relationship, which is the experience of Knowledge and the experience of God.

What is a human religion without a creation story, without a hero to worship and without a culmination of human experience? What human religion can focus on a God of this magnitude, whose sole interest is not your world alone, whose sole concern is not your daily experience, whose awareness is so complete and whose beneficence blesses those who are so unlike you? What then is the model for human behavior? What is the basis for ethics or morality in a God of the Greater Community? For this you must venture beyond a childhood religion and a child's needs. You must venture beyond the need only for rules and regulations and fantastic stories that are barely believable. You must enter into the experience and the Mystery of life, which is the doorway to God, which is at the very heart of your life and contains the very purpose for your coming here that is unique to you but which you share with all life.

In Greater Community Spirituality, there are no heroes. There is no creation story. And there is no culminating experience to bring an end to the difficulties of corporeal life. So, what is religion without these things? These things are tribal in nature. And you are not alone in the Greater Community in wanting them, in establishing them and in holding to them. Everywhere where religion has taken root and has found expression, races have based their practices and their understanding on their own time, their own history and their own temperament. But beyond this is the experience of God. Beyond this is pure spirituality. This is what you must seek now, for human religion can never embody a God of the Greater Community. So inexplicable this is because it transcends your requirements for the Divine. Therefore, you must find another way, a more mature way, a more complete approach, a true preparation.

In the Greater Community, those who have advanced have realized the nature and purpose of God in their respective worlds, but their understanding has gone beyond the comprehension of God's Will in specific matters, even beyond the concern for the well-being and survival of their race. They have gone beyond these concerns to a greater spirituality, a Greater Community Spirituality—a spirituality of all time and all worlds, a spirituality that is mysterious, that is not defined and embodied in rituals, ideals, beliefs, historical accounts or fantastic images, a spirituality that can be completely translated from one being to another with words or gestures, or without words or gestures.

Greater Community Spirituality is a spirituality of greater experience, greater perception and greater abilities. In the Greater Community, you are not saved. You are only developing. In the Greater Community, you are not condemned. You are only developing. In the Greater Community, there is no Heaven. There is only further involvement and a greater capacity for relationship. In the Greater Community, there are no local gods and demons fighting spiritual warfare. In the Greater Community, there are those who know and those who do not know. From their experience come the great difficulties that are posed in life everywhere.

You who live in a human world with human ideas, human beliefs and a human perspective have a great opportunity now to experience the Divine and Divine purpose and will for your life and time through a Greater Community awareness and through a different kind of path and direction. You need this now, for your world is emerging into the Greater Community of Worlds. And you need this now because this is the religion for all time, not only for your time. Penetrate this great threshold and you will understand the past, the present and the future in such a way that will unite them together.

This will give you strength and ability in discerning and comprehending those from the Greater Community who are visiting your world. Though they possess greater technological ability and have greater social cohesion than you, they are called to learn Greater Community Spirituality as well. Your gift to them is something very rare and precious. You have something they need. You have something that all life needs. That is why Greater Community Spirituality is being introduced into this world prior to the world's emergence into the Greater Community. This is not only given for your own adaptation to the Greater Community in order to establish a foundation for communication, recognition and understanding. It is also given to establish that you as human beings, as limited as you are in your physical capabilities, nonetheless have a spiritual gift to give—a gift for all time, a gift of true benefit. However, in order to find this gift and to give this gift, you must have a greater understanding, a greater awareness, a greater theology and a new foundation for living. This is a foundation that will liberate you in your daily life and that will make your human concerns, which are seemingly so complex and difficult, far simpler than they seem today.

What God is doing in your world is related to what God is doing in the Greater Community. If you do not know what God is doing in the Greater Community, how will you know what God is doing in your world? And how will you understand the Divine presence and experience here? You must see yourself from the outside looking in to see how you are, where you are and who you are at this time. You will need this perspective to see what surrounds you, what encourages you and what holds you back.

Knowing what God is doing in the universe can only be translated through pure experience, for the universe so far exceeds your intellectual or conceptual capacity that no language or technology could possibly describe it. And even if it could be described, you would have no way of understanding it.

However, this is not how greater awareness and greater truth are transmitted and realized. If you are willing to go beyond your own boundaries, if you are willing to go beyond your concepts, your ideas and your beliefs, then you will open a door to Greater Community Spirituality and to a greater Knowledge and Wisdom which are so needed in your world at this time. This offers you every advantage and a foundation for giving to others in the future, yet to do this, you must be very courageous. You must venture into territory where people have not gone before, into a new kind of sacred experience and into a universe far greater and more complex than anything you have had to contend with in the past. You will have to learn to be comfortable without definitions. You will have to be secure in a greater foundation within yourself. And you will have to have great companions.

This is not an adventure. This is a journey—a journey of the greatest magnitude, a journey which cannot be undertaken alone, a journey with difficulties and dangers, but a journey that is needed and that calls to you. It calls to you beyond your ideas, your goals and your concerns. It calls to you now.

This calling is an experience which seems so inexplicable, and yet it is so real, so permeating and so complete, even for you here now. It is the window through which to see a greater universe and a greater God at work.

This is the theology of pure experience—a theology of pure Wisdom and pure Knowledge, a theology that you can only demonstrate and a theology that you can only experience. It is a theology that is greater than anything that can be taught in your seminaries and schools of religion. Who can respond to such a great gift and Mystery as this? Who can enter the realm of pure experience, of greater union with God?

Let this be a calling for you who read these words. Let this call to you beyond your understanding and your ability to understand, for you will not understand these words until you have this great experience, and you will not know if these words are true until you experience their truth. You will not know their complete relevance until you yourself can embody them.

In the Greater Community, God is too large and too great to incite only faith. Faith can only bring you to the threshold of experience. Beyond this, faith is too weak and too fallible to carry you further. Here faith serves its only and most important purpose—to bring you to the gate of experience. This is the purpose of faith and the purpose of preparation. This is the purpose of religious training in your world and in all worlds. Beyond this gate is God of the Greater Community.

Leading to this gate is Greater Community Spirituality and beyond this gate is Greater Community Spirituality.

In order to realize the theology of God in the Greater Community, you must have a greater mind, a greater vocabulary and a greater range of experience. This can be translated to you, and you can translate it to others, but your words cannot capture it. It can only be transmitted from one to another through a mysterious process of Divine transmission. No one can understand it intellectually because its environment is too great and too all encompassing.

Those who want ideas alone will have to stay with their local religions, for this is too big. Those who only want to know guidelines for constructive living will find this too great and confusing, too inexplicable and too mysterious. Those who experience God in the Greater Community and those who can transmit God in the Greater Community represent individuals who have transcended the boundaries of their own racial heritage and intellectual capacity. They have become universal in their thinking. They see what others cannot see, and they know what others cannot know. This is their burden and their gift. For them, belief is not an issue because they have gone beyond the need for belief and beyond the limits of belief. Their experience is too remarkable to be translated into any broad spectrum or to any great audience. It must be given one to another. Their church and their temple is the environment in which they receive Divine transmission and communicate it to others. Their students are few. Their journey is long. Their requirements are great. Their application is total and complete.

Is such a gift possible for humanity? It is not only possible but necessary. Without this gift, the experience of the Greater Community will have a devastating impact on humanity. Without this gift, humanity's desire for power and domination will lead to catastrophe. Without this gift, you will not be able to understand those whom you will meet from the Greater Community, and you will not be able to understand the great change and the great events that are occurring in your world.

The Greater Community Way of Knowledge is being presented to the world as a means of preparing you for the Greater Community and as a means of preparing you for God of the Greater Community. It is the means for preparing you for a greater purpose in life that is related to life everywhere. The Greater Community is the greater environment in which you live and to which you must now become accountable. The Greater Community Way of Knowledge is a different kind of spirituality, but you will find that the experience which is at the very heart of this is more familiar and more confirming than anything you have ever experienced before. This experience will remind you of your Ancient Home and of those who sent you into the world. It will remind you of the greater bond of relationships that exists even at this moment that goes beyond the boundaries of your time and place in life. This is a doorway into a greater universe. It is a means for a greater ability and Wisdom in life. It is an answer to a greater need for humanity and for life everywhere.

—∞—

The perfection of this place

will only be realized

as you come to terms

with your real purpose

for being here.

—∞—

CHAPTER TWO

WHAT IS THE WORLD?

———⌇∿∿⌇———

*Y*OUR UNDERSTANDING OF THE WORLD and all things in the world will change as you advance in The Way of Knowledge. Certainly your understanding of yourself—your needs, your purpose and your direction—will change as you progress. This will give you a different perspective and a growing perspective as you proceed.

In a greater context, the world is a place where you have come to serve, to give and to reunite with those whom you are destined to meet, to know and to participate with. This definition, though universally true, is a truth that is not accessible to many human beings at this stage of development, for they are much too focused on survival and gratification to be able to see its importance. However, even as you grasp this idea and begin to experience it within your own range of relationships and understanding, it opens up a whole new panorama, a greater vista where things can be seen and known which could not be seen and known before.

The world is primarily a place to give. You learn this through giving. It is a place to associate and to reassociate. You learn this by associating and reassociating. You have come from beyond the world bearing gifts for the world. This is most certainly true, but do not fall prey to thinking that this indicates a grandiose role for you. Indeed, your role will be very specific and only in the rarest circumstances will it garner attention and acclaim. This must be a clear understanding, for here you see that the world is something very different from what you had thought before. Instead of a place to proclaim yourself and to establish yourself, it is a place to get something done behind the scenes, in secret, without recognition and acclaim. This is the way that Knowledge works in the world, and this is the way that you will learn to work in the world as you begin to experience a greater purpose and direction in life.

Before this, the world was a place in which to survive and to fulfill yourself, but now it is becoming something else. This is in keeping with the truth in the greater panorama of life that we call the Greater Community—that the Wise everywhere work with as much secrecy as possible. They contribute their gifts to those individuals for whom their gifts are destined and required.

Knowledge is rarely welcome in any society in the Greater Community except those very few that have advanced and have secluded themselves from the difficulties and tribulations of Greater Community involvements. In all other societies, regardless of the nature of their environments, their culture, their ethics, their beliefs and their standards, the Wise must exercise their gifts and their work with great caution. Knowledge finds unique expression in different societies in the Greater Community, but its purpose and its destiny are the same—to reunite you with those who have been sent to share your purpose in life so that you may fulfill your specific mission here. Then you will return to your Spiritual Family beyond manifest life, and there you will prepare for your next assignment.

There are no Heavens and Hells. There is only work to be done, and there is only success and failure in this regard. If you succeed, you advance and you progress. If you fail, you set yourself and your Spiritual Family back. Failure is not always a matter of neglect. Sometimes it is circumstantial. In this, there is no blame. However, realizing the importance of achieving success in finding your purpose in life as it truly exists and not as you would have it be is a great accomplishment. This guarantees a satisfaction and a sense of meaning that can never be found in any other way.

You are not here to condemn the world. You are not even here to repair the world. But you are here to give something, and your gift knows where it needs to go. Your gift has its own destined recipients. You cannot change this. But you can determine whether your gift can be given or not. You can determine how long it will take to give your gift. You can determine the outcome. But the final outcome is beyond your determination, for this is part of a Greater Plan. It is a Plan that does not predetermine all activities and events in life but instead sets a direction for all life and for the evolution of life. Here much variety and variance will occur, but the end result must finally in time be established.

You have a purpose in being here. This is religion. You have a message for certain people. This is faith. You are in the world to give because you have an Ancient Home beyond the world. You have a purpose that transcends your impulses for survival and your wishes for self-gratification. This purpose does not deny these other impulses and wishes, but it establishes a greater focus and a greater standard for your life.

What is the world, then, for you who have come to give? The world is a place that needs your gift. Your gift must be given to certain people at a certain time in a certain way. It is not for everyone, and it is not necessarily for those whom you want it to be for. The world is as it is because it is a place without Knowledge. It is a place of conflict. Beneath and underlying all the apparent conflicts in physical life, there is a fundamental struggle between receiving and resisting Knowledge. This struggle resides within each person. It is the struggle between Knowledge and will, between union and separation, between purpose and self-determination.

How few people in the world know that they are here on a mission and can leave that mission undefined and unexplained and yet support it wholeheartedly nonetheless. How few people can give themselves to something that is known and urgent but that seems inexplicable and beyond description. How rare are these individuals, and yet how important they are for the advancement of the world. Without men and women of Knowledge, the human race would have faded long ago. Humanity's promise, heritage and legacy are kept alive by the activities of those who work unseen and unbeknownst to the population at large. For them, the world is something very different. Its tribulations are opportunities. Its conflicts represent its calling. Its difficulties and disasters represent its condition. There is no complaint and no blame here. There is only work to be done—a great gift for a temporary place.

This understanding transcends human morality and the morality of any society or culture within the Greater Community. Therefore, its application is universal. It can permeate any situation and provide value and meaning there. It is free of the restraints and limitations of the society into which it enters, as is the person who carries such a purpose in full awareness.

The world is not a meaningless place. It is not a hopeless place. It is not an evil place. It is a troubled place. The person of Knowledge must come here to work, for this advances those in the world and those beyond the world.

Greater Community Spirituality is not a spirituality for one race alone. It is a spirituality for many races. Ultimately, it is a spirituality for the entire universe. As such, it calls upon experience rather than ideas. Uniformity in thinking is not possible in the Greater Community because of the variance in temperament, values, environment and biological development. However, the experience of Knowledge is universal, and this transcends all local customs and limitations. This has benefits beyond the horizons of your awareness. This is the source of inspiration in your life. This is the meaning of the mystery of your life.

Do not attempt to explain the Mystery or the Mystery will be lost to you. Do not give definition to your purpose, or your purpose will become only your definition. Do not claim that you understand your origin or your destiny, for to think this is to deny yourself the direct experience, which is your reward for gaining access to a Greater Wisdom and Greater Power within yourself. Allow the Mystery to be inexplicable and bond to it in your deepest experience. Hold to it with the greatest devotion. Follow it without restraint. Keep yourself in its embrace, and you will know what others cannot know, and you will see what others cannot see, and you will hear what every heart calls for—freedom and reunion with life as it really is.

Greater Community Spirituality is at the heart of every religion, and yet it is beyond every religion. It is the source of all inspiration, and yet it transcends all of the expressions of inspiration. This, then, is your Heritage—to find this, to receive this, to embrace this, and to give this according to a Greater Plan of which you are an important part. Accept the fact that your role will be small and specific. It will not be self-glorifying. In fact, it may lead away from all of your plans for self-fulfillment. And yet it contains a greater truth, a greater understanding and a greater security in life that you will not find anywhere else.

Be without judgment of the world. If the world were a perfect place, you would not need to come here. If the world were a place that functioned harmoniously, without friction or conflict, this would not be the place for you. The world represents all aspects of the human condition, from the highest to the lowest. The world also exists within a Greater Community context, which is largely unrecognized here. The world is your place to work and to give. Its pleasures are small but real. Its pains and difficulties are great. The world cannot give you what you seek, for what you seek you have brought with you from beyond the world. The world cannot answer your great questions about life or satisfy the greater yearning that resides in the hearts of all who dwell here. That requires a different understanding. It abides with something else, something we call Knowledge.

Knowledge is the source of all true religion in the Greater Community. You have the possibility of finding Knowledge, but your understanding of the world and of everything within it will need to change. You must allow this change to occur. It is not a change you impose upon yourself or upon others. It is a change that naturally occurs. What you must do is allow this change to occur and support its occurrence. Your support is illustrated in the way you live, in what you learn, in what you practice and in what you give yourself to.

Greater Community Theology is not a theology of ideas. It is a theology of experience and relationships, for these are the media through which real understanding is transmitted from one mind to another. These are the media through which greater Knowledge can be sent and embodied long before understanding has developed over time. Indeed, you may have an experience that might take years for you to understand. Has this not been true in your own experience?

Therefore, you must be very patient for real understanding to develop. You must be very open for real experience to occur within you. Then everything we are saying will make perfect sense to you. You will hear it; you will feel it; you will know it. It will seem so familiar to you in such a deep and pervasive way. Until this happens, our words will seem odd and strange, peculiar and disconcerting. Yet, they are the real food that nurtures you, not because of the words we choose specifically, but because of the intent and the strength behind them.

Truth can only be known; it cannot be understood. Purpose can only be known; it cannot be understood. The world can only be known; it cannot be understood. You may have great skill and efficiency in discerning the mechanisms of the physical world, but this does not assure that you will understand its purpose, its value or its greater meaning in life.

A great benefit for humanity in learning Greater Community Spirituality and its human translation in the form of The Greater Community Way of Knowledge is that it gives you an opportunity to look at yourself from the outside. It gives you a clear vision and understanding of yourself, your situation, your predicaments and your opportunities. When you attain this awareness, things will seem so obvious to you that before you could not understand. And yet you will be frustrated because you will see things that others cannot see, and you will know things that others either cannot or will not know. This is the price of knowing the truth. It sets you apart. Yet, this separation is temporary. It is only to reposition yourself in life in order to allow a greater understanding and Knowledge to emerge within you. This makes union with life and in life possible.

What is the world? The answer to that question must always be based on what you think you are and why you think you are here. You cannot give meaning to the world without addressing these fundamental questions of who you are and why you are here. People answer these questions unknowingly by defining their goals and by giving themselves to their priorities, without ever questioning the meaning of their goals and priorities and why they must be so.

To find a greater identity and a greater purpose in life, you must go beyond human speculation and all the self-comforting ideas that you find reassuring or familiar. This centers you in the Mystery. From this Mystery, a greater understanding of the world will arise, and your experience of it will be quite different from what it was before. Your advantage here is that the world will no longer encumber you internally. Yes, it will provide the physical context for your life and define your life to a certain extent on the outside, but the real motivating force within you will be free of the world, and with this you will become free of the world.

This is what it means to overcome the world. Here the world is not conquered. It is not banished. It is not denied or rejected. This simply means that you have found your freedom in the world, and your freedom in the world is the freedom to know, to give and to associate—not according to your habits or the demands of your external life, but according to a deeper Knowledge that is now burning within you and that is now alive within your awareness. This truth holds true in any world, in any environment. That is why it represents a Greater Community Spirituality, and that is why its application is universal.

How much human truth is universal? How much of what human beings cherish and believe is truly universal? If you could have access to the great variety of cultures in the Greater Community, you would see how limited the application of human truth is, how self-assuring it is and how limited it is. Human values, human ethics, human advantages, human endowments—how limited is their application in the Greater Community. Therefore, how limited they are in your own life. This is true because you live in the Greater Community, because your world is in the Greater Community and because you are part of the Greater Community.

Your world is emerging into the Greater Community now. It is entering a great threshold of life, a threshold that will overshadow all that you do, all that you see and all that you believe. To prepare for the Greater Community assures your survival and well-being. But even beyond this, learning and experiencing Greater Community Spirituality puts you in the position to gain maximum value and to make the greatest contribution within the reality of the evolution of life. This fulfills your purpose here, for you have come to participate in the world's emergence into the Greater Community. Regardless of your specific activities in life, whether they seem related to this great emergence or not, you have entered the world to support this because this is humanity's great need and destiny.

Within the larger context of the Greater Community, you will have an understanding that is profound and eminently useful. Here your ability to develop real discernment, true decision making, greater association and wise insight will be profound because it will not be limited by your customary thinking, by your worldly conditioning, by your painful past or even by the great assumptions that most people still hold to thoughtlessly. This puts you in a position to contribute to humanity in order to meet humanity's greater needs. Seen from this position, the world is a place to give. It is a context for giving. It is a temporary context in which to give something that is permanent.

Here you can accept the pains and tribulations of the world as part of the condition in which you must give. This acceptance is an important starting point, for if you feel that the world has betrayed you and your greater hopes and ambitions, what can you give here? If you feel that the world is an evil place that has denied the greater ideals and greater aspirations of human beings, what can you give here? Giving begins with understanding and acceptance. Without understanding, your giving has no direction. Without acceptance, your giving becomes an attack on life. You cannot help people if you attack them. You cannot help them if you are horrified by them, disappointed by them, frustrated by them, hostile towards them, angry with them or impatient with them.

The universe is great and people are small. Knowledge is great and the mind is small. These things become ever more clear as you advance in The Way of Knowledge. It is a transition from one way of thinking to another, from one perception of the world to another, from one set of abilities to another.

So far, you have learned to survive and have found various ways to gratify yourself. Congratulations! Now, it is time for you to learn of Knowledge and to learn the ways of Wisdom as they truly exist in life. This is your calling and your challenge. Do not give definition to your purpose, for your purpose now is to prepare. Your purpose now is to learn. Your purpose now is to learn The Way of Knowledge according to its reality in life, not according to human inventions.

Any truth that is genuinely true must have universal application. Small truths apply to certain situations under certain conditions. That is a small truth. But a greater truth is universal. It permeates everything. Beware, however, for a greater truth has untold ways of manifesting. The application of truth is conditioned by the situation at hand, yet the experience and the awareness of truth are universal.

The only way you will know who your visitors from the Greater Community are and what they intend to do here is through this awareness of truth and Knowledge. It would take you decades and even centuries to figure it out in your mind. You do not have decades and centuries to understand what is occurring in the world. Understanding this has bearing on your purpose for coming here.

The world presents you with a great opportunity. It is a place to work, to enjoy your work and to advance yourself and those who sent you. You who are reading these words have a great advantage and opportunity here. We are speaking to the part of you that is beyond your understanding and beyond your habitual thinking. You are being offered something of incomparable value, but to receive it and to understand it you must open yourself to it. You do not need to believe in it, but you do need to experience it. The experience will convince you; the belief will never convince you.

Those who oversee the development of the world from beyond the perimeters of physical life see the world as a great opportunity for you. They see the world as a perfect place for you to come to. The perfection of this place will only be realized as you come to terms with your real purpose for being here. Then you will look at the world and say, "Yes, this is the perfect place for me to be," without justifying the conflict, the suffering and the discord that exist here. There will be no deceit in this perception and understanding. It will be clear.

This is the theology of experience and relationships. Out of this, a greater understanding and a greater set of ideas will emerge. Greater understanding emerges from greater experience, if that experience can be applied and correctly understood and interpreted.

Greater Community Spirituality represents a greater religious tradition. It is a religious tradition of which you are a part because you live in the universe. It is a tradition that is not bound by the ideas, customs or rituals of any world. It is a tradition that is not bound by devotion to one deity or one person or one idea. It directs you towards your Creator and towards all that exists between you and your Creator—the great fabric of life that exists within the physical universe and beyond and the great fabric of relationships into which you are finding yourself to be interwoven and interdependent. Experience this with those whom you were sent to engage with and with those whom you were sent to serve, and in the most mundane situations you will realize the greatest truth.

———✦———

It is a power that

runs through your body.

It is neutral.

It is neither inherently good nor bad.

The question then is

how will you use it?

———✦———

CHAPTER THREE

WHAT IS LIFE FORCE?

———*♦♦♦*———

*W*E INTRODUCE THE TERM LIFE FORCE HERE. However, before we speak about it, we would like to bring it into a greater context, a Greater Community context. These words are familiar to some people, and there is a great deal of idealism and speculation about what Life Force really is and what it can do. But again, when we use familiar words or terminology, we must bring them into a greater context. If you can enter into this greater context, then everything that we are saying will be illuminating and very useful and valuable. If you cannot enter into this greater perception and perspective, then you will continue to interpret things according to your own interests, ideas and understanding.

Life Force is an energy which exists in all living things. This is a familiar idea to many who read these words. However, in the Greater Community, Life Force has a greater value. It is an actual power that is cultivated, used and developed by certain races for certain purposes. Because there are adept individuals in all societies throughout the Greater Community, there are always demonstrations of greater skill, greater awareness and greater ability. However, if these are discovered by the powers that rule these societies, then these powers and abilities are put to work either as a defense or as a tool for controlling others.

The discovery of greater powers, abilities and awareness becomes a liability for any society once these powers have a popular application and are seen as useful in dominating or controlling others. That is why the Wise remain hidden: to remain alive and to maintain those greater powers and abilities that they have discovered. These powers and abilities have a real usefulness in the hands of the Wise, yet once these powers become used for political or military purposes, then their usefulness declines, and they can become weapons that are used against others. This is demonstrated in many places in the Greater Community. Finer and more subtle abilities exist within all individuals, and greater powers exist within particular individuals and within particular cultures or races. These can all be exploited for political or military value. Therefore, there is a great burden in carrying Knowledge and Wisdom: the burden of keeping them hidden, knowing who to share them with and how much to share.

This is why popular teachings about Life Force are fundamentally in error. Even the good intention to share something of value with others is often born of ignorance. Power must be accompanied by Wisdom and restraint if it is to be useful and effective.

All that we speak of in the Books of Knowledge represent a mystery and a great opportunity for you, but they are not easily accessible. You must study and prepare, and you must pass certain tests in life. You must demonstrate your sincerity, your humility and your self-honesty in order to advance and to gain access to the greater powers that we speak of, which are meant for you.

Life Force is a power. It is within you, but you cannot gain control of it. It is possible to use it in certain situations, but to actually have authority over it requires a highly developed and adept mind. This is important because in physical life you have the potential for power, ability and awareness. If these are cultivated wisely and applied appropriately, they become beneficial for you and for others. However, if they are used for other purposes—if they are used for defense or if they are used for conquest, manipulation or control—then in essence they become evil, something that is inherently destructive and counter productive to the greater purpose of life which is bringing all beings towards union and realization.

Life Force is important because it represents part of your experience of being in the world. It is a power that runs through your body. It is neutral. It is neither inherently good nor bad. The question then is, how will you use it? For what purpose will you use it? Will you invent your own purpose and apply it there? Will you justify your attempt to harness it based upon your own high ideals, your great thoughts or your altruistic ambitions? If so, it will elude you and deceive you. It will corrupt you and work against you.

We speak of Life Force here because it represents power in the world. And what we have to say about the discovery and cultivation of this power applies to all forms of power in the world. Life Force can be harnessed and directed. It is neutral, so it does not have a will. If it is cultivated according to the guidance of Knowledge, the greater Knowing Mind within you, then like all forms of power, all abilities, and all forms of awareness, it will find a good purpose here.

Here you must stop and ask yourself these questions: "Why do I wish to know about this? What does it mean for me? What are my ambitions regarding it? Am I willing to train and prepare slowly and gradually in order to find these greater abilities that are being spoken of here?" Ask yourself these questions, but do not give a ready answer. Instead, abide with these questions so that a deeper understanding may emerge within you over time.

All that is great in life will elude you if you seek it for selfish purposes. All that is genuine and meaningful will turn sour if it is sought to fulfill your ambitions or personal goals. Thus, the Wise remain hidden to nurture their development, to give their gifts appropriately and to protect themselves from the usury of the world. The more you know, the more discreet you must be. The more you have, the more discerning you must be. The greater your capability, the more restraint you must exercise. This requires great self-purification.

In the Greater Community, Life Force has been harnessed successfully by individuals and small groups of individuals who serve a greater network of the Wise. This network is called the Harim. This word, which is from the Septoral language, speaks of those who uphold Knowledge in all worlds. Their purpose is not local or ambitious. They represent a universal purpose that bonds them with others very different from themselves. This has created an association of the Wise who are unlikely ever to encounter each other face to face in manifest life. It extends the whole network and fabric of genuine relationship beyond the visual realm. Here Heaven and earth overlap. Within these overlapping boundaries, there exists a greater bond of relationship, a greater awareness and a greater experience of life.

Knowledge within you will guide you to utilize all aspects of yourself appropriately and harmoniously and will lead you to develop certain aspects of yourself for certain specific purposes. It will not guide you to cultivate all aspects of yourself because this is unrealistic. It will not ask you to develop all of your capabilities to a high functioning level because this is not possible. However, it will direct you to develop certain inherent abilities and certain skills that are relevant to your specific purpose in the world at this time. This is why there can be no ambition on your part if you seek to gain access to Greater Community Knowledge and Wisdom.

Even if your motives are pure, should others discover your growing abilities, they will attempt to use you for their own purposes. Some will idolize you; some will try to follow you; some will glorify you; and still others will try to steal from you. Some will try to destroy you. Many will malign you.

This truth comes as a great shock to the developing student of Knowledge who discovers early on that their quest for Knowledge is not shared by others, even those whom they love and value. Later they discover that their development alters people's perceptions of them, and people begin to act in very strange ways around them. Eventually, they will see that their gift, which is now slowly emerging within their own awareness, must be protected and safeguarded and given with great specificity to certain individuals at certain times. This requires tremendous restraint, for each person is eager for power and control to offset his or her sense of insecurity in physical life. Ambition exists within each person. Within the student of Knowledge, it must be discovered and arrested in all of its manifestations.

It is not power that you must focus on; it is your approach to power. It is not your abilities that you must claim; it is your understanding of them that must be cultivated. Once this has been accomplished, and this indeed may take a great deal of time, then things can be given to you. Then they will bear fruit within you, and they will find their rightful recipients within the sphere of your relationships. You will give to some and not to others. You will speak to this person but not to that person. You will give your gift here but withhold it elsewhere. This understanding is not comprehensible to the casual observer or even the critical observer, for they see things only according to a set of assumptions which they themselves have not challenged or faced.

Life Force within you can exert an actual physical effect. It can have an impact in the physical environment. In the mental environment, it can take the form of thoughts, forces of energy, powerful and self-sustaining ideas, and so forth. It is a power. Life Force is not the same as Knowledge because Life Force is not intelligent. It is like clay—you shape it, you form it and you use it for specific purposes. It is subtle, so most people are unaware of it. It is pervasive, so it is very effective. It is everywhere, so it can be harnessed and used. It abides in all living beings, so its application is universal.

Should you be directed to develop Life Force within yourself, you will have to learn great restraint. It will turn against you if you use it for selfish purposes to fulfill your goals or ambitions. Here it will turn against you even if you want to use it to help humanity. Unless Knowledge is your guide, your counsel and your restraint, you will create discord, confusion, despair and failure. You cannot use the power of the universe for personal reasons and hope to achieve anything of real merit or value. This is a truth that is universal. It affects all intelligent beings everywhere. With power and control come great responsibility and the need for restraint. When these are lacking, power is destructive. When these are present, power carries on a greater and more beneficial effort that can have great and lasting impact wherever it is applied.

Should you become a real student of Knowledge, you will begin to feel things consistently that you only rarely felt before. You will be able to experience life on a more subtle level as you prepare in *Steps to Knowledge.* Here you will need true instruction because you will need to identify and clarify your ambitions, both those that are known to you and those that will emerge within you as you develop. Here temptation can be very great. Here you cannot teach yourself. Here you must give yourself to your instructor and trust your instructor to guide you and to prepare you, to hold you back and to send you forward.

In the Greater Community, Life Force is a power that is used. It can have great influence over the unknowing. Its equivalent in the mental environment is the power of projected forms of thought. In the physical environment, Life Force exerts an actual force that moves things and creates an impact and a reaction. Someone can knock you down with Life Force even if they are standing across the room. Someone can weaken you physically using Life Force even if they are across the street.

Life Force is not as effective in the physical environment as it is in the mental environment, where thoughts can be directed at an individual thousands, even millions, of miles away and have an impact. This is true because in the mental environment there is no resistance except the resistance of countering ideas. In the physical environment, there is a great deal of resistance, such as the resistance encountered by a moving object. In the mental environment, there is nothing that affects the velocity of a moving thought except a countering thought. And a countering thought must be born of a mind that is aware of what is impacting it and can arouse within itself power in the mental environment to counter, obstruct or prevent the accelerating thought from reaching it. We call this mental screening. It is a great ability. You cannot use this ability constructively unless you are selected by the Wise and prepare for a very long time. You must begin to learn about Life Force now because it represents part of what affects you individually and what shapes your world.

As Greater Community influences gain a greater stronghold in your world, their abilities, their power and their awareness will exert an ever greater impact on all aspects of your life. Some of these are very manifest, but many are quite subtle. Often they cannot be seen. However, they can be discerned because you can feel them.

Why is this important in the context of spirituality? Because it represents the world into which the Creator has sent you. Given a real understanding of your purpose and a real experience of its meaning, you will see that everything fits within this theological context because of the nature of your origin and your destiny—where you have come from and where you are going. The world is a place that you are in temporarily. Therefore, where you have come from and where you are going provide the real meaning of your existence here.

Life Force is power that few have ever discovered and fewer still have ever learned to use constructively. There are those in the Greater Community who can use it in certain situations, but this does not mean that they can control it. There is a very great difference between use and control. For example, you use electricity, but the ability to control it, redirect it and guide it represents a greater set of skills and abilities. You use the power of the sun to grow food, but can you harness the power of the sun? Can you control it?

Let us give you this understanding: No one in physical life can control the mechanism of the universe. No one in physical life can control time. They can use time, but they cannot fully control it. The Wise know the limits of control and exercise their abilities appropriately. The foolish think that there are no limits, that everything is there for them to acquire, to conquer or to obtain. No one individual or group of individuals can gain control of the physical universe because everyone exists within limits.

It may appear that you have great power and ability compared to other people. However, seen in a larger context, you have significant limits. Knowing your limits represents an aspect of Wisdom. Knowing what you can develop and what is beyond your reach represents an aspect of Wisdom. These are learned as you proceed in The Way of

Knowledge because here you are beginning to distinguish greater powers from lesser powers.

You cannot control Knowledge, the Knowing Mind within you. You cannot direct it to give you what you want. You cannot focus it to produce the results you want. You cannot use it to influence others. Why? Because it is more powerful than you are. You can enter into relationship with it; you can reclaim it in your awareness; you can learn to reassociate with it by taking the steps to Knowledge, but you cannot control it. You can only control your expression of it, and this is within your range of responsibility. However, do not think for a moment that this is a small responsibility. It is actually very great and represents consummate learning in the human environment.

It is an interesting fact of life in the Greater Community that the Wise are all very similar, and the unwise are all very different from each other. The Wise from your world and the Wise from other worlds have so much in common. However, the unwise are so distinct. The Wise in all worlds have a means of communicating with each other through Knowledge, yet the unwise cannot recognize or communicate with each other. The Wise see what is the same; the unwise see what is different. The Wise identify with what is the same; the unwise identify with what is different.

In order for humanity to have any advantage in the Greater Community, certain individuals here must become wise within a larger context in life. And others must support these individuals because for every individual that advances, it takes a great deal of support from others. This is how Knowledge is kept alive in the world. And this provides a means for Knowledge to be communicated in the world through a network of relationships all supporting a central focus. This is how greater things are communicated throughout the Greater Community, throughout all manifest life and indeed even beyond manifest life.

Real Wisdom is passed on through a network of relationships. Like water seeping downward through the soil, Wisdom finds its real channels and its path of least resistance. It creates pathways where Knowledge can be passed on, transmitted and initiated from person to person through a means that is both wonderful and mysterious.

The pursuit of Knowledge and Wisdom is not an individual quest; it is a collective effort. For anyone to advance requires meaningful involvement with many other people. Developing this understanding indeed is part of the education of going from a singular approach to a community approach, going from a singular viewpoint of life to a Greater Community understanding of life. This is a part of your education. This is a part of the transition from being lost in your individuality to being embodied in the Greater Reality.

Life Force means something different at either end of the spectrum, and your understanding of it will change as you pass through the spectrum on the way to a Greater Reality. Indeed, all that we are presenting in Greater Community Spirituality is important because it takes you to a Greater Reality. It cannot be used within an individual reality. The Greater Community Way of Knowledge invites you to find escape from your own isolation, escape from being lost in your own individuality and escape from being a prisoner of your own mind. It invites you to rediscover your intrinsic relationship with all life and the specific purpose which is yours to reclaim and to contribute in this life, at this time, in this world.

You will need Life Force to progress, to advance and to carry on your preparation and your contribution. The extent to which you will need to use it and how you will need to use it depends on the role that you are here to play. Your role here is predetermined, but how it will be carried out and the time it takes to carry it out—especially the time it takes to discover it and to prepare for it—can vary considerably. In this, your decision making has great importance, and indeed you will determine if the outcome can be achieved. What greater responsibility would you ever want to assume for yourself?

People who think that they can create their own destiny and who call this their freedom have no idea of the burden that they are placing upon their own shoulders. This burden is great because it guarantees failure. You cannot control your greater destiny, but you can experience it, and you can find a way to express it. In this, you will have to make many decisions; in this you will have to assume greater responsibilities; in this, you will find your power; and in this, you will assume authority in your life.

You are the captain of your ship, but it is not up to you to determine where it is sailing and for what purpose. Even what your ship contains is beyond your authority. Consider these words carefully and do not make a mistake here. To become the captain of your ship is a responsibility and a power that few people have ever assumed. To become a true captain means that you are aware of everything concerning the protection, maintenance and well-being of your vessel and that you have respect for its secret cargo and its true destiny. While many people proclaim that they are the captain of their own lives, they have no idea what this means.

In the Greater Community, personal freedom has a different context and a different value. Advanced technological societies are highly organized. Individuals are not free to do whatever they please whenever they please without regard for others. The Greater Community is a competitive environment on a scale and a magnitude that you cannot even imagine. Therefore, to become effective and competitive in this environment, and, beyond this, to gain Greater Community Knowledge and Wisdom, you must over time reassess all of your values and assumptions. Personal freedom is chaos without Knowledge. It is the source of everyone's mental and physical illness. Contrast will show you this as you learn to associate with those who are beginning to discover a greater purpose and meaning in life and as you yourself begin your own discovery of this.

The contrast will be marked. You will see yourself going in a different direction from everyone else. You will see yourself valuing experience more than ideas, insight more than assumptions, patience more than acquisition and affinity more than possessions. You will travel a different path, and the discrepancy between your growing understanding and the assumptions of your nation, of your culture, of your group and even of your family will become greater and greater. Such is the burden and the promise of discovering Knowledge throughout the Greater Community.

Life Force is within you. You can feel it at this moment. It is breathing your body; it is moving your blood; it is keeping your nerves alive; it is sparking your mental awareness. It is here right now, and it will grow in scope, meaning and value for you as you progress in The Way of Knowledge. It will grow as you leave your ideas, beliefs and assumptions at the outer gate of the temple and enter in where True Wisdom and Knowledge can be imparted to you.

—∞—

You live life at two levels.

You live life at the level

at which you think,

and you live life at the level

at which you know.

—∞—

CHAPTER FOUR

WHAT IS KNOWLEDGE?

⟶◈◈◈⟵

IN THE GREATER COMMUNITY, KNOWLEDGE is the essence and substance of all religious experience. It transcends the expressions of this experience in terms of theology, devotional ritual and spiritual practices, which vary considerably from one world to another world. However, the essence of spirituality—the motivating factor in religion, the real call of religious experience—is Knowledge.

Knowledge represents your bond and your intrinsic relationship with all life. Yet Knowledge has a specific mission for you in this life—a mission which you are encouraged to discover, to accept, to integrate and to fulfill. In other words, Knowledge is not everything within you; Knowledge is your connection to everything. Knowledge is intelligent; it is here for a purpose. Knowledge is the part of your mind that is spiritual and permanent. It is the part of your mind that knows who you are and why you have come here, who you must reach and what you must accomplish.

Knowledge is within you now, but you cannot lay hold to it. It is not there for you to acquire and to use. Rather, you have an opportunity to come back into relationship with Knowledge. Here your personal mind, the mind that is conditioned by your world, and your Impersonal Mind, the mind that you have brought with you from beyond the world, reunite in a meaningful relationship based upon a purpose in the world and upon relationship with the world and with people who support that purpose.

All of these definitions are valuable, but to experience their value, you must consider them deeply. If you say, "Well, I like that definition," or "I don't like that definition," or "This sounds right to me," or "This does not sound right to me," you are merely trying to relate to your own past judgments, evaluations and experiences when encountering something new and revolutionary. If you do that, you will not understand the meaning of what we are presenting. You will only be exercising your former beliefs, ideas and evaluations, and no new learning will occur. Stretching beyond your own ideas and assumptions and reaching out for something which is greater that transcends them is an act of courage, integrity and commitment to your personal development and to true contribution in life. This is the road to Knowledge.

Knowledge is with you. It is in you, but you cannot reach for it and grab it, take hold of it and use it for yourself. Rather, it represents the promise within you that you have a greater identity and a greater purpose in the world. It represents the promise that there are greater relationships within the world which you can find and develop given the correct understanding and the realization of an underlying purpose in life which is yours specifically to fulfill. Here your definition of your purpose must remain undefined, for in truth it is something that will come together very slowly. You cannot simply identify it and say, "This is it. This is why I am here. This is what I will do." Many people do that, but that is reckless. It only reveals their impatience and their ambitions. The real discovery of Knowledge and purpose is something quite different.

It is very important to give Knowledge a practical definition in the world, for Knowledge must lead to action. As an idea or an ideal, its value is very limited. As a motivating force that leads you, guides you, and even at times impels you to do certain things that transcend your personal interests, Knowledge has a meaningful definition. This is the experience of Knowledge.

You may have difficulty with the word God and with other kinds of words that have been implanted in religious traditions with which you are familiar or from which you have developed since childhood. However, Knowledge is the very core of your spirituality. You reunite with God through Knowledge. You reunite with yourself through Knowledge. You reunite with others through Knowledge. Knowledge is the medium.

Therefore, we have different definitions, and they all seem somewhat distinct. Why is that? It is because Knowledge is so great and has so many facets. Knowledge is at the very center of intelligence in life, here in this world and throughout the Greater Community. You cannot simply define it by one aspect. Knowledge is the Great Presence that stands behind all the manifestations of life. You see it here, and then you see it there. It looks different here than it does over there. Then, you experience it anew, and something new comes with it. Knowledge is the greater part of you living in manifest life. It is translating the Will of the universe into your mundane worldly experience. As you are able to come into proximity to Knowledge, to pay attention to Knowledge and to open yourself to Knowledge, its translation can be given to you with increasing frequency and depth.

You will welcome Knowledge within your heart, for it will be known to you, and it will resonate within you. It will resonate in a part of you that you rarely experience. It will resonate all the way down to the core of your being. Even if your mind is protesting against it, even if your fears are aroused, and even if you are confused, angry or resistant, it will be true for you because it is true. This is communication; this is being; this is purpose; this is identity that transcends all worldly thoughts, beliefs, cultural identifications and political associations— even your personal will. This is Knowledge.

To begin to understand the reality of Knowledge, we must look at the evidence of Knowledge. This evidence can be found in your experience. It is the experience of being moved to do something or moved not to do something. It is the experience of irrational restraint. It is the experience of foreseeing something and knowing something and then having it happen. It is the experience of being moved to go somewhere, to do something, to associate with someone, or to disassociate from someone.

This represents the deeper movement of your life. It is not something that is impelled by your ideas, emotions or feelings. It is something deep within you that moves you at your foundation. This is the evidence of Knowledge.

When individuals are deeply moved to do something that sets them on a different course in their lives and in a different direction from where they were planning to go before—this is evidence of Knowledge. When individuals feel that something wrong is going to happen and then act to avoid a dangerous situation—this is evidence of Knowledge. When individuals extend themselves to others in a profound way, bridging the gap between their divergent personalities with such impact that they are both changed—this is evidence of Knowledge. The experience of affinity with life and affinity with another, the experience of a greater motivation in life to exert a greater effort or to reach a goal that must be accomplished, however undefined in the moment—these are the evidence of Knowledge.

Now you might say, "Well, you are talking about intuition." No, we are not talking about intuition. Intuition is the outer expression of Knowledge, like the snow flurries before the storm. So much greater is Knowledge than intuition. Some people think intuition is part of their personal survival mechanism. They do not realize that Knowledge is the Greater Source within them. Knowledge is so much greater than the slight expressions that are called intuition that you must not confuse the two. Knowledge is alive; it is intelligent; it is thinking at this moment. It is not simply a reflex that you have within your mind or your body.

You live life at two levels. You live life at the level at which you think, and you live life at the level at which you know. It is to bring you into life at the level at which you *know* that is the purpose of true religion in all of its forms. This reunites you with your Creator and with your greater purpose for being in the world. This brings you back to Knowledge, for God can only be known. Your purpose can only be known. Your true relationships in life can only be known. Your true impulses can only be known. Your ideas about them are secondary and, as is often the case, can only interfere with the recognition of Knowledge. You can believe in all these things. However, belief must have real experience as its foundation, or it becomes self-deceptive.

Knowledge is living within you at this moment. You live in your thoughts and your ideas, in your sensations and in your perceptions of the world around you. You are governed by forces, both physical and mental, that you cannot account for, but this happens only at the surface of your life. Deeper down are the real currents that move your life, the currents of Knowledge. Knowledge moves you slowly into position so that you can discover and learn those things that will enable you to take the next step in your life. Knowledge is moving you towards realization, towards understanding and towards certain individuals who are destined to meet you and to be with you, if you can find them and if they can find you.

Because something is predetermined does not mean that it will happen. This is very important to understand. You can miss your opportunity to discover your purpose and to discover those people who are meaningful to your purpose, and they can fail to do so as well. In reality, this happens all the time. You can comfort yourself and think, "Well, another opportunity is right around the corner." But this is not the case. If you could see your life from a larger perspective, you would see how important these few opportunities are and why they do not come around very often.

Knowledge is moving you towards a destiny and an accomplishment in life, in spite of all your personal goals, wishes, fears, ambitions, associations and activities. Never think that all the things you want come from Knowledge. Never think that all the things you aspire to have, to do or to be come from Knowledge. Here you must become very honest, candid and open with yourself. You must become committed to the truth beyond any other advantage. This is necessary even to begin to reclaim Knowledge. You must honor the greater need and the greater impulse that are moving you beyond your own definitions. This begins your journey in The Way of Knowledge. This gets you started.

Knowledge does not offer you riches, fame, love and pleasure. It offers you something so much greater and so much more valuable that when correctly seen and really seen, you will see there is no comparison to the other things which dominate people's attention, ideas and activities.

Knowledge is religion in the universe. It is the part of your spiritual experience that is translatable between you and others, amongst other cultures in this world and between worlds as well. It represents a translatable and universal spirituality—a universal way of communication, recognition and association. Another who may not share your biology, your environment, your temperament, your values, your social conditioning, your aspirations, your concerns or your technological abilities can be reached and can reach you through this greater medium of life called Knowledge.

Something that seems so evasive, so rare or so ephemeral is in actuality the very essence of life. And, in like manner, the things that seem so grand, so powerful, so overwhelming, so magnificent and so dominating are the very small things of life. This recognition represents a great reversal in thinking and a great breakthrough in understanding.

Knowledge is an essential emphasis when we speak of the Greater Community because Knowledge is the only part of your mind that cannot be influenced, corrupted or controlled. Your personal mind can be and is corrupted, influenced and controlled—by your media, your government, your primary relationships and so forth. However, Knowledge within you is incorruptible. You can misapply it and misinterpret it, but you cannot corrupt it. It is Divine. It is beyond your reach. The world cannot corrupt it, for it is beyond the reach of the world. That is why it is the source of your freedom in life. That is why it is the source of your true integrity in life. And that is why it can carry out your mission without your mission being perverted or destroyed. You may try to pervert or destroy your mission, but at the level of Knowledge, it is still intact.

When we say that you cannot grab hold of Knowledge and use it, we mean that you cannot spoil it and you cannot violate it. If you try, you will feel a great discomfort. You will feel tremendously ill at ease with yourself. This discomfort is something that is pervasive in human experience. Even without knowing what Knowledge is or where it lives or how it functions or what it knows, whenever you do something that goes against the direction of Knowledge, you will feel this discomfort, this disassociation from yourself. You will feel ill at ease. You will feel this not because Knowledge is punishing you in any way, but because you are going against something that is known within you. This produces a very profound and permeating discomfort. No amount of therapy, pleasure, escape or preoccupation can free you from this discomfort. You must bring your life into harmony with Knowledge within you. This you can experience, and your experience will be the evidence that you are either succeeding or failing in this regard.

The discomfort that results from being at variance with Knowledge is very deep and profound. It is not something at the surface of your mind. Many people are so compromised in their activities, their values and their pursuits that they have adjusted to this discomfort. This discomfort represents how they feel and how they live. This discomfort accounts for all the desperate attempts at escape, addiction, avoidance, self-deception and other forms of dishonesty that are so manifest here.

However, beneath all of this is Knowledge. You may call it Spirit. You may call it Spiritual Mind; but it will transcend your definitions, whatever you call it. The Way to Knowledge is the way to Divinity and to the realization of your greater purpose and meaning in life. In the Greater Community, this takes on an even greater meaning. Here Knowledge will enable you to transcend your ideas, your customs, your beliefs and the ideas, customs and beliefs of your own world in order for you to gain something more complete, more universal and more translatable. In a Greater Community context, you must focus on something that is fundamental that you share with all other forms of intelligent life. This exists at the level of Knowledge, not at the level of intellect, personality, culture or custom.

The Greater Community Way of Knowledge represents religion in the Greater Community. Therefore, it represents a greater context for religious experience and expression everywhere in the world. If you take religion away, you have spirituality, for religion is all that is built upon spirituality in an attempt to sanctify it, to recreate it, to validate it and to assure its furtherance in your experience. Knowledge is the source of your spirituality, and it has been placed within you. It is a gift, and we are reintroducing you to it. It may seem new to you though it has been with you all along.

To value Knowledge and to accept its reality and to move towards it, you must reach a certain threshold in life. Here the world must disappoint you enough so that you will question whether it can satisfy you at all. Here you reach a threshold in your own life and in your own way where you come to know that there is something greater in your life that is waiting for you, that is calling for you, that is given to you and that abides with you. And you know that no matter what you do in life to acquire pleasure, wealth, fame, acquisition, recognition or anything else, nothing can compare with re-experiencing this deeper and profound sense of self and purpose in life. Everyone is moving towards this threshold, the beginning threshold where Knowledge is recognized.

Many people think that they are very intuitive and that they have always been intuitive. However, this does not mean that they have reached the threshold where Knowledge becomes really important and worthy of their time and effort. Many people think intuition is something that is just feeding them as they go along, as if they were part of a spiritual welfare system where you just collect as you go. This is very pathetic. You will never find the source of your purpose or inspiration with this approach, and you will never take responsibility for what you yourself must learn and do to begin to walk The Way of Knowledge and to take the steps to Knowledge.

Knowledge is related to your ability to know. We also call it the Knowing Mind. However, the problem with presenting it as the Knowing Mind is that many people think that they have a Knowing Mind that they can tap into at any moment. This is not the case. Knowledge reaches you. What you can do is prepare yourself for Knowledge by learning to become still and receptive, by learning to suspend your judgment and by setting aside your preferences, your compulsions, your ideas and your beliefs long enough so that something greater can be revealed to you. You prepare yourself for Knowledge. You cannot lay hold of it, grab it and use it for yourself. This is for your protection. Something great lives within you. It is not yours alone to own and to possess. It is something you share with all life. Whether you have had a religious upbringing or no religious upbringing, no matter what faith you were born into, you have Knowledge living within you.

If Knowledge can find expression in your life, then a greater value, a greater meaning, and a greater purpose can be demonstrated through your experience. The impact of this upon others will be profound and life changing. The expression of Knowledge can change another's life forever. Nothing you can do for others, even feeding them if they are hungry, can compare with this gift. However, you yourself do not give it. You allow it to be expressed through you, and the gift is then given to another.

In the Greater Community, Knowledge is as rare and valuable as it is in the world. And, of course, there is much deception about who has it and what it is, as there is in this world. Knowledge is the most valuable and precious gift and ability you have. It will enable you to recognize and to discern others. It will allow you to see what others cannot see, to know what others cannot know, to say what others cannot say and to feel what others cannot feel. Knowledge brings you to the forefront of life—your life and life all around you. It restores your body and renews your mind and brings all the divergent feelings and motives within you into harmony and into a balanced approach to life. Nothing else can integrate you but Knowledge. No idea, no ideal, no method, no teacher and no power can do this except Knowledge.

The evidence of Knowledge can be found if you look for it. Amongst all the other manifestations of life, you will find the evidence of Knowledge if you seek for it. Knowledge does not display itself; it does not make a show, yet it is always there. You can find it if you look, but you must look, and you must look with open eyes—not with greedy eyes or self-seeking eyes, not with eyes seeking self-validation or self-glorification. Indeed, as you seek it, you will likely have to give up even your spiritual ideas and beliefs because Knowledge will be beyond them.

Never think that you fully know what Knowledge is and what it will do. To do so is to close your mind to Knowledge. Knowledge is an involvement moment to moment. It is an opening in yourself based upon a deeper need and a greater trust. Claim Knowledge for yourself and you will lose it. Open yourself to Knowledge and it will return to you.

With Knowledge, you will understand the Greater Community presence in the world. You will have insight here. With Knowledge, you will be able to see the outcome of a relationship before it even begins. With Knowledge, you will be able to see destiny in certain things and in certain activities. Knowledge will lead you here and prevent you from going there. Knowledge will engage you with this person but not with that person, all without judgment or condemnation. What could be more natural to you, to your experience and to the very core of your being than the experience of Knowledge itself? So fundamental is this that most people miss it entirely. It is like a sound that is always sounding, but people cannot hear it because they are only listening for other things.

To come to Knowledge, you must prepare for Knowledge. This you cannot do alone. To learn Knowledge at the level of the Greater Community, you must learn a Greater Community way to Knowledge. You cannot teach this to yourself by reading books or by taking different practices or ideas from different traditions. Formulate your own approach and you will stay exactly where you are. Choose a path that you did not invent for yourself and you will go somewhere you have never gone before, and you will find something that you have never found before. Let Knowledge carry you forward, not your preferences, ideas or ideals.

This represents real spiritual development in the world. It is this development that is advancing your race, that advances all other races and that keeps Knowledge alive in the world and throughout the Greater Community. This is the purpose of the Creator—to keep Knowledge alive in the universe. To the extent that this can be done, all beings everywhere have the possibility for advancement towards reunion in complete harmony with life itself.

———◦⁓◦———

Purpose is entering the door

that begins a greater journey

in life.

———◦⁓◦———

CHAPTER FIVE

WHAT IS HUMAN PURPOSE?

*URPOSE IS SOMETHING YOU WILL UNDERSTAND as you climb higher on the mountain of life. As you gain a greater vantage point, you will understand more of the journey itself, by looking behind and by being increasingly able to anticipate what is up ahead. Purpose is realized by taking the journey, not by establishing a favorable or fascinating explanation or a definition for oneself. Purpose is not a justification. It does not compensate for anything. Purpose is something that is waiting for you to discover. You can only discover it by taking the journey, by following the way, by learning as you go and by gaining the greater perspective and understanding that one acquires as one matures in The Way of Knowledge.

As we have said before, you have come from someplace and you will return to that place. You have come bearing gifts for the world. Your greater purpose is embodied in this idea. Because of your origin and your destiny, you have something greater to give to the world, something that the world cannot give to you. Your gift is hidden within you like a secret cargo, but you cannot gain access to it until you have advanced. Then it will begin to emerge, slowly and incrementally, all on its own.

The impatient, the ambitious, the zealous and the fanatical cannot travel this way, for they cannot abide with a greater journey. They cannot be without definitions or explanations because they are too unstable to do so.

Your calling in life is very specific. It involves engaging with certain people for specific reasons at certain junctures of your life. The greater purpose that you share with everyone is to keep Knowledge alive in the world and to bring something from your Ancient Home into the world. This is a definition that you can abide with because it will not limit you and it will not deceive you, but go no further in your definitions. Allow the manifestation of your purpose to take place naturally, as it will if you follow in The Way of Knowledge. Your purpose now is to prepare to gain a greater understanding of the world, the world's evolution and the world's destiny. Within this larger context you will gain a new vantage point for understanding your role in the world and your reason for coming here.

Your life must be fulfilled. It must be justified. The world is a difficult place to come to. It is not a vacation spot. It is not a place where you are sent for punishment. It is not a place where you are sent for pleasure. It is a place that needs your gifts from your Ancient Home, and for this reason you have come. Your gifts are very specific, and they can be given without making a great show. Except in rare cases, you will not receive acclaim, glory or fame for giving your gift. This is appropriate. If you could gain a greater understanding of the world and what the world really is, what the world's need is and what the world's predicament is, you would see what a great advantage this is. You would understand why the Wise remain hidden and why they must learn to do so even to become wise.

The Creator is at work in all places and in all dimensions, reclaiming the separated through Knowledge. God's work goes on behind the scenes although it is active and quite apparent if you can perceive it. It does not make a show of itself, and, therefore, it receives a minimum of resistance and contamination from the worlds and the cultures that it serves.

Knowledge is like that. It works behind the scenes. It does not need recognition. It does not need glorification. It does not need for you to bow down to it like a slave. However, it does call to you to respond and to open your mind and your heart to it so that you may reunite with the greater aspect of yourself that bonds you to all life everywhere. Like a parent calling a wayward child back into the family, it calls you back. It calls you home, and as you progress towards it, however unknowingly, it protects you and it guides you. Though most of its gifts go unnoticed and unheeded, its presence and its beneficence are showered upon you nonetheless.

To find this Grace within yourself represents part of your preparation. Your purpose now is to prepare. It is not to make wonderful definitions for your life. It is not to justify your errors. It is not to make everything feel good or look good. Without preparation, your purpose will not be realized. There are many forms of preparation. All of them come from beyond you. If you make your own way, you will lose your way. If you choose only what you like and disregard the rest, then you will stay where you are, lost in your own mind, concealed from life and cut off from the greater movement of life which you are in truth here to serve and to participate in.

Your purpose is not to escape the world. Your purpose is not to run home to your Creator. Your purpose is to give what you came here to give, to reunite with those whom you are intended to reunite with and to contribute all that you have brought with you—that secret cargo that you carry even at this moment. Your purpose begins with preparation. That takes you towards realization and contribution. All the while you are giving. These great stages represent the milestones in your development. Do not think that you have already prepared, for the preparation is much greater than you realize. And the preparation continues.

You are here in the world for very specific reasons. They are not your personal reasons. You are here to contribute to and participate in a greater order of reality that exists within the world and beyond the world and even beyond the physical manifestation of life. How can you determine what that is? If you had access to and understanding of all things, then perhaps you could see and define your own role within it. However, you cannot do that, so do not attempt it because you will deceive yourself in the worst way.

Your purpose now is to prepare. If you must learn Greater Community Knowledge and Wisdom, then you must prepare in The Greater Community Way of Knowledge. You cannot make this up for yourself. And if you receive the curriculum, do not tamper with it; do not editorialize it; do not select what you like and disregard the rest, or you will not move beyond where you are. It takes a different understanding and a different movement in life to carry you into a greater awareness. With greater awareness comes a greater ability. This all comes from Knowledge. Here you are asked to follow, to respond and to learn the great lessons in discernment, discretion, communication and affinity. These lessons are inherent in the preparation itself. From the first step to the last, you will be learning these things, and life will be your laboratory.

Realize that this preparation is not for you alone. It is to enable you to contribute your gifts so that you may complete your service in the world and return to your Spiritual Family. Here you return with your gifts given, with everything contributed, without anything left undone here. This represents real accomplishment. How few in the world can identify this and claim it for themselves. To really understand your purpose, you must have an understanding of what God is, what the world is, what life force is and what Knowledge is.

At the beginning of the preparation is a process of undoing. So much that you believe in, so much that you admire, so much that you cannot tolerate, so much that you resent must be cleared away so that you can have the opportunity to have a new and direct experience. This is not a process of adding to your former thinking and conclusions. Therefore, do not come seeking validation. Instead, come seeking education. Education by its very nature is designed to take you into new territory, to take you beyond your former boundaries and assumptions and to expose you to new ideas and experiences. This is the very essence of education, and this is what we mean when we say that you must first prepare.

Without preparation, you will not achieve anything. This is obvious in many other areas in your worldly existence, and it is equally true in this area as well. Many people seek, or claim that they seek, for greater Wisdom, greater understanding and greater relationships, but few will prepare. Something in you must motivate you to prepare and must move you to prepare beyond your concerns and your anxieties and beyond your preferences, your doubts and your fears. Trust this. This comes from Knowledge. Knowledge will bring you to Knowledge. Your goals, your ambitions, your aspirations, your fantasies and your dreams can only stand in the way of this great homecoming.

As you come to realize that your purpose is not for you alone, then you will realize that you must not allow yourself to become self-possessed or self-absorbed. Indeed, the great liberation is a liberation from this self-absorption which returns you to life with an open mind and with all of your faculties fully activated. Those who are self-possessed cannot see beyond their own mental states, feelings, thoughts, emotions, changing attitudes, fixed beliefs and so forth. What can they bring to the world but their own confusion and their own isolation? Your first freedom is freedom from your own mind. This is freedom from your past, which represents your mind at this moment. This is your personal mind; it is not the Greater Mind of Knowledge. This is the mind that the world has conditioned. This is the mind that you must utilize now in a new way.

Knowledge gives you a reprieve from the prison of your own thoughts and attitudes and from the confines of your own emotions and beliefs. It does this without destroying your mind; it does this without harming you in any way. It gives you a new experience, an experience in present time without past associations. Having this experience is part of your preparation. Here you must be willing to go beyond your ideas. Here you must be willing to be without conclusions and without fixed ideas about what the world is, about what you are and about what truth is.

For many this is very difficult. You may feel quite insecure when you enter these states of unknowing, but in reality this is coming into the clear within yourself. This is being without resolutions but with an open and inquiring mind. This is not a passive approach. It is highly active because here you must be very attentive, very focused and ready to act.

Often, when people speak of purpose, they speak of the end result instead of the process of reaching that result. This, of course, is quite meaningless and has no lasting value. People claim what they believe they are now or will become, and they consider this to be a definition and a declaration of their purpose.

Do not deceive yourself with these fantasies. The ones who will succeed are the ones who focus on their preparation and allow the course of their life to unfold without determining its result and without determining what it will look like, how it will be and so forth. Here you must develop a great and growing faith in yourself, in the beneficence of those people who assist you, in the Unseen Ones who guide you and help you and in the power and presence of Knowledge within you. Without this trust, you cannot begin, and you will not be able to proceed. However, because these are living realities for you, you can proceed and you must proceed. But you must leave your need for self-assertion and self-validation behind.

You are entering new territory. You do not know what it means. You do not know how it is going to look. You do not know what will happen next. This is being open to life. This is being present to life. This is being without assumptions. Here the mind can truly integrate itself in present time and escape the prison of its past associations.

We give you great encouragement to begin preparation in The Way of Knowledge. To learn Greater Community Knowledge and Wisdom, we give you great encouragement to begin The Greater Community Way of Knowledge, which is a specific preparation for those whose purpose resides in understanding the greater context of life and the greater movement of the world. You will know if this is for you. Knowledge will initiate your preparation and will reaffirm your preparation in times of doubt and in times of false confidence when you believe you have attained something.

Purpose is a process; it is not a definition. It is not a validation. It is not a form of self-comfort. It is something that awaits you. It is a great journey. It is a door that is open to you now, a door that you can pass through. It is a journey where you do not lead yourself alone, but instead become a part of the greater education that exists throughout the universe. The Creator is at work everywhere, reclaiming the separated through Knowledge. This is the Creator's purpose. Your purpose is to give what you are designed to give, according to your nature and your true abilities. In this, your life becomes fulfilled because everything you have done can now serve a greater purpose.

This journey requires phenomenal self-honesty. This awaits to be learned. It is not something that you possess at this moment. Humility, honesty, openness, discernment, restraint, discretion, tolerance and compassion—these are qualities that result from preparation and advancement in The Way of Knowledge. These things are what provide inspiration and true ability in life.

This is purpose. Purpose is entering the door that begins a greater journey in life and staying on that journey in times of happiness and in times of distress. This is purpose. Leave aside all magnificent definitions and all glorious spiritual images. This is fantasy material for people who cannot make the way, who cannot journey up the mountain, who will remain below talking about its heights and its magnificence, but who really have no way of knowing its reality.

Your purpose is the same as everyone else's. However, your calling is specific. It is a specific set of tasks with specific people and in specific relationships for certain purposes. That is a calling. But for a calling to be genuine, to be real and to really bear fruit in life, it must be fundamentally based within the greater purpose that you share with everyone.

How do you know that you are engaged in true preparation? Because you are giving yourself to something that you cannot control and you cannot understand, but which you find to be increasingly beneficial as you proceed. This is very concrete, for much of your preparation is very concrete. It is not wandering around blindly, speculating and having big ideas. Instead, it is engaging in a process of development that has been provided for you by your Creator and by your Spiritual Family to initiate you in this life into the greater calling and purpose for which you have come. Only through this discovery will your life be fully justified and fully realized. Here you will enter a greater range of relationship and understanding which will make you a person of incredible value in the world.

The world is a hungry and lonely place. It is full of fantasy and folly. Its suffering is profound. Its confusion is deep. Its violence is sickening. Its possibilities are great. Who can see these things but those who realize that they have come from beyond the world to give something? They realize this because it is something they can feel. It is not an emotion; it is something they feel. They feel that they have come here for a reason. It is something that they cannot yet define, but they cannot make it go away either. Something greater is calling them. This is purpose. Eventually, if they respond to this, they will begin their preparation. This is purpose. If they stay with their preparation and advance within it, without trying to alter it or change it, they will begin to gain greater insight and understanding. This is purpose. If they continue and do not fall prey to the misperception that they are advanced, then Knowledge will slowly germinate within them, and their perception and understanding of things will change. Their awareness of the mystery of life will grow more and more profound, and their ability in life—in their relationships, in their career, in all their activities—will deepen. This is purpose. At some point, they will give themselves to something that involves other people in service to the world in one capacity or another according to their nature and their design. It will be natural for them to give themselves in this way, as it would be unnatural for them to decline it. This is purpose.

As we describe this process of preparation in a very general way, do not think that you are near the end. Do not claim that you are anywhere in the process, for how can you tell? You cannot pull yourself out of life and examine your life. You do not have that vantage point yet. Accept that the journey is great. It is marvelous. It is at times difficult. But in all ways it refines you. It washes away that which is nonessential in you and reveals that which is permanent and meaningful. Your real purpose and calling become apparent when all that hides and conceals them has fallen away, and what is left is what is real, and that becomes welcomed and embraced.

Your great impediment here is your fear of the real and your longing for fantasy. Reality is not harsh; it is redeeming. It is not cruel; it is revitalizing. It is not crushing; it is restoring. This is a reality of a greater nature than what your eyes perceive and what your hands can touch. This is a reality that will bond you not only to life in the world but to life in the Greater Community as well. This will prepare you for your encounters with those from the Greater Community. For you and for your children these encounters will grow in scope and magnitude. How few will be prepared, but these few must be prepared, for that is their purpose.

You do not need to feel an affinity with the Greater Community or even to believe in it to come to the understanding that your purpose is related to it. Everyone's purpose is related to it, directly or indirectly, because this is the world that you have come to serve. This is the time that you are here, and this is the condition of the world and the evolution of the world at this time. Though your specific calling may seem to have little to do with the Greater Community, you are serving the world in its emergence into the Greater Community. You are fostering goodness, Wisdom and the reality of Knowledge in the world through your own demonstration. This is your purpose.

Come, then, without definition. Come, then, without the need for self-validation. Come to the open door to Knowledge. It awaits you now.

The Greater Community gives you

a great opportunity for liberation as a race.

The gravity of its impact,

the problems that it will present

and the challenges it will give to humanity

will either defeat you or redeem you.

This is the greater problem

which will unite people everywhere,

for everyone will be in the same boat now.

The differences between you

will not matter.

CHAPTER SIX

WHAT IS THE
GREATER COMMUNITY?

—⟋⟍⟍⟋—

*T*HE GREATER COMMUNITY IS THE ENVIRONMENT in which you live. It includes your world and all the worlds in its vicinity. It is a vast region of space where intelligent life is interacting with each other, representing a great network of relationships between societies and between individuals in societies, a greater cosmology and a greater universe. For this, it is necessary to have a greater perspective, a greater understanding and a greater religion.

It is difficult for those who only see their own personal culture and immediate environment to realize the importance and significance of Greater Community Spirituality. The significance isn't merely in the scope of its teaching, its perspective and its understanding, but in the tremendous practical advantages that it gives you in daily life in your own world and in the very small affairs with which you are normally preoccupied.

The Greater Community here serves as a context—a context for seeing, for understanding and for knowing. It provides an opportunity to see beyond the limits of human thinking, human preoccupations and human beliefs and assumptions. This gives you a tremendous advantage. Thus, the emphasis here is not on what is beyond your realm, but on how to understand your realm within a larger context. What is occurring in other worlds and between other worlds is not your concern. Only very little of what is going on in the Greater Community will have any direct impact on humanity. However, the impact that is being exerted on your world from Greater Community forces is quite sufficient to create the need to learn a Greater Community Spirituality and a Greater Community Way of Knowledge.

Gaining a more universal understanding and perception is the emphasis when we speak of the Greater Community. In the Greater Community, there are many forms of intelligent life and great diversity in cultural ethics, preoccupations, concerns and activities. Yet what is common to all life everywhere that has evolved into the stage of intelligence is the presence and purpose of Knowledge.

Knowledge in the Greater Community is Greater Community Knowledge. The ability to receive Knowledge, to accept it and to apply it represents Wisdom, not only worldly Wisdom, but Wisdom in the Greater Community. As you were taught to see yourself in a very small way, we take you beyond yourself into a larger universe. Then, as you look back upon yourself, you will see what you could have never seen before. And you will recognize your environment more clearly than you ever could have previously.

The Greater Community is made up of a great diversity of life representing many different kinds of physical environments and many stages of individual, cultural, political and spiritual development. The range of this diversity is not your concern. However, the fact that it exists and that you will encounter its reality is profound indeed and gives rise to the great need that we are fulfilling in our presentation to you.

In the Greater Community, there are many worlds where intelligent life has evolved. And there are even more worlds and locations that Greater Community forces have colonized for resource acquisition or to seek new and more safeguarded environments. Worlds such as yours are quite rare and are therefore highly prized and regarded by those in the Greater Community who are aware of them. Indeed, your world has been used as a biological storehouse and resource for millennia by several different races.

You might ask, "Why hasn't a Greater Community force come to colonize the world and taken it over?" There are several important reasons for this. The first is that the great biological diversity that you enjoy and that represents such splendor in your world poses a great dilemma for advanced races, many of whom have evolved in more sterile environments. Living here is difficult because of the biological diversity itself.

Another disadvantage to your world is that human beings live above ground, which is not preferred by most advanced races. Underground settlements have proven to be far more effective and accommodating, especially when you are actively engaged with other Greater Community powers. This gives you greater security and a greater opportunity to protect your physical resources and your population at large. However, living underground isolates you from biological elements in the outer environment, thus making you more susceptible to illness and attack by other kinds of organisms. This presents an interesting truth in the Greater Community: The more safe and secure you become, the more vulnerable you are.

Therefore, while your world is splendid in its diversity and in its abundance of plants and animals, it also poses a great difficulty for Greater Community visitors to dwell and to abide here with any degree of freedom and mobility. Yes, they can visit you and travel about. Yes, they can do marvelous things. However, they cannot live on the surface very effectively. That is why there is a great attempt now to interbreed with humanity in order to gain this adaptive biological advantage. Mix Greater Community social cohesion and intelligence with human physical endurance and you have a race that, indeed, can abide within the world.

These ideas might seem startling, but from a Greater Community perspective they are quite obvious and apparent. Because you have not functioned within this larger context consciously, these things may seem frightening or difficult to comprehend. However, you must now accept that you are not alone and that you are certainly not at the pinnacle of development in the Greater Community. This is both humbling and refreshingly honest. This gives you the advantage and the motivation to learn, to progress, to overstep your former limitations and boundaries and to gain new abilities and understanding, which your visitors will give you, either intentionally or inadvertently. The conditions of the world require this. This is the world that you have come from your Ancient Home to serve. And these are the things that you must now learn and apply.

The Greater Community offers humanity redemption, but not in the way that you might think. It offers redemption because it poses a greater set of problems and occasions to which you must rise and to which you must now dedicate yourself. This provides escape from the terrible dilemmas and limitations that bind humanity and keep it in a desperate state of survival and self-preoccupation.

Solving greater problems gives you the opportunity to gain greater intelligence, greater ability and greater Wisdom. Only greater problems can do this because their resolution is necessary and because they require greater things from you. It is rare when a human being can develop these qualities without tremendous external demands. The external demands now are here. And though the risks are great and the problems are tremendous, the opportunities are unparalleled.

To meet these greater problems, you will need the Greater Power which the Creator has given you. You cannot rely on conventional wisdom; you cannot even rely upon your intuition. You must seek the Greater Power that is within you that can help you accelerate your development and meet a new set of requirements for adaptation, survival and accomplishment. In this, the Greater Community offers you redemption by requiring greater things of you and by calling upon a Greater Power within you. This is how humanity will advance. This is how all races in the Greater Community advance. And this is the evidence of the Creator's work, for the Creator does what works, even if it is incomprehensible to those who are destined to be its beneficiaries.

Therefore, do not seek understanding first. Seek involvement and experience. Knowledge within you knows exactly what you must do in life, what you must aspire to and what you must accomplish. It cannot be confused or distracted by the pleasures or the terrors of this world. It is not ambivalent. It is not doubtful. It is not beset with painful memories of the past or a dismal view of the future. It is relentless in carrying you towards your fulfillment and your purpose, for they are one. Fulfilling your purpose represents your work in the world and the purpose for your coming here. The Greater Community is the context for understanding this now, for indeed humanity is in the process of emerging into the Greater Community. You have come to participate in this and to support its successful establishment.

Thus, the Greater Community is your context. It represents a greater life, requiring a greater Wisdom from you and the establishment of greater relationships in your life. This is the evidence of God's work in the world, which is largely beyond human appreciation. You have not advanced far enough to look back and see the overall impact of this. You do not see how important it is for humanity's survival, how important it is for humanity to meet the great environmental and political challenges that it faces within its world and how important it is for humanity to meet the even greater challenges of successful engagement with races from the Greater Community.

The Greater Community represents a new understanding of Divinity, Divine purpose and human accomplishment in physical life. It is an entirely new threshold through which to pass. In fact, it represents many new thresholds of understanding. For now, the Greater Community must be equated with the physical universe, but in truth it is not limited only to the physical realm of life. It includes the greater and more refined dimensions of intelligent life and intelligent interaction. It is a consummate experience of life and of the presence of life in which you are immersed.

When we bring you to the Greater Community, we bring you to your life as it really is, in all of its fullness, magnificence, diversity and depth. We do not take you from your world and place you somewhere else. We do not put you in alien environments. We do not give you alien viewpoints and alien understandings. Instead, we bring you to your life as it is and as it will be. And we call upon you to meet life as it is and to prepare for life as it will be.

What is theology but the recognition of Divine involvement in physical life? Speculating about what God is, what God looks like, where God lives or how God functions is clearly a pointless endeavor. The answers to these questions exist in the realm of Mystery far beyond human understanding and concepts, far beyond your ability to understand at the level of ideas and intellect. This is the realm of pure experience. It is the realm of affinity and relationship. It is the realm where greater purpose is to be found, experienced and fulfilled. Therefore, we take you beyond your understanding into a greater arena of life in which you already live to encounter the forces which are already there for you to encounter, to give you a greater presence of mind and a greater facility to deal with life's mundane problems and to enable you to rise to meet the great challenges which you face in your world at this time. As we do this, we encourage humility, open-mindedness, faith, perseverance and clear discernment.

When we speak of the Greater Community, we are not advocating that you leave the world and travel to some distant place. We are not preparing you for space travel. We are not even encouraging space travel. Space travel will occur because that is part of your destiny and evolution, but that is not what is being encouraged here. You do not need to go to another world to realize you live in a Greater Community, for the Greater Community is at your doorstep. It is looking into your windows. It is in your neighborhood. It is here. It represents splendor and terror, wonderment and beauty, grave problems and dilemmas, just like your world but in a larger context and to a larger degree.

Meet these greater challenges and you will be able to solve the problems that are endemic in your own world. A greater set of problems will enable you to solve lesser ones. This is the ability you need to cultivate now. The Greater Community is redemptive because it creates necessity for you. It is not simply a problem that will exist at some distant time in the future. Greater Community forces are in the world now and are determining the direction of world evolution. The Greater Community represents your destiny and your fate, your dilemma and your greater promise. Success and failure here are critical, and that is why we give Greater Community understanding and Greater Community preparation such tremendous emphasis.

In this book, we present the theology of the Greater Community, which represents the will and the work of the Divine in physical life. To sit in the world and to speculate about what God is up to is not the work of theology. To recognize the work of the Divine and to involve yourself with it wisely and appropriately is what theology is all about. Theology is about understanding and action. If the understanding does not lead to action, then real understanding does not exist. This is the great difference between Wisdom and idealism. Wisdom leads to action, and idealism leads nowhere. It has no direction. You cannot act upon it effectively, for it is not going anywhere. Theology is visceral. It is real. It is here. It is the movement of the world and the movement of the Divine within the world and within the Greater Community as a whole.

The Greater Community is redemptive to you for another very important reason. It is your great opportunity to see into the larger arena of life, to see the grandeur of life and the expanse of life. In this, you will gain a greater appreciation for why you have come into the world and for who sent you. The Greater Community context gives you this opportunity and this requirement. You see, God redeems you by giving you something important to do, something greater than your personal preoccupations, fears and concerns. This is how your value is restored to you. This is how your gift is discovered. And this is how your existence in the world is justified and blessed.

You have been given a greater task and a greater understanding to learn. This is a greater mountain to climb that will make all the small hills that frustrated you before seem truly small and insignificant in comparison. Here you will escape your addictions and dilemmas because you are taking on something greater in life. Here you will escape fear and self-protection and all of the miseries that attend them by moving in a certain direction, by working within a larger context to gain a greater understanding and by using this larger context to resolve the little dilemmas that could only frustrate and obstruct you before. For all these reasons you are blessed to live in the Greater Community and to have the need and the opportunity to learn Greater Community Spirituality and all that it means for your well-being, your development and your continuance as a race.

The Greater Community offers you the requirement to unify your race, a requirement that you desperately need in your world, a requirement that is a necessary part of your evolution and that will make great accomplishments possible both now and in the future. Those things that overshadow you and that call you out of your individual preoccupied life call for the very things that the world needs from you and for you. No matter at what level, in what avenue or in what context your contribution is made, it is to serve this greater movement of humanity. The greater your understanding, the greater the gift that can be given.

Therefore, we present to you the Greater Community as it really is, not as you want it to be, not as it is hoped for, not as it is prescribed by the religions of your world, but as it really is—with all of its inherent problems and its magnificent opportunities.

Redemption is based upon accomplishment. This is the appropriate understanding to have. Therefore, when you pray for peace, for healing, for education, for Wisdom or for equanimity, what you are really calling for is a means for you to gain access to Knowledge, the Greater Mind that you possess, which joins you and bonds you to all life everywhere. You are calling for greater requirements to be given to you. Asking for peace or equanimity, Wisdom or Grace means that you are asking to be given those things that make the fulfillment and experience of these things possible. However, if you ask for escape from life or a reprieve from life or the avoidance of life, you are asking for nothing. In this case, should your request for peace and equanimity be granted and an answer given, you will not understand the answer. The opportunity is to be found in resolving the problems of life and in facing the problems of the Greater Community as they have bearing on your world. Accomplish something here and cultivate a greater awareness and understanding, and you will have a reward that could never be obtained otherwise.

The Greater Community is your new home. It is not new, but it is your new home while you are in the world. You do not live in a village any more, a little municipality or even one nation alone anymore. You are a citizen of a whole world. The Greater Community requires you to have this understanding and this identity because from a Greater Community perspective, human beings are all the same. They are all alike. The differences between you are insignificant. No matter where you are born, what language you speak, where you go to church or what kind of food you eat, from a Greater Community perspective you are a member of the human race. You are a human being. You are a citizen of this world.

This perception of yourself is necessary for your development because you *are* a member of one race and one world. Your race needs to become unified, even with all of its diversity—its idiosyncrasies, its cultural distinctions and its ethnic divisions. You are still a human being, a member of one race, of one world. Gain this awareness and great things can be done through you. The Creator can work through you. Your purpose can be experienced, and its contribution can be given. Only the Greater Community can offer this to you. You cannot gain this if you are bound to your culture, to your race, to your nation, to your family, or to your daily affairs.

As you learn over time to gain a Greater Community perspective and understanding, you will realize what needs your attention and what problems and difficulties you must set aside or avoid. Then your life will become simple, direct, magnificent and demanding—all the things that lead to accomplishment and to true satisfaction. Life asks a lot of you because your prayers for peace have been answered. You live in a demanding situation because your need for Knowledge and self-integration is so pressing. If you regret that the world is the way it is, you will miss its opportunity. If you regret having to consider or accept that your world is emerging into the Greater Community, then you will miss the answer to your prayers. God gives you something to do that takes you out of your misery and requires that you demonstrate a greater Wisdom and intelligence, both for others and for yourself.

This is the way because in these greater activities, greater relationships are fostered and greater abilities are called upon. You are freed from the past and are called into the present to something greater where you are needed, where you are destined to be and where your contribution is required. This is fulfillment. The Greater Community is calling this from you because you live in the Greater Community, because you are part of a race that is emerging into the Greater Community and because forces from the Greater Community are engaging with the world and are encountering people everywhere. Do not try to understand this, for your understanding cannot encompass its full meaning. However, you can experience it and recognize its value and its meaning for you specifically.

If you can accept that you have come from beyond the world to serve the world, then you will realize that the world you have come to serve is offering the conditions that will bring forth that which you came to give. If you can accept this, then you will stop condemning the world and start looking for its opportunities and allow it to call from you that which you came to give. This calling is natural and the response from you will be natural, more natural than anything else that you can think of. If you can accept these things, then you have entered the path of redemption, accomplishment and fulfillment. It is a long path, a path with many challenges and great learning requirements, but it is a path that will set you apart from others to such an extent that you can gain a greater understanding and a greater ability. And others will benefit from your accomplishment and from your education.

Your preparation for the Greater Community represents the greatest and most vital education that can be fostered and extended in the world today. This education is the only thing that will enable you to solve the growing global problems of the world that seem so overwhelming and that your societies seem so incapable of facing and so poorly equipped to resolve. Preparation for the Greater Community is the most essential thing. It involves all aspects of learning. It requires that the student of Knowledge become effective at solving problems on a small scale so that problems on a larger scale can be recognized, attended to and resolved.

What is the Greater Community? It is your answer. It is what you have come to attend to. Working in your own specific way, you will play a part in the world's evolution and will fulfill your mission here and the mission of those who have sent you. This is the great promise that we offer. This is the great promise that is born of the world's emergence into the Greater Community. And this is the great promise that Knowledge within you must respond to, for in this it has no choice.

—⸙—

Wisdom is knowing

how to do

what you came here to do.

—⸙—

CHAPTER SEVEN

HOW IS WISDOM ACHIEVED IN LIFE?

———~~~———

ISDOM IS UNDERSTANDING HOW TO APPLY Knowledge in the real world. Wisdom is cultivated by following Knowledge and by developing skills in the world. It is based upon the cultivation of discernment and discretion, two very fundamental aspects of your education. Let us explore what Wisdom is, and then we shall discuss how it can be developed most effectively.

Wisdom deals with the application of the Greater Power which lives within you at this moment and which seeks to express itself through you. Gaining access to this Greater Power and learning of its grace, its intelligence and your intrinsic relationship with it represent the focal point of your education in life, the highest expression of your purpose and the reclamation of your greatest relationships, both with your Creator and with others who live with you here. Learning how to gain access to Knowledge, how to receive Knowledge, how to accept Knowledge, how to interpret Knowledge, how to apply Knowledge and how to become a vehicle for its expression in life requires the cultivation of Wisdom.

Knowledge lives within you at this moment, but your ability to receive it, to relate to it and to express it requires the development of a whole new understanding and approach to life. Here you are not taken away from the world. Here you are not elevated beyond physical life but are brought into the world with a greater purpose and mission. This purpose and mission remain mysterious. You cannot define them although you can give definition to their expression. However, even their expression cannot capture their full meaning and importance for you and for others.

This requires a different kind of education. Learning to deal with the tangible world in a practical way and to open yourself to the mystery of your life, with reverence and humility, represents a new threshold in learning. It is passing through this threshold and the many thresholds beyond it that will generate Wisdom in your life—the ability to know what must be done and the skill to learn how to do it and how to carry it forward effectively.

Wisdom, then, represents the ability to translate Knowledge into the finite world. This is your function—to be a vehicle for creativity and creation. This is the highest expression of your mind and your body—to be vehicles for the Greater Power that lives within you, which represents the essential and immortal aspect of yourself and of everyone who lives here. Wisdom is an experience, an experience of openness and recognition, an experience of being in contact with two realities simultaneously—the reality of your physical life in the world and the reality of your divine life, your spiritual life, which represents your intrinsic relationship with God and with all of God's messengers.

Becoming an intermediary represents an expression of real purpose in life. However, this requires a very unique kind of skill. It requires a remarkable openness to certain things while distancing yourself from many other things, for you cannot be open to everything at once. There are many things that are competing for your attention, and there are many things that will overwhelm you should you open yourself to them. There are many kinds of relationships available to you and many kinds of involvements with people. Where you place yourself and what you open yourself to is an expression of your development in Wisdom.

Here we must speak of discernment and discretion. Discernment is knowing what something is, as it truly exists at this moment. Discretion is the ability to hold Wisdom within yourself, to hold an awareness within yourself without sharing it with others inappropriately. Discernment is knowing what you are dealing with. Discretion is knowing how to communicate with it. Both of these require the willingness to be instructed, the willingness to learn, and the willingness to revise or unlearn things that have proven to be counter-productive for you. This requires restraint. This also requires that you hold in abeyance many of your needs—the need for recognition, the need for validation, the need to express yourself, the need to be accepted by others, the need to overcome your adversaries, the need to be unique or special and the need to have all of your wishes fulfilled. These needs must be overcome in order for you to have this greater presence of mind and security in life.

With Wisdom you will know the right thing to say to the right person in the right place at the right time. Until you are with the right person in the right place at the right time, you remain silent and observant, without condemning yourself or anyone else. Here you wait for that moment when your gift must be delivered, and you are prepared to give it in whatever form is appropriate. You may have to wait a very long time for this moment and exercise tremendous patience and forbearance. The ability to do this represents Wisdom—knowing what something is and knowing how to deal with it effectively.

Wisdom is not something that you possess alone. It represents a relationship—your relationship with the Greater Power in your life and with Creation itself. Wisdom must be able to guide and instruct you in areas which are beyond your understanding and capacity. Your understanding and capacity are growing slowly. While you are integrating this learning and understanding, you must be open to be shown things and to have things demonstrated to you.

Here you learn to rely upon Knowledge within you and upon Knowledge in the universe, which is God. Here you do not need to rely upon your fears, your passions, your needs or your compulsions, or upon the needs or compulsions of others. Now, you are governed by a true and Greater Power within you and are not swayed and dominated by the vacillating wishes and interests of the world around you. This represents freedom. This is what it means to overcome the world—to have a new foundation in life and a greater authority, which is your true authority in life, and to become an authority for your own mind and your own body. Then, everything is set in the correct proportion—your body, your mind, your spirit, your Creator. All are set in the right relationship, each with its proper range of authority. Do not think for a moment that you will be weak, helpless or passive in this relationship. Indeed, you will be asked to assume greater responsibilities and a greater authority in your life than you had ever considered possible.

Governing your body and your mind is certainly a great challenge. It calls upon Knowledge, which is the very essence of who you are, to guide and to manage your activities effectively. You are the captain of your ship, and you must manage everything that occurs within it. However, you do not assume to direct your ship, to justify it or to determine its origin or its destiny. This must come from a Greater Power because this responsibility is beyond your capacity. Being in right relationship with your body, your mind, your being and the being of life itself, which is God, represents Wisdom.

We cannot give you a simple definition of what Wisdom means, for it is too great for this. Anything that is great and meaningful in life is beyond definition. What can be done here is to describe its aspects and its expressions in different ways. You have experienced Wisdom before in those moments when a greater understanding overtook you, when you found yourself experiencing a remarkable objectivity and openness, a clear vision and a directed mind. Perhaps this was only for a moment. Perhaps you clicked into it and then clicked out of it, but within this moment you had an experience of Wisdom and an experience of how to be in the world.

Knowledge and Wisdom are different although they are related. Knowledge is complete and intrinsic within you. As a student of

Knowledge, you learn to gain access to Knowledge, to learn of its meaning and purpose in life and to reclaim your relationship with it, your union with it and your mission with it. Wisdom is something you learn through activity in the world. It must be learned. Knowledge cannot be learned; it can only be reclaimed. Wisdom is something that you learn. It is relevant to your life here. Knowledge is relevant to your life everywhere. In other words, Knowledge is already complete within you, and you are learning to come into proximity to it and to reclaim your relationship with it. Wisdom is something that you develop as you go along. It is a set of skills in learning how to be in the world. It is related to your worldly experience, and in that regard it is temporary.

The ability to experience Knowledge and the ability to experience greater purpose, meaning and direction in life rest upon the cultivation of Wisdom. Here a partial understanding is indeed dangerous, for you may know one thing, but what you know is incomplete, and you may be tempted to use it for selfish purposes, for self-defense, for acquisition or for domination over others. Without real Wisdom and the understanding of how to use what you know, Knowledge will remain latent within you and will not become an effective force in life. This is why the reclamation of Knowledge is slow and why it is a very gradual process with many steps in learning. You must understand and integrate what you know and allow it to direct your life very slowly. It does not happen all at once, for you do not yet have the desire or the capacity for Knowledge in a complete sense. This desire and capacity must be gained gradually over time.

Knowledge will change your life and give you a new foundation, a new understanding and a new vision. It will change the direction of your thinking and give you a whole new set of ideas upon which to build a new and greater understanding and ability in life. This represents fundamental change, change at the very center of your being in the world. It must happen gradually because it rests upon Wisdom, which is the ability and understanding of how to be in life and how to be a medium in life for a Greater Power and a Greater Reality.

Becoming wise in human affairs seems to be a formidable task in and of itself. However, becoming wise in dealing with life in the Greater Community represents a whole new threshold in learning and a greater challenge and opportunity for you. Here we are not speaking only of human life, where Wisdom is being applied in a very limited context. We are speaking of the Greater Community, which is a much greater context for you. This offers many new challenges and places a greater requirement upon you to learn The Greater Community Way of Knowledge and to develop the Wisdom necessary to experience it and to express it.

Why is Wisdom important for you? Because it will harmonize your life. It will establish the priorities of your life and bring you back into right relationship with yourself and with everyone around you. Consider these words. Consider how great this gift is and how essential it is for your well-being, your advancement and your contribution in life.

What could we offer you that is greater than this? We could offer you Heaven itself, but Heaven is what you will find when you go Home to your Spiritual Family. What you need now is to gain a real foundation for living in the world and to discover the real purpose which you have brought with you from your Ancient Home. This is what you need while you are in the world. Here you must find the right people in your life that you will need. Here you must develop an understanding of how to carry Knowledge and Wisdom in a world that cannot recognize Knowledge and Wisdom and does not even want them necessarily.

Your gift is meant only for certain people in certain situations, and even these people must be ready for your gift. Everyone else can help you in mundane ways, but your gift is meant for certain people. Knowledge will speak to them but will remain silent with everyone else. Perhaps this will only be one or two people in your life. Perhaps it will be hundreds or thousands. You cannot dictate this; you can only accept it and learn what it means.

Who you need to communicate with and what you need to offer are determined by your nature and design in the world, which give real meaning to your individuality. You as an individual are designed to fit within the context of life as it is and as it will be. But can you hold yourself back and learn to wait for those special moments to give yourself to those unique people that you are destined to be engaged with? Can you allow a Greater Power to express itself through you without trying to use it to fulfill your needs or your ambitions? Can you be this open and receptive? Can you be this patient? Can you have this forbearance? Can you hold yourself back or stop yourself from becoming engaged with people for other reasons and purposes?

Beyond the mundane requirements of your life, you need only adhere to this Greater Power and its mission, realizing that its meaning and purpose in life far exceed your understanding. However, you can experience what this Greater Power means for you individually. It represents a fundamental experience for you. It cannot be given to you all at once. You do not yet have the capacity for it, and you do not yet have the Wisdom to experience it or to express it.

Knowledge and purpose in life will indeed seem a great burden to you until you can learn to position yourself with them correctly and become a vehicle for their expression in a constructive way. Life gives many demonstrations of people who experienced something with great meaning but could not express it or contribute it in a constructive way. They tried to use it to gain power or advantage. They tried to use it to attack others. Irresponsible leadership, fanaticism, demagoguery—all of these things are expressions of the great error of attempting to have Knowledge without Wisdom, of attempting to know something without knowing how to carry it in life.

How do you develop Wisdom? This requires a preparation, an association with those people who can share this preparation with you and a commitment to contribute the fruits of your preparation to those people who need it. This will take time, for you must learn many important lessons along the way. You cannot rush out and have this experience with whomever you want. You cannot apply it to solve every problem that you see. You cannot use it to validate yourself or to justify your involvements with others. Here you must have faith and great patience with your preparation. And as we have faith and great patience with you, you must also learn to have faith and great patience with others. You must wait for them as we must wait for you.

This faith and patience, along with your preparation, will enable you to bring a greater Wisdom and a greater understanding into the thousand involvements of your everyday life. This is Wisdom—knowing how to do what you came here to do. It will take a lifetime for you to learn this completely, as it will take a lifetime for you to fully learn how to express what you came here to do. Can you be patient and have a great understanding grow, step by step, stage by stage? Can you wait and allow your life to become clear and evident to you, without trying to fill in all the gaps, without trying to assign value where value has not yet been realized and without trying to use your growing understanding as a means to fulfill all of your desires? This is the great challenge in education: to learn what is important, to learn what is unimportant and to be able to tell them apart in all of their manifestations.

You may think you can know everything or have access to all Knowledge, but if you cannot undergo the preparation, if you cannot carry the responsibility, if you cannot patiently learn to express Knowledge correctly and appropriately with the right people at the right time, then your awareness will become a great and intolerable burden for you. It will disassociate you from the world rather than enable you to come into the world as a representative of a Greater Reality.

Ambition in learning can be very destructive here. Many have failed because of it. We want to safeguard you against failure. We want you to take the slow and careful path of learning. Many have failed in attempting to learn greater Knowledge and Wisdom. In the attempt to learn Greater Community Knowledge and Wisdom, many will fail as well. They will fail because of their impatience. They will fail because of their ambitions. They will fail because of their unwillingness to learn the essential lessons and to integrate themselves correctly and appropriately according to their nature and to the greater truth which they are attempting to realize and to express. They will fail because they will associate with the wrong people in the wrong ways. They will fail because they will attempt to use the truth themselves, without allowing the truth to guide and to direct them correctly. They will fail because they have not yet learned to discern the voices within themselves and the relationships that surround them. And they will fail because they are indiscreet, because they say things to the wrong people at the wrong time. All of these lead to failure.

To safeguard against this failure, you must learn a Greater Community Way of Knowledge. This provides the slow and sure way while others rush by you attempting to have what you are learning to have, attempting to be what you are learning to be and attempting to understand what you are learning to understand. You must take the slow and steady path. This will assure your success. If you follow the steps to Knowledge, you will learn the way to Knowledge. However, if you rush ahead or if you make outrageous assumptions about your abilities or about your role in life, then you will falter and fail. The one who is taking the real steps to Knowledge and is learning them correctly will pass you by. And you will become broken down by the side of the road, unable to participate and unable to move forward.

All education has the risk of failure and misappropriation. Therefore, you must learn The Way of Knowledge and you must learn The Way of Wisdom, which is how to carry Knowledge in the world. Wisdom requires many things, and these things take time to develop. You must take this time to develop and not try to control the learning process or make outrageous assumptions about what you can do, what you have and who you are. Who you are must be revealed to you over time, through demonstration. What you have must be revealed to you over time, through demonstration. And who sent you here and what mission you are a part of must be demonstrated to you over time.

These things will be demonstrated through contrast—the growing contrast between the experience of Knowledge and the experience of being without Knowledge, the contrast between the experience of acting with Wisdom and the experience of acting without Wisdom, and the contrast between acting with certainty and acting with ambition. Learning this contrast will set you apart and give you a new foundation in the world. To serve humanity in a real way, you must be set apart from its foolishness and from its errors, from its fears and from its aggressions. You cannot go where everyone else is going and have any possibility of learning the real purpose and meaning of your life. Realizing the contrast between this and what everyone else is doing or appears to be doing will enable you to become wise.

Therefore, commit yourself to learning the way to Knowledge. Commit yourself to taking the steps to Knowledge. And commit yourself to learning how to wisely receive Knowledge and how to carry this greater power, ability and relationship in your life. If you move too fast, you will falter. If you move too slowly, you will falter. Over time you will find your pace in learning, and then you will be able to increase your pace and accelerate your advancement. You cannot do this based upon your will, your wishes or your ambitions. You must do this based upon a growing understanding and ability within yourself. Knowledge will indicate how fast you can go, and Knowledge will enable you to accelerate your pace as your learning increases and expands.

Knowledge is your foundation now, not your mind. Your mind will find its proper engagement in learning to deal with the particulars of life and in learning to solve little problems. However, fulfilling your greater needs and your greater requirements and finding your greater destiny and your greater relationships with other people—all of these must be guided by a Greater Power within you that represents your true nature and association with all life. This is Knowledge. Yet being able to receive Knowledge, to accept its benefits, to carry out its greater responsibilities and to meet its greater opportunities requires a new approach to life. It requires a new way of being in the world, a new foundation for relating to others, a new experience of yourself, a new sense of being in time, a new experience of having a body and a new sense of having responsibilities to the world and to those who sent you here. Together these represent Wisdom—the art of being in life with a great purpose and a great mission.

Consider these words, but do not think that you can fully understand them. These words are meant to take you into The Way of Knowledge, not to define The Way of Knowledge. You must make the journey, not simply try to understand it. You cannot understand it until you make the journey yourself. Making the journey is a path of learning Wisdom. As your Wisdom grows, as you gain this new foundation, this new ability and this new experience in life, Knowledge will emerge within you. And you will be able to receive it, to follow it and to express it with those people for whom it is intended, according to your nature and design and according to the greater purpose that you are learning to serve.

—◦◦◦—

Greater things are revealed

to those who experience

a greater need.

—◦◦◦—

CHAPTER EIGHT

WHO IS WISDOM
MEANT FOR?

—~~~—

*T*HE ANSWER TO THIS QUESTION IS CLEAR, but it may take a very long time to understand what it means and what it will require of you. Wisdom is meant for you—you who have been drawn to a greater experience of purpose, meaning and direction in life, you who have not been able to be content with the little satisfactions that preoccupy most people. It is meant for you who feel a deeper yearning for truth and who entertain a vague but persistent feeling that there is something important for you to do in life—something that is unique and significant, something that you have not been able to find at your universities, in your books or through your conversations, something extraordinary, something that most people are not even aware of. It is meant for you who have felt this inner need and this inner prompting that have set you apart from others and that have made you impatient with the superficial things of life. It is for you who feel an affinity with all life and who have a sense that your life and your purpose extend far beyond the immediate circumstances of your individual existence here. It is meant for you who feel and long for a deeper affinity with another, who seek relationships that are meaningful and permanent, relationships that have a greater context and a greater capacity for self-expression and for shared affinity.

The Greater Community Way of Knowledge is meant for you. It is meant for you who are reading these words, you who have shown a spark of interest, you who have already taken some initial steps towards something great and mysterious in your life. Wisdom is meant for you who have already tasted its beneficence, its grandeur, its grace and its simplicity—an experience that sets it in contrast to all other things in life, making them dull and mundane in comparison, an experience of certainty, open-mindedness and greater relationship with life. And even though the experience of Wisdom might have only lasted for a moment, it still abides with you now as a tiny but significant reminder that you have come from a greater life and that you will return to a greater life. It is a reminder that you are here to do something important and that you must meet certain people in order to accomplish your task. The inner prompting towards this continues even now and has brought you to open the book that reveals a greater Wisdom and purpose in your life.

You may ask, "Is this meant for everyone?" The answer to this is no, for not everyone can receive it. If everyone could receive it, the answer would be yes. Why should something be meant for someone who will not, within this life, gain access to it? Remember, we have said that God does what works. Greater things are revealed to those who experience a greater need and who have already set in motion a process of moving towards Knowledge by becoming honest about their affairs, about their feelings and about their deeper inclinations. If this has not already happened for a person, then he or she may not even be able to begin the reclamation of Knowledge or the study of The Greater Community Way of Knowledge. This is not to say that those people who have had these preliminary experiences have made great progress, but it does mean that they have already begun a process that can enable them to experience truth, to recognize its value and to set it in contrast to all other things that compete with it.

The experience of truth—the experience of being united with yourself, being honest with yourself and having integrity within yourself—however limited and circumstantial it may be, is an outstanding experience. This experience is established in contrast to all of the compromises, the avoidance, the compulsions and the fearful activities that govern the minds of so many in the world today.

Wisdom is meant for you because you have arrived at these words. This is not to say that your success is guaranteed. This is not to assure you that everything will work out perfectly. This is not to reward you for great accomplishments. It is only to acknowledge a beginning and a real potential. If you value the words that you have read so far in this book, then you have already arrived at the beginning of a new perspective.

The experience of truth and reality is in such contrast to all other experiences that you will come back to it again and again. Perhaps you are afraid of this experience; perhaps you think it will rob you of your pleasures and your interests. However, in spite of these fears, which are unfounded, you will return to the experience of truth because you will be able to experience reality here. As you experience reality, you will see how empty and unfulfilling all other pursuits are. You will see how, after great expense and involvement, they produce such small rewards. The price of these pursuits is so high, and the rewards are so small. Escaping the experience of being cheated by life and the experience of cheating life itself represent a great freedom and a great opportunity.

Wisdom is meant for you. A great journey lies ahead for you—a journey that will be challenging and remarkable, a journey that will affirm your deeper nature, a journey that will free you from the bondage of your own ideas and obligations to others, a journey that will take you beyond dependency into a truly independent state and beyond this into a state where you can become interdependent with others. It is in this stage of interdependence that real relationships are established and true devotion can arise. If you truly want what you know, then you will know what you want. However, if you only want what you think, you will enter deeper and deeper into confusion and will invest yourself ever more heavily in those things that can only confuse and frustrate you.

Wisdom is meant for you because it is an answer to your prayers. The opportunity to gain access to Knowledge, to learn Greater Community Spirituality and to develop Wisdom is the answer to your deepest needs. Move towards this and your lesser needs will become resolved in the process. Then you will not have to devote so much time and energy to their resolution. Tell the truth about something great and you can tell the truth about everything around it. The truth grows in this way because it stands in contrast to everything else. Experience your own reality as the result of being honest with yourself and others and you will never want to lose this experience. You will return to it again and again, even in situations where there is great challenge or risk of loss.

Wisdom is meant for you who can understand these words and respond to them. You must be the first recipient. Do not think of your friend or your brother or your sister or your mother or your father whom you would like to restore or change in some way to make them easier for you to be with. Wisdom is not for them; it is for you. Everything we say is about you and for you. Do not look over your shoulder. Do not point across the street. Do not think of someone else who is having difficulty in their life right now and think, "Oh, this would be so good for them." No, this is for you. They may not be ready for this. They may not be interested. This may not be their way. They may not even have a way for a very long time.

In our presentation to you, we present things that are both within the range of your experience and beyond it. Because something is beyond the range of your experience does not mean that it is not important or relevant to your needs and to your future. It simply means that it is not related to your past. We want to take you into the future and prepare you for the future. The preparation will speak of things you know already and of things you have never thought of. If you say, "Well, I cannot relate to some of these ideas," what you are saying is that they do not relate to your past and past interpretation. Of course not! They do not relate to your past because they are here to liberate you from your past. If you took everything we said and you said, "Oh, I know this. I know this. I know this," you would be using everything we say to reinforce your past. Our mission is to free you from the past so that you can live in the present and prepare for the future, which will enable you to live in the future.

This is meant for you. Receive this. Learn to become a receiver. You are not ready to teach this to others yet, for you must be engaged in studying *Steps to Knowledge* and advanced as a student of Knowledge in order to translate and transfer this to others successfully. You know, many people want to go out and share everything they learn as soon as they learn it. The problem is that they have not really learned it, and so they cannot demonstrate it. If you want to inspire others, if you want to show them something that has really been effective in your life, then you yourself must demonstrate it. This demonstration is far more powerful and effective than any words that you could say or any illustrations that you could create. That is why we say that this is for you. The gift is for you. It is not for anyone else. It is for you.

Why would you read about Greater Community Spirituality if you were dedicated to reinforcing your former beliefs and ideas? Regardless of your former beliefs and ideas, the teaching and the preparation in The Greater Community Way of Knowledge will take you beyond them. Then you will not be encumbered by them, and you will be free to live in the present and to see things as they really are, not as you want them to be or believe them to be.

Some people think that you only see what you believe. They think that if you change your ideas, you will see something else. This ignores the reality that there is life outside of you. Life is happening. It is not all about you. It is not the result of your own thinking. You interpret what you see, but this only means that you are either able to see what is in front of you as it is or you are not. We are teaching you to see, to see things simply, as they really are—without self-glorification, without self-avoidance, without self-protection and without falsification of any kind. See yourself as you are today. See others as they are today. See the world as it is today. All without condemnation. To see without condemnation, you must see without idealism. You must see without the need for you, for others and for the world to be as you want them to be. Insisting on these things leads you to condemnation because the world, others and you yourself will disappoint you. They will not live up to your expectations. To see things as they really are, you must let them be as they really are, without attempting to put happy faces on them or sad faces, without attempting to make them beautiful or hideous. This can be done.

To bring you back into relationship with yourself, with others and with the world, you need this kind of vision. This vision will be the by-product of the reclamation of Knowledge within you. Knowledge deals with things only as they really are and leads them towards their purpose and fulfillment without any deception, glorification or condemnation. This experience is possible for you because Wisdom is meant for you.

You may ask, "Why isn't this meant for everyone?" The answer is simple but again hard to understand. Potentially, truth is for everyone, but today it is meant for those who can receive it today, and tomorrow it will be meant for those who can receive it tomorrow. Perhaps you cannot receive the truth today. Then you come back tomorrow, and you can receive it. The Way of Knowledge is the return to truth and the reclamation of all meaningful relationships. It is offered to everyone, but few will respond, so it seems like it is offered to them specifically, which is not the case.

We make everything practical, plain and simple. Therefore, we must emphasize that this is meant for you. You must learn to receive the gifts. Perhaps they are not like the gifts that you have thought of or have sought after or have invested yourself in—those things that have only required you to give more and have put you deeper in debt within yourself. We offer a different kind of gift, a different way of living—a way that calls upon your ability and requires its expression. We do not only give you ideas, for ideas alone are not enough. What we give is a message that calls you out of your dilemma and provides a means of escape from those things that could only belittle you, confuse you and isolate you. We give this because Wisdom is meant for you.

If you can receive Wisdom and learn The Way of Knowledge, then you will be able to give to others. Then certain people will be able to receive from you. In this way, a greater meaning, purpose and direction in life can be given to everyone, moving through the channels of relationships as they exist throughout your world and throughout the Greater Community.

If you can receive the gift, you will demonstrate that you have received it. It will work within you, and it will find an expression through you according to your nature and your design. It will bless you and empower you and give you depth of insight and understanding. It will give you patience and forbearance. It will teach you that you live a greater life. Through this long and wonderful process of development, you will give to others—others you can see and others you cannot see. Your life will become more and more a demonstration, and your ideas will have more potency because they will ring true. These are not temporary ideas; they are permanent ideas. They are lasting. They are meaningful.

The path is not difficult so much as it is exacting. Like following a footpath through a dense jungle, you must watch your steps carefully and be very attentive to your environment as it changes. You cannot go running ahead, proclaiming yourself or your ideas, trying to improve people or situations. You must follow the way carefully and slowly. In this way, the dangers of the jungle will not affect you. In this way, you will foresee danger and difficulty and will find a way to avoid them or to change them if that is possible.

If you can receive, you can give. Until you have received and learned The Way of Knowledge, you cannot give it because it is not you who will do the giving. It is Knowledge itself that will do the giving. This is the great difference, and it will make all the difference in your experience and in your expression of truth.

How is Knowledge transferred from one to another? It is ignited invisibly. We speak to Knowledge within you, not to your mind. If you are connected to Knowledge and can experience it, you will feel the depth and impact of what we are saying. This is how Knowledge is transferred. This is how Knowledge is ignited. This is how true initiation takes place. There are outer things to do, of course, and they require much time and energy. However, the Mystery—the transference of Knowledge and the reuniting of ancient bonds—is something that is beyond the intellectual understanding of anyone. It must be experienced.

You can speculate. You can fantasize. You can theorize. But the Mystery can only be experienced. Therefore, to learn The Greater Community Way of Knowledge, to learn what Greater Community Spirituality means and why it is so essential for you and for your world, you must begin to have this experience. It will happen in increments, depending upon your desire for it, your resistance to it and your capacity to feel it and to carry it. As your desire and capacity grow and as your resistance lessens, the Mystery will take on greater and greater dimensions, and its rewards will grow for you. Your responsibilities will grow as the Greater Power within you grows. In time, it will speak through you and move through you.

Wisdom is meant for the world, but it must be given to individuals, and they must prepare and be able to translate it into the existence, the language and the images of daily life. Pure truth, pure Wisdom, pure affinity and pure relationship cannot be received here yet, except by a rare person here and there. And even these individuals must undergo tremendous development. This is because people's desire and capacity for truth and honesty, relationship and affinity are so very limited. It is also because people everywhere have dedicated themselves to things that they must learn to outgrow. This takes much time, and there are many failures, but the possibility of success is there.

If you follow the way and if you learn the lessons as you go, without adding anything or subtracting anything, you will make the journey. You will pass through the jungle, and you will find the mountain and the way up the mountain. You will proceed in moments when you have vision and in moments when you do not have vision. You will proceed when you can see your goal and when you cannot see your goal. This is meant for you. You may disqualify yourself. You may reject the gift. You may give it other meanings or you may assign terrible associations to it. However, the gift is pure, and you must be pure of heart to receive it.

To deny a calling in life says nothing about the calling but everything about you. You must be ready, and you must have the experience of truth. People lie to themselves. Their deceptions are in layers and become so deep that even the truth is just a fantasy to them. It is just an idea, something they cannot rely upon or experience. Truth always brings you back into relationship with life, with others and with yourself. Fantasy and deception always take you away. There is fantasy about everything, even about the truth.

Many people will attempt to use The Greater Community Way of Knowledge to acquire power, to assure themselves of love and money, to gain advantages in life, to dominate others and to proclaim themselves, but they will not learn The Way of Knowledge. It will escape them entirely. They will only have ideas about it, ideas that they find to be comforting or self-inflating. However, the essence and the meaning, the purpose and the truth of The Greater Community Way of Knowledge will escape them entirely. They will use the words but be lost to the meaning. You will see this.

Until you can value truth, choose truth and abide with truth, fantasy will be projected upon everything. Everything will be determined to be useful according to whether it substantiates and furthers your personal aims. How can anything real be found if this is the motivation? Here there will be no vision, no understanding and no comprehension. Things will not be seen as they are. They will not be valued as they are. Real opportunities will be lost, and dangerous opportunities will be chosen.

Every failure started out as a good idea—something that would lead in a preferred direction, something that would further a personal cause. Let your failures in life, then, disillusion you and sober you, temper you and open your eyes. Accept your failures. Call them failures. They *are* failures. Let them renew you. Let them clear your vision. Let them free you from future failure. Let them give you discernment. Let them teach you discretion. Let them take you back to truth, which is what you needed to begin with. Things can be known at the outset. Truth is available because Knowledge is within you. This is your gift to receive as it will be your gift to give.

We have spoken of greater things in this book and will speak of greater things yet. We keep things in a larger context because you need to think about things in a larger context. This will show you how little your fantasies, your goals and your objectives are in contrast to the needs and requirements of the reality in which you live. This is redemptive. This will free you from the bondage of your mind. This will show you that your prison door is open and you need but step outside. Life exists outside.

To be free of the mind is to gain new eyes, to gain new ears, to touch with a new sensation and to see things with a clarity that could only escape you previously. Wisdom leads to this liberation. Yet it does not lead to one great enlightenment experience. It is something that builds every day and gives its gifts every day. It leads you on to meet greater challenges and opportunities which you could not meet before.

People only have so much time and energy for problem solving. If that time and energy is devoted to little things, it will be used up. If it is devoted to greater things, the little things will get resolved in the process. Little problems require little amounts of energy, and bigger problems require larger amounts of energy. By solving bigger problems, you will feel valued because you are doing something important.

People suffer because their lives lack meaning and necessity. Thus, God gives meaning and necessity. Meaning is found in real engagements with others which serve a real purpose that serves the evolution of the world. Whether this involves feeding people, building bridges or teaching The Greater Community Way of Knowledge, it all serves the same purpose. Service must happen at many different levels—at the personal level, at the family level, at the community level, at the national level and at the level of humanity.

We bring to you a challenge, an invitation, an affirmation and a recognition. As vast as it is and as great as it might seem, Greater Community Spirituality—when it is really experienced and when it is really employed—gives you a greater ability to deal with what is in front of you right now. You see what is small, and you recognize it as small. You see something that is great, and you recognize it as great. You do not call everything great; you do not call everything small. You recognize what is great and what is small, what requires a little of your time and what requires a great deal of your time.

Time well employed is time fulfilled. Time not well employed is time lost and wasted. You have only so much time in life; you have only so much ability in life. Where are your time and ability invested? Where are they given and what purpose do they serve? What part of you do they satisfy? Your personal mind, which is at the surface of your mind, is never satisfied. It must have more of everything. Its experience of happiness is momentary. It requires constant stimulation and acquisition in order to feel any kind of self-assurance because it only identifies with what it owns, both its physical possessions and its ideas, which its physical possessions are meant to validate.

Satisfy Knowledge within you and your life will be fulfilled. You will be given a new life, a greater life, a life that is simple and meaningful, a life that is powerful and effective, a life where you have real companions who are devoted to you and to whom you are devoted. And you will escape the great majority of the miseries that imprison everyone.

If you can make this journey and if you can choose this journey again and again, you will advance. If you quit, you will not advance. The journey is the way. You will only know it is the way if you travel it. Do not stand at the beginning and say, "Well, I'm not sure. Is this the way or should I do something else? Something else looks better. Something else looks quicker. Something else looks more pleasurable." Do not be deceived. You can only find the way if you travel it. The Way of Knowledge cannot be understood by standing outside of it and judging it. When people do that, they are only attempting to validate their ideas. Travel this journey and you will find out where it takes you. Where it takes you is to the truth that lives within you, to the truth that lives within others and to the truth that lives within the world. Then Greater Community Spirituality will make perfect sense to you because it will be obvious.

Once you gain this vantage point, you will see how clear it is and you will also see why you could not have seen it before.

God's first purpose is to unburden you in life so that a greater gift, a greater opportunity and a greater calling can be given to you. If your hands are full of your own necessities, how can you receive anything else? If your mind is filled to the brim with stimulating and exciting ideas, how can any real insight emerge or be given to you? First there must be an emptying out, a simplification, an unburdening. You don't have to carry all of this baggage through life—the baggage of your possessions and your ideas. You keep what is needed and what is truly meaningful, and other things are simply given away because they are seen as burdensome. Nothing is taken from you. There are no thieves on the path to truth. Truth only gives and restores, verifies and confirms what is true in your relationship with everything, and most fundamentally with yourself.

Who is Wisdom meant for? It is meant for you. Through you it is meant for others, and through them it will be passed on again. This is possible because Knowledge lives within each person and because Knowledge is recognized, valued, confirmed and experienced within the context of real and meaningful relationships. Though the world seems incomprehensible and dedicated to self-deception, dishonesty and destruction, the reality of Knowledge that lives within each person lives today at this moment. It is this reality that must be confirmed. It is this preparation in The Way of Knowledge that must be given and shared. Then what seemed impossible before becomes apparent and achievable. Then what seemed confusing and complex before becomes a simple path through a dangerous jungle.

The path you will follow is a simple path, but you will need to watch every step and be attentive to what is around you. In this way, you will move into life and through life, and you will have direction. You will be able to see everything around you with a greater understanding. And you will be able to see that which can move and that which cannot move, that which can advance and that which cannot advance, that which has purpose and that which does not have purpose. This can only be found by traveling the way. Therefore, the way is the answer.

—⚬∿∿⚬—

God works behind the scenes.

God gives opportunities.

God gives work, redemptive work.

God gives problems to solve

and directs you

towards the world's needs.

—⚬∿∿⚬—

CHAPTER NINE

HOW DOES GOD PARTICIPATE IN THE WORLD?

---❧❧❧---

$\mathcal{G}$OD'S PARTICIPATION IN THE WORLD is very pervasive but not easily recognized. People have great expectations of God once they accept that God is a reality. They expect God to solve their personal problems, to save them from their own calamities, to restore their loved ones when they are sick, to prevent death and difficulty for those whom they love, to bring about peace and equanimity amongst warring tribes, to effect sweeping change without upsetting anyone's concerns or priorities and to bring about miracles great and small, yet in such a way that no one is offended, no one is challenged and no one has to change. Given these kinds of expectations, which permeate your cultures and are part of most of the world's religions, it becomes very difficult to appreciate who God is and how God functions in the world.

Let us, then, give a new approach and a fresh understanding. However, before we do this, let us say that when we give a simple idea, it will not be simple to understand. The simpler the idea, the more difficult it is to integrate it, to experience it and to apply it. Therefore, what seems easy can be more difficult. The quick and easy way can be the most difficult. A simple idea is more difficult to fully penetrate and to comprehend. Let us give you a simple idea now.

God is reclaiming the separated through Knowledge. Said in another way, God is calling upon you, and you have an opportunity to respond, to respond at a deep level. God is calling upon God within you—the part of you that is a part of God, the part of you that is in intrinsic relationship with God and with all life, the part of you that contains your greater purpose, mission and destiny in the world, the part of you that can recognize your true allies, your true partners and your true endeavors in the world. If you're not in touch with or aware of this greater aspect of yourself, which is Knowledge, then God will seem very confusing and very complex. God will even seem contradictory. You may think, "Well, God promises peace, but where is the peace? God promises comfort, but where is the comfort? God promises reassurance, but where is the reassurance? I cannot see it around me; I do not feel it within me, so God must either be cruel, confused or weak."

God reclaims you within the context of relationship. You reclaim God within the context of relationship. Here you come back into relationship together. Your relationship with God was never over; it was simply denied and forgotten and other things came to take its place. You come into the world like an abandoned child. Through your experience here, you have an opportunity to recall the memory of those who sent you, members of your Spiritual Family, and their relationship with you, and the memory of your relationship with the Source of all relationships.

We teach the reclamation of Knowledge. This is experienced through the reclamation of relationships with others, for alone you cannot know anything. Alone your Knowledge will not be validated or verified. To be fully experienced, it must have an impact within the context of a real relationship—not a relationship with an idea, a theory or a principle but a relationship with another.

God works through Knowledge in you. God does not interfere because God is not really welcome here. People expect great things of the Divine—miracles, tremendous compassion and forgiveness—but they do not want any interference. Nobody wants a savior until they are desperate. Nobody wants freedom until they feel they are truly imprisoned. If God answered all your prayers, you would have to allow God to take over your life. God will not do that.

You can have a life here that is imaginary or a life that is real. God brings you back to the life that is real, the life that you can know, the life that you can embrace and devote yourself to. Without this there is no real devotion, there is no real commitment, there is no real understanding and there is no real security.

God does not intervene. To fully understand this, you would have to have a complete understanding of God. This is far beyond your capacity at this time and in this context of life. However, you can gain some appreciation for this when you see how much you do not want your plans and goals to be interfered with. Like adolescent children, people want to be able to do what they want to do with little or no interference. It is only when they get into trouble or are endangered or imperiled that they want intervention from their parents. They want their parents to bail them out or to rescue them or to pay their expenses, but this does not verify or recognize a real relationship. This is a form of dependency and rebellion. And there is a great deal of this dependency and rebellion in the world. This is made ever more complex by the fact that people use religion and their claimed relationship with the Divine as a justification for all kinds of acts of cruelty and attack. Thus, real religion is maligned, abused, compromised and invalidated because of its use by the ambitious and the fearful.

You cannot come to God as a beggar or as a thief because God does not know you as either of these. You must come as part of Creation, recognizing your own authority and your own place in life and recognizing the greater context into which you fit and of which you are a part. It takes a new kind of education to teach this to you and to help you to reclaim this awareness. To sit on the sidelines and expect or demand or appeal or cajole the Divine to intercede at your will, at your command, to be your servant and to fetch things for you, is so clearly ridiculous and so ignorant and presumptuous that you can see how false this is. You can see how nothing of any real value and merit can come from this approach and behavior.

God is at work in the world, working through Knowledge. God does not leave somewhere else and come here because God is God of the Greater Community. This is obvious. However, in the world's religions, this is not realized. Often it is assumed that God is preoccupied with this world to the exclusion of everything else. It is believed that there is God, the world and you. Everything else is just part of the background to this great drama between the human and the Divine.

However, God is God of the Greater Community, not only the Greater Community we have described but of all life everywhere. God does not come to pay special attention to the planet on which you live. God does not drop responsibilities elsewhere and become unusually concerned or preoccupied with human affairs, human demands or human expectations. God is at work everywhere reclaiming the separated through Knowledge. And the reclamation must come through Knowledge because Knowledge is what redeems you to yourself and to life.

Your personal mind cannot know God. Your personal mind can only yield to Knowledge within you, and Knowledge within you yields to Knowledge in the universe. Then everything is set into right order. And with right order comes real relationship. With real relationship comes a steady flow of communication. This is what enables you to be a contributor in the world. Then, you are not merely an individual running around trying to make things happen and trying to acquire things for yourself. You become a translator and a communicator for something greater. This is mysterious; it is beyond definition, even beyond the theologies of your world. It is pure. It is untainted. It cannot be used or harnessed for political or economic goals. It is everywhere. It is natural. It is pervasive. It cannot be corrupted by human interference. Human interference can only mislead the perceiver, but the essence of God's work is beyond human contamination and beyond the contamination of any race anywhere in the Greater Community. Understand this and you will be able to have a different approach to your relationship with the Divine and to the Divine presence and activity in the world.

How does God work in the world? What does this mean? What are some examples of this? God seeks to reclaim you unto yourself and to bring you back into your true relationship with life as it exists here and now in order to enable you to find your place in the world and to fulfill your specific role here. God amplifies Knowledge within you and calls you to return to Knowledge and to develop a relationship with Knowledge and a reverence for Knowledge. This restores your self-esteem. This also validates your authority, which you must exercise in order to approach a greater authority. You cannot simply give up your authority and try to yield to a Greater Power. This can never be effective.

If you are to represent the Divine, you must become a representative. You cannot come as a beggar. You cannot be passive. You cannot simply give yourself over. People try to do that because they are either too lazy or too unfocused to actually prepare for the role that they need to fulfill. They simply want God to do everything for them. This, of course, is impossible, for they must do most of the work. It is their efforts, their abilities and their accomplishments which they must experience, not God's.

Giving up all of your authority—thinking you cannot make a decision about anything or anyone, denying your own perception and experience and giving everything over to God—looks like a wonderful freedom and a wonderful escape, but it is not the way that will restore to you your true ability and your true value. God does not need glorification. It is you who need validation in the world. God is not driven by the ego desires that motivate people to establish their own self-importance. Do not think that God thinks like you or God will seem terrible and contradictory, cruel or impotent.

The disappointment and confusion that people have about the Divine is based on the projection that the Divine is thinking about life and about them the way that they are thinking about life and about themselves. God functions at the level of Knowledge, which is a different kind of mind and intelligence from your personal mind. It is not conniving. It is not treacherous. It is not self-indulgent. It is not selfish. It does not use others for personal advantage. It is not competitive. It does not debate. It does not wonder. It is not confused. It does not need to make decisions. It acts because it knows. And between times of action, it is silent and present. It has absolute certainty and is infinitely patient.

Knowledge will protect you—your personal mind and your body—but it will not prevent you from hurting yourself. Like God, it will not interfere when interference is unwelcome. Knowledge will provide all of the stimulation and all of the signs you need to make wise decisions and to choose wisely in your relationships. However, if you do not heed these signs and signals, if you do not listen, if you do not follow and if you are not able to respond, then Knowledge will not come and punish you. It will not criticize you. It will not banish you to hell. It will not condemn you, and it will not judge you. Knowledge will allow you to fail. Perhaps then you will come back to it again with greater sincerity, feeling a deeper need.

Knowledge is completely honest. It is without conflict or deception. Your personal mind has conflict and deception. When something that is purely honest is dealing with something that is dishonest, it requires great tact and care. If you want to know how God is working in the world, then follow the way to Knowledge, find your relationship with Knowledge and learn over time through many experiences how Knowledge is working in your life. Then, within the range of your real experience and not in the context of your speculation, you will come to see, understand and appreciate the incredible grace, power and pervasiveness of God's presence in the world.

You could say that God is working from the inside out, yet this is only partially true because God has agents in the world. God has emissaries—some of whom you can see and some of whom you cannot see. The Unseen Ones travel here and there, and they work with certain individuals who are showing great promise and with certain individuals who are well advanced on the path to Knowledge. They give their assistance in such a way that their presence goes largely unrecognized. This is God working in the world.

God works behind the scenes. God gives opportunities. God gives work, redemptive work. God gives problems to solve and directs you towards the world's needs. God does not come and fix things up for you as if you were a helpless little child. God teaches you how to fix things within your own realm, within the realm of human invention. Human life is a human invention. It is not a Divine invention. Human culture, human ethics, human beliefs, human economics, human politics, human relationships, human involvements—these are all human creations. They are not Divine creations. To bring Divinity into your creations, you yourself must introduce it. God is not in the middle of your dilemmas. God is outside of them. God calls you to leave them and offers you a way out, a way that restores your true abilities and your true relationships with yourself, with others and with the world.

God's way is wise and effective. Yet unless you become wise and effective, how can you appreciate it? At moments when you are wise and effective, you will appreciate it. At other times when you are not being wise and effective, you will either deny it or think it is something else. You know, many people think that God is using everything as a lesson for them as if God is pulling all the strings. When something good happens, it's a blessing from God. When something bad happens, it's a punishment from God. When something cruel or tragic happens, well, people are disappointed, and they secretly resent the Divine for being cruel and heartless. Then they try to justify it by saying, "Well, it was coming," or "They deserved it," or "Someone deserved it," or "It had to be," or "It is beyond our comprehension and we don't know."

God does not work in the world like this. The world contains a set of forces that are working on their own. God is here to teach you how to negotiate these forces and how to utilize them effectively. God is not pulling all the strings, determining everything that is happening to you today and everything that will happen tomorrow. The world is in motion, and all the myriad forces within its mental and physical environments are in motion. God is involved in present time in the world without controlling everything.

Rarely is there direct intervention. When this happens, it happens because it is welcome, because it is needed and because it would further restore relationship to the person or persons receiving it. Beyond this, God lets everything happen. The tragedies that you see around you and throughout the world do not represent the work of God. The world is a dangerous place. It has many risks. Anything can happen here. You need to be aware. God would teach you to be aware. God would teach you to have vision. God would teach you how to protect your mind and your body, how to develop your skills and how to use them effectively and constructively. This is God's work in the world. Without this relationship, you would be on your own, and you would suffer for this. However, there is greater assistance and assurance available to you. It is not a false assistance and it is not a false assurance. It is real. And it will work through you and for you if you welcome it and are open to it, if you are sincere and if you do not try to use it for your own personal goals or advantages.

God is at work everywhere in the world through Knowledge. God knows you. You can only know God. Believing in God may be preliminary to knowing God, but believing and knowing are not the same. Many people claim they believe in God, either because they believe or because they are afraid not to believe. However, to know God is to come into relationship with God. This takes a very long time. Here many things are unlearned, and new things are learned in their place. Here many old ideas are cast off, and new realizations emerge. Here old problems are approached in a new way. Here little things are kept little, and great things are kept great. Here you learn to say yes to certain things and no to others. Here you give up your allegiance to guilt, to compulsion, to the need for approval and to the need to take advantage of others in order to respond to a greater certainty that is slowly emerging within you.

God does not interfere because you need to experience your own value and relationships within the context in which you live. Whenever you experience real affinity or recognition with another, you are validating God. Whenever you do something that you realize is necessary and you do it for reasons that you cannot justify or understand, you are validating God. Whenever you heed an inner warning and take the necessary steps and follow what you know, you are validating God. This is an experience, not an idea. This is fundamental. It is not merely a belief, a convention or a convenience.

In coming into meaningful relationship with another, you will feel God. In telling the truth where truth needs to be told, you will feel God. In experiencing gratitude for something that has been done for you, even on a mundane level, you will feel God. This is how God is recognized and experienced. The rewards of this experience aren't only the experience itself but the relationships that are established, the actions that are taken, the difficulties that are avoided and the contributions that are made.

God wants you to work in the world to make good things happen here. God is not asking you to leave the world and to become mesmerized with God. God is saying, "You have important things to do. You came here to do them. I know it and you know it, so do what you know." You cannot return to your Ancient Home now. You have work in the world. You are learning about Knowledge, you are learning about The Way of Knowledge and you are preparing to take the steps to Knowledge.

Advance here and you will see that God is working in the world, and you will not hold God responsible for the mechanisms of life here. You will not hold God responsible for the tragedies that occur. You will not hold God responsible for human error. You will not hold God responsible for the creation of religions, beliefs and authorities. You will realize that God is working within you and engaging you meaningfully with others. This can only be appreciated as it is experienced.

You may consider yourself a religious person or not, but you still have an opportunity to reclaim your relationship with God through the reclamation of your relationships with others. As you experience Knowledge within yourself, you will verify the true relationship of your body to your mind and your mind to your spirit. As you experience true affinity in relationship with another and experience a greater purpose together, you will validate and verify your purpose for coming into the world. This is how the memory of your Ancient Home is restored to you. This is how you return to Knowledge within yourself. And this is how you feel the presence of God with you, the presence of your Teachers, the Unseen Ones, and the presence of your true companions in life—those who have gathered to help you to carry out your mission and your purpose as you slowly realize what it is and where it needs to take you.

We are not asking you to believe but to know. There is no devotion in belief. People believe because they are afraid not to. People believe because they think they must. However, no devotion, no commitment and no relationship come out of belief. Belief is always weak and faltering. It is easily assailed by the difficulties of life. The only value of belief is to restore to you your conviction that Knowledge is alive and well and that your faith in it is justified. The value of belief is to fill in the spaces between those moments when you experience Knowledge and real relationship. Belief and Knowledge, however, are not the same. Real devotion and commitment can only arise from Knowledge because Knowledge is completely devoted and completely committed. It is committed to God. It is committed to carrying out your purpose in life. It is committed to the well-being of others. It is committed already. Returning to relationship with Knowledge, you will learn to become committed to Knowledge as Knowledge is committed to you.

Any relationship where commitment has not been established and accepted is a relationship that has not yet established itself. Think how rare real devotion and commitment are in human relationships. People need each other, cling to each other, control each other and won't let each other go, but this is not devotion or commitment. Devotion and commitment are something that come from within you. They are a natural outpouring of your spirit. They are an expression of Knowledge. They are a recognition of your place and role with another. They emphasize a greater purpose beyond your personal interests. They emphasize your well-being and the well-being of the other person and demonstrate this. Think how rare this is in human relationships where people attempt to use each other for personal reasons, and think of all of the unhappiness and all of the difficulties that result.

Relationships based upon Knowledge are very different. You will not have many of them. They will be unique, and there will be a great contrast between them and all the other kinds of relationships that you have experienced—relationships for convenience, relationships for advantage, relationships for pleasure, relationships for acquisition. There is no devotion, no commitment, no recognition and no real affinity in these relationships. How different is a relationship based upon Knowledge and what a different result it creates. When you experience real devotion or when you recognize it being experienced genuinely by anyone else, you will see the evidence of God in the world. Devotion is the highest expression of love. It is love's most complete expression. It is where a person chooses to give themselves to someone to carry on a greater purpose and to serve something more magnificent than their own personal interests—whether it be raising a family, carrying on a form of work in the world or fulfilling a mission in service to humanity. At whatever level it is expressed, this is something rare and wonderful in life. This is the evidence of God's work.

While many people are expecting or demanding God to come forth for them and to give them what they desire, you can begin to see behind the scenes the real work of God—the work of God that restores people's relationship with themselves and with each other. All the great things that have been given to humanity are the result of relationships that are meaningful and purposeful where devotion has been experienced and expressed. Great individuals—great creators, great inventors, great scientists, great spiritual leaders—all had tremendous relationships behind them, both in the visible and the invisible realms. Their ideas did not come from them. They came from beyond the world and were translated through them into the world in a form that could be recognized and used.

What is genius but a mind that is connected to a Greater Mind? Being smart or witty, clever or quick, are not signs of intelligence. People will say, "Well, my friend is doing such a foolish thing, but he is such a bright person. He's such a smart person." But that person is doing something very foolish or damaging. Is this an expression of intelligence? No. Intelligence emerges from Knowledge. It is the ability to see, to know and to act. It is the ability to carry on an activity or action in the world effectively. Intelligence is Knowledge and Wisdom working together. It is the truth and the mechanism for expressing truth working in harmony together. This is an expression of intelligence. You have this intelligence. It is born of Knowledge within you. And you can experience it. It demonstrates a Greater Power and a greater possibility for humanity.

As we are telling you these things, perhaps you will realize that advancement for humanity, in whatever field you might consider, has been the result of the efforts of a relatively small number of people who were committed, who were devoted and who had great allies. This is the evidence of God's work in the world. In spite of all of the calamities and all of the tragedies, all of the addictions and all of the difficulties that prey and prevail upon humanity and human relationships, the work of God carries humanity forward. If God were not in the world, humanity would simply destroy itself. There would be no motivation for greater things. There would be no yearning for truth. There would be no real kindness. There would be no real dedication or recognition. Humanity would destroy itself.

God is like the air. Everyone breathes the air, but few pay any attention to it. Everyone is sustained every moment with every breath. Their bodies depend upon each breath in order to live in the next moment. Cut off this supply of air and the person dies quickly and everything comes to an end. God is like that—so pervasive, so present, so supportive and so nourishing. And yet God is not recognized, God is not understood, God is not revealed and God is not experienced. God is, of course, greater than the air that you breathe. However, this example can help you understand what we are saying. What we are presenting here is beyond the normal range of human understanding. You must stretch, open yourself and reach high to have this awareness. This leads to the true experience.

Become a student of Knowledge. Learn The Way of Knowledge. Take the steps to Knowledge. Let Knowledge rearrange your priorities. Let Knowledge straighten your life out. Let Knowledge guide, direct and protect you. Let Knowledge foster a greater intelligence within you. Let Knowledge direct you in your relationships and in your evaluations. Become still like Knowledge. Become penetrating like Knowledge. Become insightful like Knowledge. Become devoted to others like Knowledge. Find your true allies. Find your purpose. Allow your true work in the world to emerge as other things are set aside—willingly, happily and with relief.

As you make progress here, God's presence in the world will become something that you will feel and know, rather than something that you struggle to believe in. And in spite of all the tragedies and difficulties that you and others may face and all of the tribulations of physical life, you will know that God is with you. You will know that you are headed towards God, and you will know that you have something important to do. You will know this because God is in the world.

—⁓⁓—

Do not look at the mountain and say,

"I know a better way up this mountain!"

You have never been

on this mountain before.

—⁓⁓—

CHAPTER TEN

HOW DO YOU PREPARE?

——⁓⁓——

*E*DUCATION IN THE GREATER COMMUNITY WAY OF KNOWLEDGE is quite unique. It calls upon a different kind of intelligence within you and creates a pathway to this intelligence that is quite distinct from your normal forms of education. Here you do not set about to remember facts and figures, equations and details. Here you seek to wed your intellect with your deeper mind, the mind we call Knowledge. Here the emphasis is on developing stillness and the ability to focus on things objectively— two very high functions of the mind.

Because Knowledge does not think like your personal mind, there has to be a bridge built between them. Building this bridge enables Knowledge to communicate to you and enables you to receive its guidance, its blessings and its protection. Without this bridge, you will feel like you are split between your personal mind, which thinks one way and wants certain things, and Knowledge, which thinks in a different way and has a greater purpose than the personal mind. Building this bridge represents the purpose of education in The Greater Community Way of Knowledge.

To prepare, you will need several significant things. First, you will need the correct preparation. You cannot use human spirituality, human philosophy, human idealism and human motivations to attain a

Greater Community understanding of Knowledge. Instead, you will need a unique form of education, which we are providing for you here. Human wisdom and human understanding will only take you so far. This is a greater mountain to climb. You will need a special focus, a map and a pathway in order to undertake the great preparation in The Way of Knowledge. In addition, you will need the correct curriculum, instruction, attitude, companions and way of evaluating your progress.

As we have mentioned, the curriculum is vital. You must take the correct way up the mountain or you will lose your way; you will come to a dead end and find yourself meandering about, not certain where you are going. The curriculum that we are providing is designed specifically to enable men and women to gain a greater understanding of life—a Greater Community understanding and perspective, which establish a greater vantage point from which to see yourself and others with compassion and understanding.

If you alter the curriculum or try to marry it to other things you are accustomed to or to things that you appreciate, you will not find the correct way, and you will not progress. You must follow the way as it is given—without altering it, without deleting anything and without adding on things that you learned before. In fact, here you must really begin as a beginner. Forget what you have learned. Leave aside your ideas and your philosophy. Do not try to make this new education the same as something else. Do not try to make it continuous with something else. You cannot learn a Greater Community Way of Knowledge based upon a previous education. You must start from the beginning and be a beginner. This approach is the wisest one, for this enables you to proceed with an open mind and to escape the limitations that your assumptions, beliefs and attitudes will certainly place upon you.

The correct curriculum requires the correct attitude. The correct attitude is one of a beginner. If you have a beginner's mind, you will have an open mind. Here you will be able to see things as they are and not as you think they must be or prefer them to be. Here there is a great distinction between an education in Knowledge and the education that you have found in the world. In the world, you always build upon what you have learned in the past, adding new things as you go along. As you advance, you become more selective in what you learn because you want to validate what you have learned already. Thus, the intent of education, which is to learn something new, to experience something new and to be able to do something new, becomes lost because increasingly you will attempt to validate the past. Here you will become more fearful and anxious about the future, less willing to see things as they really are and less open to new ideas, new experiences and new capabilities. Here the mind closes down upon itself. It often does this with the belief that it is open and accessible when in fact it has become such a filtering mechanism that very little new information can come to it, either from within or from without.

How different is The Way of Knowledge. How different is the preparation in learning Greater Community Knowledge and Wisdom. Here you must start from the beginning and constantly set aside things you think you understand, things that you believe in, things that you believe have to be in the world and things you hold true about yourself, others and life in general. You must keep opening yourself to something new. What you will experience will confirm Knowledge within you and open new arenas of experience to you. Here you will find yourself venturing into the unknown with only Knowledge and the strength of your companions to assure you. This open attitude is essential throughout your preparation. As soon as you think you fully understand the curriculum and can define it for yourself and others, your progress will stop. Here you can make some very dangerous and unhappy conclusions.

Learning a Greater Community Way of Knowledge is a great undertaking and preparation. You cannot study it for a few weeks or a few months or a few years and master it. That is why we say there are no masters in the world. There are only proficient students. Therefore, seek to become a proficient student, which will indeed make you seem masterful to others. However, as soon as you think that you have arrived and that your education is complete, your studenthood will come to an end, and your mind will begin to close in upon itself. You will stop where you are and begin to slide backwards.

You can see the evidence of this in the self-proclaimed leadership of many people who profess to know great things and have great methodologies. However, unless their minds are fresh and open, unless they are pliable and can adapt to new experiences, these people become increasingly fixated upon the past and increasingly defensive about their own position and understanding. As a result, they become increasingly selective about what they will experience and less and less open to life, to relationship, to Knowledge and to real Wisdom.

The correct attitude must also include the willingness to correct anything that obstructs the reclamation of Knowledge—those beliefs, those attitudes, those ambitions, those cherished needs and those personal demands that infringe on and limit your ability to experience life as it is, as it will be the next moment and as it is destined to be in the future. This takes great courage and a desire for honesty. Indeed, this far exceeds most people's definition of and boundaries for honesty. Here you must continue to push the boundary of honesty and come back to what you know, which is distinct from what you want or believe. This is an act of personal integrity and a statement of real honesty.

You must love the truth more than anything else, and your love of the truth must grow. You must be able to feel the truth as distinct from other forms of stimulation—self-validation, pleasure, fulfillment or anything else—for the truth has its own experience, which is unique. As you are able to identify it, value it and experience it again and again, you will want to return to it. Here you learn to make your own wise decisions, and as you learn to make your own wise decisions, you will be able to help others to make wise decisions for themselves.

Because the preparation is so great and requires so much time and patience, we encourage you to go slowly and consistently. We encourage you to practice daily but without a sense of urgency or impatience. There are many things you must learn the first year. There are many things you must learn the next year, the year after and the year after that. You cannot see what is up ahead for you to learn.

Beginning students always think that they are on the verge of accomplishment. Intermediate students think they are on the verge of mastery. Advanced students realize they are on the verge of simply learning the next step. This represents a mature attitude, an attitude that recognizes the challenge, the difficulty, the need and the reward. You must advance far enough to gain this mature approach. Advanced age in life does not guarantee this mature approach. Advancement in The Way of Knowledge and advancement in true preparation are the only things that can assure this. This will show you the true lessons in life and how difficult they are to learn, how necessary they are to learn and what the results of learning them are. Your experience will confirm this.

This will put you in a position to wisely counsel others. This is why only an advanced student in The Way of Knowledge can teach The Way of Knowledge. Many people want to pass on everything they are learning as soon as possible, and this is understandable. However, do not claim real comprehension, for the Mystery will exceed your understanding, always. When you can be immersed in the Mystery, you can represent the Mystery. Then you can teach in a whole new way. Then you will understand why the preparation in The Greater Community Way of Knowledge is unique among all other forms of education. Yet even in the uniqueness of this education—its unique goal and the greater dimensions of reality that it will expose you to—it holds in common many things that you have learned already in the world. Let us illustrate this now.

Education requires a wise instructor, someone who is competent and who understands the learning process at hand. You can only take yourself so far. Even when you try to teach yourself simple and mechanical things, you make yourself vulnerable to grave error, and it takes much more time and energy to advance. It is better to assign yourself to a capable and competent instructor. If you attempt to learn the way yourself, you will take a very slow and difficult path. In fact, many people choose to do this because they are too afraid to work with an instructor, or because they have grandiose ideas about themselves and think that an instructor is not necessary and that they can learn on their own. Some people do not want to commit the time and resources to their education substantially enough to engage with an instructor, when a true instructor will in fact save them time and energy and preserve their resources for the future. You have learned this already. To learn an athletic sport, to learn an art, to learn any kind of skill requires wise instruction. Someone must show you, and someone must correct you as you proceed and try things out for yourself.

Your education has also taught you that you must practice what you seek to learn. How obvious this is and yet how much it escapes so many people who attempt to find a quick and easy way to bypass the years of work that are required to build an awareness and to lay a foundation for Wisdom. People say, "Give me the answer. Show me the method. Give me the secret. I can use it. I understand it. I will not fail with it." How foolish this is and how unwise.

For example, if you want to learn a technical skill, you must practice and study. You must have a good instructor. You must have your direction and purpose clarified as you go along. You must take a path where you can mature in your skill and understanding. Reading a book or going to a class can only introduce you to the preparation. They are not the preparation itself. Only a book that contains the actual practices can take you into the preparation and further you and advance you there. Yet you will still need instruction. You will still need to associate with those who are wiser and more advanced than you are. And you will need to associate with those who are less advanced than you are. Those more advanced can pass on their Wisdom and help save you time and energy. Those less advanced can benefit from the results of your accomplishments and thus validate and verify the importance of your endeavor.

Your education has already taught you, then, that you need wise instruction and that you need to practice. Your practice must be consistent, diligent, patient and effective. Do not think that you can master things that are important in a short period of time. If you do, you will end up taking the long and difficult road. Do not look at the mountain and say, "I know a better way up this mountain!" You have never been on this mountain before. You do not know what it is like at its higher altitude. You do not know what the requirements are. You do not know what impact the environment will have on you. You do not know the way. And yet how many people scramble feverishly, trying to carve their own way and end up getting stuck, unable to proceed.

Your education in the world has shown you another truth that is applicable here. You must immerse yourself in your preparation in order to advance, to comprehend and to learn the application of whatever skill you are attempting to understand and to become competent at. You cannot dabble with this and dabble with that and do a little of this and do a little of that. If you are to become a student of a Greater Community Way of Knowledge, it will require all of your attention. Not only will you have to master and understand human Wisdom, you will have to learn Greater Community Wisdom. However, every little bit that you advance towards a Greater Community understanding will make you more effective, more capable, more gracious and more compassionate as a person. You will be more able to help others with the simple problems in life and with the greater problems in life.

You need this immersion. You cannot study and engage in this preparation while trying to learn three or four other things that you also think are very important and then try to bring them all together. Paths go off in different directions. You cannot follow them all at once. There are many ways up the mountain, but you must follow one and stay with it. If you get onto another track, well, you don't know where that one goes.

You do not know where you are going in life, but Knowledge within you knows. Knowledge will engage you with those who are wiser and those who are less wise. And when you are ready, Knowledge will bring you to the preparation and the curriculum of study that you will need in order to advance.

Knowledge will lead you to those individuals who can become the real companions in your life, companions in a greater endeavor in life. These relationships transcend the personal emphasis that people give in their relationships. These are greater relationships where devotion and commitment, deeper understanding and greater validation can be found. You will need these companions because you cannot learn The

Greater Community Way of Knowledge alone, for the truth is you are not alone. You must learn this truth, and it must be demonstrated to you in the most tangible ways possible.

Many people, however, still want to go alone. They do not want to become involved with others because they are afraid to join anything. They do not want to be around anyone who is more advanced because they do not want their limitations, their weaknesses and their false assumptions to be revealed to them. They would rather go alone, making their own decisions and having their own conclusions. How hopeless this is.

Life is bringing you back into relationship with yourself, with others, with the world and with God. How can you advance if you refuse to enter relationship, to share your understanding, to have your errors corrected and to enter into a different and greater venture that far exceeds what you alone can know and understand as an individual?

Knowledge within you requires Knowledge within others to bring about any kind of positive results in the world because Knowledge is fully revealed within the context of relationship. This is where things are known and verified. This is where things are acted upon and given meaning in the world. This is an expression of Wisdom. To think that you can learn and accomplish things on your own is not wise. You as an individual can do very little, but the truth is you are not alone, and you must learn this truth.

Knowledge will engage you with those whom you need to be engaged with. It will bring into your life those that you need to meet. Some of them will demonstrate error to you, to help clarify things for you and to sober your mind. Others will come with the capacity to join you in your journey. There will be a greater dimension of relationship here, something you could never have found before—something that gives permanence, meaning, a deeper resonance, a greater capability and a joining of two resources of mind into the meaningful direction of relationship.

Both in learning things in the world and in learning The Greater Community Way of Knowledge, you need the ability to evaluate things correctly. This must come from maturity. For example, if you are learning to play the piano, in order to evaluate yourself correctly, you must become fairly advanced in your study. You must be able to see clearly what is correct and what is not correct. This will be based largely upon your experience with an instructor who has taught you these evaluative skills. This will be based upon your own failures in performance and in practice, which have shown you where you need to improve. Eventually, you will be able to hear the errors yourself and see where the improvement needs to be made.

Only an advancing student can develop these kinds of skills. A beginner cannot. How can beginners fully evaluate what needs to be improved in their development? They may realize that they are not doing very well. They may know that they are not very accomplished, for they are constantly coming up against their disabilities and making many gross errors. However, to refine and perfect their study requires a mature approach. Gaining a mature approach requires time and energy and will be the result of their sharing themselves with those who are more advanced who can teach them these evaluative skills and give them a greater sensitivity.

Developing these skills also depends upon whom you share your study with. They will demonstrate both error and accomplishment to you in ways that you can see and understand. For example, a student of piano must listen to many other students' attempts to play in order to gain a more critical ear and a deeper sensitivity to what is harmonious and to what is not, to what is effective and to what is not. This refines their awareness and sensitivity.

How true this is in learning The Greater Community Way of Knowledge. In the Greater Community, advanced races have recognized that no individual can have complete Knowledge or Wisdom. Everyone needs what is called Verication, which is a process of reviewing decisions and conclusions with Knowledge. Verication is necessary because everyone is capable of making terrible mistakes. Everyone in physical life needs this. Anyone who attempts to claim ultimate Wisdom or who thinks that they can correct themselves effectively on a consistent basis is making a grave and serious error and is demonstrating that they have not yet gained true maturity in their understanding and studenthood.

In the Greater Community, Verication is essential for success. It both requires and develops relationships of real meaning and value. It requires that you be committed to the people who are committed to you. It requires that you be committed to Knowledge together, that you serve a greater purpose together and that you have a greater enterprise, a greater goal, together.

We teach this and we emphasize this because nothing great can be done alone and all errors occur because someone is acting without Knowledge. Here the quality of your companionship and your desire for truth are fundamental for your success. One bad advisor can damage or obstruct your progress and lead you astray. Choose well here. How can you choose well? Those who advance in The Way of Knowledge must be advancing in their maturity and understanding. Yet those who cannot or will not advance are doing so for personal reasons. Be aware and be careful with them.

As you become more skillful, you will need a higher and higher quality of Verication. You will need stronger and stronger companions. You can give to those who are less developed than you are, but you cannot rely upon their Wisdom. Here your relationships become more and more important. That is why we say there is no mastery in the world, because when people think of mastery, they think that they can reach an end point in education where they become infallible. Here demagoguery, totalitarianism and fanaticism of all kinds bring unhappiness and misery upon people in the world.

Your errors become more costly as you become more advanced, and you will need to be more guarded against them. Here is where you will need a community of Knowledge—a network of relationships that are able to vericate for you and bring you back to Knowledge to offset your personal conflicts, which will still be plaguing you as you advance. Here your interdependence with others will become the foundation of your relationships, and here interdependence will become fully established.

As a master musician needs to associate with other master musicians, you must seek to associate with those who are advanced in Knowledge, for they can vericate for you. They will be able to understand your nature and your purpose, your difficulties and your challenges, things which others will not be able to see and fully comprehend.

These are some things that you have already seen in your own education. Perhaps you have not fully experienced them, but if you look and see, you will understand that the correct curriculum, the correct attitude, the right instructor, the right companions and the ability to evaluate your own progress are all essential. If you have ever gone beyond a beginning level in learning anything, you have seen that there are new thresholds in learning and new requirements for learning. We call upon your experience and recognition here, but we don't expect you to fully understand the meaning of this within the context of learning a Greater Community Way of Knowledge. Remember, if you think that you can learn this great preparation without wise guidance, without the correct curriculum, without the right attitude, without good companions and without evaluative skills, you will be deceiving yourself.

The Greater Community Way of Knowledge is not something that you learn in a weekend, or a week or a month or a year. It is not something that you can fully comprehend in a book. It is far greater. It is so much greater, and yet its greatness is what returns greatness to you. Seek to do what is easy, comfortable and familiar and you will stay right where you are, bound to the past and bound to all the deceptions that have plagued you in the past, unable to proceed, unable to advance, unable to learn and unable to accomplish what you came here to accomplish.

Your calling is great because your purpose is great. Your purpose is great because your nature is great. Your nature is great because your Creator is great. Do not be discouraged, then, but allow yourself to be challenged and challenge yourself. You came here to learn. You came here to accomplish something. Why take the easy and comfortable way? That only leads to a great failure at the end of your life, a failure that will cause you much distress and unhappiness throughout your life. There is no comfort in comfort. There is no escape in escape. There is no relief in passivity. There is no luxury in luxury. Unless you can fulfill your mission and purpose here, a misery will attend you that no amount of pleasure, luxury, avoidance, comfort or passivity can allay.

Prepare, then, with the right curriculum, the right attitude, the right instructor, the right companions and the right evaluative skills. The correct attitude is based upon your feeling your deeper need, which is necessary even at the outset. You need to learn, and your learning must take you beyond the conventions of human education, which are limited and specific. To learn something greater about life and to do something greater in life require a different kind of preparation.

We have mentioned some of the things that are similar between learning things in the world and learning The Greater Community Way of Knowledge. How about those things that are different? The difference here is that you will enter Mystery. Here you cannot take your prior learning with you. Only a little bit of your prior experience can help you now. Here you cannot rely upon your philosophy. You cannot rely upon your sense of who you are. And you cannot rely upon your ideas or your ideals. All that you can rely upon is the remembrance of how things are learned and what is needed in learning. Here you shift your reliance from your ideas to reliance upon Knowledge itself. Ideas seem tangible. You can control them. However, Knowledge is not tangible. You cannot control it.

Entering the Mystery takes great faith—faith in yourself, faith in Knowledge and faith in the Greater Power of the universe that has sent you here. This faith is necessary at the outset. It is the thing that you need before real certainty can be developed and relied upon on a consistent basis. Here you learn to rely upon the Mystery and not upon tangible things. Here you ask the Mystery to give you that which you need in the tangible world rather than asking the tangible world to give you what you need to function in the world of Mystery. Here your education is very different, and your experience is very different. Instead of adding on and adding on more information, more ideas, more experiences, more methods and more conclusions, you keep opening yourself to the unknown. You keep asking Knowledge to take you into new arenas, and you do not attempt to govern or control the process.

Your discipline here needs to be in learning to discern the way—discerning the lessons that have to be learned, discerning the relationships that you come in contact with, and discerning your own motivations as you proceed. This is a great enough requirement in and of itself. How few have been successful here. So do not ask for more, and do not expect more. When we give you a challenge, it will be quite sufficient in terms of engaging your time and energy. It will be quite sufficient in relieving you of the burdens, complaints and confusion that belittle you and keep you bound to old ideas and old ways of doing things.

Learning The Greater Community Way of Knowledge takes you to a greater certainty within you. You cannot rely upon your ideas or your conclusions, for they may be true in this moment but not true in the next. They may be applicable in this situation but not applicable in that situation. They may have served you well before, but they may be ineffective in what you are facing now. Therefore, in learning, do not rely upon previous conclusions.

Become a beginning student. Open yourself. Assume nothing. This makes you really available. This makes it possible to give you instruction. This makes it possible for you to learn from instruction. This teaches you what you must learn in order to help others in life. And you will see from your own experience as you progress that those who are full of presumptions, ideas and beliefs about themselves and life are inaccessible and ineffective in learning new things.

Therefore, learning a Greater Community Way of Knowledge requires courage because you must risk your ideas. You must risk your conclusions. And you must be willing to proceed even at times when you feel very uncertain about yourself or what you are doing. The Way of Knowledge takes you from one stage of certainty to a greater certainty and then on to an even greater certainty. These are all thresholds of experience. As you pass through one, you go through a period where you feel like you do not know anything. This is where new experiences and new understanding can emerge, but you must allow this to happen.

It is like the farmer planting the fields. After each harvest, the field must be plowed under, and everything looks bleak and empty. There is no produce. There is no harvest. There is no evidence of any bounty. Everything must be replanted and started all over again so that next year there may be new and different harvests, and life may continue.

This is how it will be in your education in The Greater Community Way of Knowledge. Instead of accumulation, there will be release and freedom. Education that only accumulates ideas, beliefs and experiences gluts the mind and prevents it from learning new things. An education in Knowledge, however, keeps opening your mind. It is as if you were going from a smaller room of understanding into a greater room of understanding, and from that great room of understanding into an even greater room of understanding. As you pass from the familiar environment of your current understanding into a greater context, you will feel like you do not know anything. You have not yet defined yourself within this greater context. You do not yet understand its dimensions. And you do not know what awaits you there.

It is openness, courage and greater motivation in learning that will carry you through. Here you will find a great truth in life: Only Knowledge can take you to Knowledge, and only Wisdom can take you to Wisdom. Your personal reasons for following The Greater Community Way of Knowledge will run out when you see that it will not give you more money, more love or greater advantages in life—advantages that you define in terms of your own personal goals. Here you will have to choose again, and what will enable you to keep going is Knowledge itself. Then you will see that your former goals were small and selfish and could never satisfy you. Yet you can only see this as you advance and become mature in your evaluative abilities. When you have become honest and objective with yourself, then you will have reached a state of maturity in your evaluation. This is a great accomplishment in and of itself and will take a long time to achieve. However, its rewards are so great, so valuable and so lasting that there is nothing else in the world that can compare with it.

You have before you a mysterious preparation. However, like all forms of education, it requires certain fundamental things. Here you can call upon your previous experience to remind yourself of what is essential, what you must choose and what you must accept as a student. Beyond this, however, you are entering into a new realm. Only a Greater Community Way of Knowledge can teach you Greater Community Spirituality. Here you must be willing to go beyond the boundaries of human thinking, human beliefs and human assumptions. Here you will enter into a new and greater arena of learning in life where your previous assumptions and beliefs do not hold and do not fit. You must leave them at the door before entering a greater room, a greater context and a greater experience.

It is the ability to be empty and open and to cast away ideas that you have relied upon that will enable you to truly advance and become a light in the world, a light that can shine ever more brightly. What are ideas but expedient things that have temporary value? What are beliefs but things that can help you see and function better in life as it is occurring now? Yet these things must be changeable, or they will prevent you from being open to life and will work against you once their usefulness is over. Like a set of clothes, they wear out and you must have new garments, and these garments must be appropriate for the conditions that you are facing and for your experience of yourself. Do not look at your garments and say, "This is who I am. I am how I dress." Do not do that. Likewise, do not look at your ideas and beliefs and say, "This is who I am because this is what I believe. This is who I am because this is what I think." Your thoughts will change and will need to change. Allow them to change. They are temporary expedients. They are like prescription glasses that help you see, yet as your vision changes, you will need to get a new prescription. If you don't, your ability to see will decline, and you will become ever more blind to the world.

What is permanent within you is Knowledge. Your intellect is a vehicle for Knowledge. It is temporary. Knowledge is the permanent and the immortal part of you. To find a permanent life, you must venture beyond your temporary life. To find a permanent intelligence, you must be willing to pass through your temporary intelligence. Accept what is permanent and what is temporary here. This will give you great freedom and flexibility in life. It will enable greater things to be learned because your mind will be growing in its scope and capacity, your desire for education will be growing, and you will be a person who is fresh and young at heart instead of old and defensive.

All these things are part of your preparation. Use what you have learned, but let your ideas and conclusions be flexible. Let your understanding of yourself be flexible, for it will most assuredly change and expand as you advance in learning a Greater Community Way of Knowledge. Your sense of yourself will go from being a member of your family to being a member of your community or network of friends to being a member of the world and finally to being a member of the Greater Community. What a tremendous expansion this is and what a greater vantage point in life this will give you. How far you will be able to see then. How much you will be able to know. And how great will be your assistance to others who seek to learn and to know. You cannot fulfill your purpose as you are now. You cannot understand your nature as you are now. You cannot see the world as you are now. And you cannot discern your relationships as you are now. To do these you need a greater vantage point. You need to be far above where you are now so that you can look down and really see the lay of the land.

Therefore, the answer to your desire for truth, honesty, resolution, peace and accomplishment—however you may wish to express and define it—must be a means for you to reach a greater vantage point in life. You cannot stay where you are and simply have answers or good ideas. You must move to a different position in life. You must have a greater intelligence within you. You must have a deeper point of reference, a deeper awareness within yourself. Using the analogy of the mountain, you must climb above where you are now to look and see where you are and to understand your situation. Then you will be able to move forward.

To advance, you cannot stay at the bottom of the mountain and fantasize how it will be and imagine yourself going up and being at the top. The experience will always be different from imagination. The experience will be its own initiation. Stay at the bottom of the mountain and you will never know the mountain. Stay in your thoughts and your ideas, and you will never understand what real purpose, meaning and direction in life are. Protect your ideas, and they will hold you where you are, but Knowledge will take you beyond your ideas to a greater understanding, a greater vantage point and into a greater arena of life.

We offer the path to the Greater Community. You are able to learn this, and you can understand this even being a citizen of your world. You do not need to travel about the universe, for there are indeed many races who do travel about the universe, but they have not learned The Way of Knowledge. They see, but they do not know. And they are prone to the same errors as you are, even though their comprehension of the universe is greater and their technology and methods of transport are more advanced. We are speaking of something that will give you an advantage in your life in the world and an advantage even in the Greater Community. In the Greater Community technology is not the prize. Power is not the prize. Advantage is not the prize. Domination is not the prize. The prize is Knowledge and Wisdom. This is fulfillment. And this is what you need in the world right now.

—⟊⟊⟊—

You have a pressing need

to elevate yourself,

to unify your race,

to restore your environment

and to speak as one voice

in the Greater Community.

—⟊⟊⟊—

CHAPTER ELEVEN

WHAT IS YOUR PREPARATION FOR?

———✥✥✥———

HE GREATER COMMUNITY WAY OF KNOWLEDGE is a very great preparation. It is great because it meets a great need in the world. You have come into the world at a time of tremendous change and challenge. It is not an easy time to be in the world, but if contribution is your purpose and intention, it is the right time to be in the world.

You have come at a great turning point. It is not the beginning of a new age. It is the beginning of a great transition, a transition from tribal culture into a world community and into interaction with the Greater Community, of which your world is a small part. You have not come here to live a normal life under quiescent circumstances. You have not come here to retire, to go into repose or to live a life of quiet meditation. You have come to serve a world whose needs are immense and pressing and whose time has come for a greater encounter with life beyond its borders.

Perhaps you consider yourself to be unfortunate because you have come at such a time. However, if you think clearly about everything we have said thus far, you will indeed see that life is giving you exactly what you need to redeem Knowledge within yourself and to reclaim your true power and ability. You do this not necessarily because you want to but because it is needed. Great things are never achieved because people want them. Great things are achieved because people need them. Want and need are very different. There is not enough power, dedication, determination and perseverance in wanting something. There must be a *need* within you—something you must do, something you must have, something you must accomplish. It is this greater incentive that gives you true power and ability and keeps you on track regardless of the circumstances or situations that you might encounter.

You have come at a great time. You have come to give important things. Congratulations! The Greater Community Way of Knowledge is given to you to enable you to prepare. What you are preparing for is greater than what your parents or your grandparents had to face. Therefore, a new teaching and a new vision must be given for you to fully appreciate the situation that you are encountering here. You cannot rely upon your ancestors' gathered Wisdom and learned experience because you must have an even greater capacity now. Therefore, when we speak of the great preparation, we relate this to the greatness of the time in which you have come.

Do not seek for the world to give you what you want, for that is the path of disappointment and disillusionment. Instead, seek for the opportunity to contribute something greater to a world that needs what you have, for indeed you have what the world needs. The world has what you need only insofar as it can give you the opportunity to give, to engage yourself fully and to avoid the little preoccupations, addictions and difficulties that keep people in chains here. Your role will not be grandiose; it will be simple. In almost all circumstances, you will work behind the scenes quietly and without recognition. This is necessary to protect you and to protect your gift from contamination, misuse or exploitation by others.

What are you preparing for? You are preparing for a world that must establish a world community. You are preparing as a race to encounter intelligent life from beyond the world and to become engaged and involved, inadvertently, in a larger scheme of affairs, conflicts and interactions that are occurring in this part of the Greater Community. You are like villagers in a distant forest who all of a sudden find themselves in the midst of greater interactions between exploring and invading nations. Your village will never be the same. You cannot return to an earlier, more isolated existence where human beings only had other human beings to contend with. Now your problems are greater, but your opportunities are greater as well. Therefore, your incentive to learn and to develop must be great.

This is not a time for confusion, ambivalence or complacency. This is a time to meet a greater challenge. This is a time to prepare yourself for things you cannot even comprehend. This is a time to follow Knowledge and to regain your true power and direction, which are yours to reclaim and which are needed now for you to begin the preparation.

You are preparing to be in a world in great transition. It is not a world where everything will be torn apart. It is not a world where nature will destroy itself or the world will be dashed and devastated. It is not a world where angels will come and rescue humanity. Leave these fantasies and these fearful and hopeful dreams aside. Be clear, open and honest. Be attentive to what is happening so that you may see things as they really are and experience their reality.

You are preparing to be in a world where humanity must unify itself. It must do this because this is its evolution. Its evolution is being fueled by greater forces both in the world and in the Greater Community which will determine the direction and development of your race. Your evolution is being determined by the Greater Community, for you are in preparation for the Greater Community. The world is emerging into the Greater Community, and the Greater Community is involving itself in human affairs every day to a greater and greater extent. This will require the unification of human societies. Even if the Greater Community were not involved here, even if you had no contact whatsoever, eventually human societies would have to unite for their mutual survival and for the restoration and protection of the world.

However, the fact is the Greater Community is here, and this is accelerating your development at a rapid pace. Each generation now must face new difficulties and global problems that are growing greater every day. Your parents were not concerned with what you must be concerned with. Now you must be concerned with the well-being and survival of your planet. These are greater concerns, and they are affecting you in every way. They are requiring greater adeptness, intelligence and attention.

The fact that you are beginning to give this your attention is indicative of the predicament that humanity is in at this time. As we have said, humanity is always furthered by the dedicated actions of a few people, so do not look to the general public to make the difference. Look to yourself and to others like you who are responding to a greater need and who see a greater problem and a greater promise for humanity. It is a greater promise for humanity to become a unified society. Only in this way will humanity be able to meet its global problems. Only in this way will it be able to assure any well-being for its citizens, wherever they are. And only in this way will it be prepared to deal with forces from the Greater Community, which are themselves unified and determined.

A fragmented, divisive, warring set of nations, cultures and tribes in the world will have no power or efficacy in the Greater Community and will be subject to all forms of manipulation and subterfuge. Because, for the most part, your visitors are concerned with the preservation of your world, even those who are not beneficial to you do not want to see you destroy yourselves because you would destroy much of the environment with you. Those who support you wish to see you advance and become productive and meaningful participants in a larger arena of life. They wish to see you advance, and they also wish to see your environment protected.

In the Greater Community, environments are often considered more important than the races that inhabit them or use them. An environment as beautiful, as rich and as diverse as this world is, is a great prize, a gem, a biological storehouse in the universe. In the Greater Community, such environments are the most highly valued. There will be great effort to preserve these environments if they are threatened by their native races or by any other race that might seek to use and to dominate them. This represents the ethics of many of the advanced races in the Greater Community.

Therefore, you have a pressing need. You have a pressing need to elevate yourself, to unify your race, to restore your environment and to speak as one voice in the Greater Community. This seems like a great challenge—perhaps impossible, you say, and not achievable. Humanity has never done anything even close to this. So why would it rise to the occasion now? What will give it the strength and fortitude to enable it to achieve something that seems almost insurmountable given human nature and behavior at this time? What will do this is the presence of the Greater Community.

The Greater Community will have a very important impact on people once they become aware of it. From a Greater Community perspective, human beings are all the same. Therefore, this gives you the incentive to bond together, to share your resources and wisdom, to collaborate for your defense and for your well-being. The deterioration of the world's environment and the growing interdependence of world economies will also foster this. However, nothing will have so great an impact on human motivation as the fear of survival itself because most people are concerned primarily with survival. Not enough of the human race has yet raised their awareness and their motivation to a higher level.

Ultimately, union and contribution are the greatest powers in the universe. However, for a race such as yours in your stage of development, concern for survival and well-being are what will raise people to a greater level of participation and cooperation. This indeed has been demonstrated over and over again in your history. We are not saying that this is right or wrong. We are saying that this is the way it is. Greater Community Spirituality functions at the level of what is, not what should be. It leads to that which is the destiny of all life, but it begins where things are at this moment.

It is your evolution and your destiny that you will encounter and become engaged with the Greater Community. The Greater Community represents many different races with different motives. Many of those that you will encounter will not be interested in you at all. They only want to preserve your environment for their own use. Others seek to have a meaningful relationship with you, while some are looking at the possibility of trade and diplomatic relations. However, some wish to exploit you. They consider you brutish and self-destructive, and they seek to gain whatever they can from you before you destroy yourselves.

There are many different attitudes and points of view here because the Greater Community is vast and diverse. Some races are spiritually developed; many are not. However, for any of them to be able to reach your shores, they all must have greater technology and a greater social cohesion. Moreover, they are all powerful in the mental environment, which means that they will be able to affect your thinking more than you will be able to affect theirs.

The Greater Community is what you are preparing for. Of course you don't see this, at least not yet. From where you are looking, all you see are the immediate things of your life. And what you speculate may happen tomorrow is based upon these things. However, when you have a greater perspective and can see further afield and can see what is coming on the horizon for humanity, then you will have the incentive to prepare and to educate yourself and others.

The world's emergence into the Greater Community will be very gradual, but the effects of this emergence will be profound. At this moment, there are Greater Community forces seeking to genetically bond with human beings to protect the environment and to plant their incentive and their Greater Community intelligence within the human community. At first, this might be seen as good because it could give you greater possibilities for awareness and genetic development. Yet it is bad because it preempts your decision making. In effect, it takes control of you. No one wishes to be dominated, even if it holds some good possibilities.

In the Greater Community, you will be dominated, unless you can develop sufficient awareness and discernment. We are not speaking of technology here. We are speaking of Knowledge and Wisdom. Your visitors are not more advanced in Knowledge than you are although they hold far greater capabilities technologically and possess a greater social cohesion and determination than exist in the world at this time. You must prepare for them as they have already prepared for you.

You are preparing for nations within the world to meld into each other and for cultures here to clash. The future will be strife ridden and very difficult. No longer will nations be able to mind their own business and avoid each other, for if one nation fails, others will be impacted. If one nation destroys its environment, other cultures will feel the full impact of this. Greater and greater world cooperation will be needed and required. You will not see all of this in your lifetime, for you are in the early part of the transition, but what you contribute here now will determine the quality of life for your children and for the generations to come.

You see, in the Greater Community and in life itself, individuals do not live for themselves alone, as they seem to do in this world at this time. They live for all life. What you have today is based on the giving of those who lived before. All of your technological conveniences, your art, your music, everything that has been made and produced, your freedoms and your disabilities—all are the legacy of the giving and lack of giving of those who lived before you. They made possible the life that you have today, as you must make possible the life of those who will live beyond you. From a greater perspective, this is the context in which your mission and purpose can be understood. This is what fulfills you at the level of your Being. All other forms of fulfillment stimulate the mind and may give it a temporary sense of peace and purpose, but they do not affect the greater and deeper part of you. They do not lead to anything lasting and meaningful.

What you give today will be felt tomorrow. What you contribute in this life will determine the life of the generations to come, and they will thank you or curse you depending on what you gave and how your giving was accomplished.

You do not live for your generation. You live for the future. The future is determining the present. This is a great truth in Greater Community Spirituality, a truth that will be difficult to understand at first, for it represents a higher awareness and perspective and a greater vantage point from which to view life and to participate in life. You are here for the future. Knowing this enables you to see what you need to do today. This brings you into present time because life at this moment is for this moment and for the moments to come. You live for now and yet you also live for the future because your gift is for the future.

Many of the great gifts that will be given in your generation will not be felt by your generation but by the generations to come. This is how humanity is furthered. This is how life progresses. Look at your plants and animals. They give themselves so that they may give to the future of their kind. The trees lay down their leaves and eventually their whole life so that they might create soil for future trees to grow. Plants and animals give their seed so that future generations may evolve and have the opportunity to live and to give something to the world.

Consider this carefully, but do not make premature conclusions. This is a great idea to consider. It is an idea that takes you out of your personal mind and puts you into a greater state of mind where you can see your life within a larger time frame. Here you will see your life in a larger context and as part of a greater order of being in the universe.

You are part of a great transition. Your generation and the generations to come are part of the great transition from being an isolated and divisive race to becoming a unified race that is capable of interacting with the Greater Community. Even if the Greater Community were not present in the world today, your failure to take these steps would lead to the destruction of your environment and the loss of your opportunity to live in this world. Two great tragedies. The possibility for that failure now is great; the risks are high. That is why you must now see your life in a greater way. You must see yourself not just as a person struggling to be happy and to get along, but as a person who was sent here on a mission—a mission which is yet to be realized, a mission of great importance both for the present and for the future, a mission that restores your greater power and your greater relationships to you.

Greater Community Spirituality sees life within the context of the Greater Community as a whole. Greater Community Spirituality does not focus exclusively on your world. It is not dominated by your world's attitudes, beliefs, customs or history. It sees your destiny because your destiny is obvious. Intelligent life in all worlds must unite at some point for their survival and well-being. They must unite in order to be able to contend with the Greater Community, with all of its divergent forces and greater problems. This is what you must prepare for. In preparing for this, your life will come into harmony and will become unified. This is the promise of a Greater Community preparation, a Greater Community Way of Knowledge. This is what it means to experience and to express Greater Community Spirituality—a spirituality not merely of ideas and speculation, but a spirituality of real life, both now and in the future, a spirituality both for the present and for your destiny.

You are preparing for the Greater Community. If you prepare consciously and wisely, you and future generations will have a greater opportunity to live and to realize the great rewards of being part of a Greater Community of life. However, if you fail to be aware of the need for preparation or if you do not prepare wisely or effectively, then life will become more harsh and difficult, and the challenges will seem abrupt and overwhelming. You will be taken by surprise, and you will not be ready. This is why you must become sober about yourself and your life. This is why you must rise above your preoccupations and your petty interests and concerns.

You must hear this message with your heart, and you must feel this message in your heart. If you think about it, you may want to dismiss it because it seems either too uncomfortable, too strange, too alien, too challenging or too difficult. You may then say, "Why worry? Why bother? I won't worry about it. I won't think about it. God will take care of everything." God has sent *you* to take care of everything. Do not sit back and think that the Divine will come and save you. You have come to help save the world, to give humanity a future and to give your race a greater opportunity—an opportunity to unite, to develop and to become stronger, wiser and more capable, an opportunity to outgrow its tribal divisiveness, its religious fanaticism, its violence, its selfishness and its self-indulgence.

This is the gulf that exists between a primitive race and an advancing race in the Greater Community. You are still a primitive race, but life is requiring that you pass over this gulf and learn to become an advancing race in the Greater Community. That is why Greater Community Spirituality is being presented now, and that is why preparation in The Greater Community Way of Knowledge is necessary. You must outgrow your primitive tendencies. You must go beyond your history. Your history is nothing to be proud of. However, you can see in your history a great movement towards unification, towards world inhabitancy, towards solving world problems and towards humanity achieving a greater awareness, education and responsibility.

You are a citizen of your world. From a Greater Community perspective, you are not an American or a Chinese. You are not an Indian or a Russian or a Polynesian. You are a citizen of one world. The differences that you hold among yourselves are meaningless, and they must be outgrown in order for you to advance. This is necessary. You must feel this and see this. We are giving you a vision of where you are going and what you are preparing for. This is directly related to the purpose for which you came, which is not a personal or a selfish purpose. It is a mission to give—to give to the world now and for the future. You can feel this and see this. It is available for you to feel and to see because the movement of the world can be felt and discerned. Even though the world's movement is huge and seemingly incomprehensible, it can be felt.

This is why your preparation is great. This is why your preparation is necessary. This is why your preparation will restore you and redeem you to your real purpose and meaning in life. Where you have come from, you are important. When you are in the world, you are not important until you find the importance that you experienced and that you knew before you came here. This places you on an equal footing with all others who have been sent here for a purpose. However, your contribution is unique, and this is the meaning and value of your individuality.

You will not take this journey alone. Your contribution will not be yours to claim for yourself alone. Instead, it will be part of a greater collaboration that you will make in meaningful relationships with individuals and with small groups of people. This sets everything in motion in very specific ways because this represents the Greater Plan for life, a Plan that was always intended for humanity and which now is entering a new stage.

If you read and understand human history with this greater perspective, you will see it has always been geared towards ascendancy in the world and participation in the Greater Community. However, in the Greater Community you will not be dominant. And unless you can educate yourself and learn Greater Community skills and abilities, you will be dominated because the strong dominate the weak in the Greater Community, as they do here on Earth. To give you a real power that few even in the Greater Community possess, we bring to you The Greater Community Way of Knowledge—The Way of Knowledge as it exists in the Greater Community. The Way of Knowledge is being given through secret and mysterious means to individuals everywhere, in all races, cultures and worlds. This represents the work of the Divine. Beyond the tribal interpretations of any young race in any world, this represents pure Knowledge and pure spirituality. It is unalloyed with the traditions of any world to which it is sent. Thus, it represents a real challenge in learning and a great opportunity for true understanding and greater ability.

You have come for a great purpose. Therefore, you need a great preparation. You need great companions. And you need a great heart. This is your gift and your destiny. It is this that you have come to be a part of. And it is a blessing that it is so.

—◦◦◦—

You were assigned to each other

before you came here—

not to fulfill each other as people

and not to satisfy each other's

personal wishes, desires or needs,

but to initiate, inaugurate,

support and nourish a greater purpose

and mission which transcend

your human interests.

—◦◦◦—

CHAPTER TWELVE

WHOM WILL YOU MEET?

—⟜๑๑⟜—

𝒥N YOUR LIFE, YOU WILL HAVE MANY GREAT ENCOUNTERS. In order for you to recognize them and to value them, you must be prepared for them, or you will miss them and they will not come to be. We have said previously that you will need great allies in learning a Greater Community Way of Knowledge. You will need great allies in finding your purpose and discerning your purpose amongst the many attractive things that the world seems to offer.

Knowledge is leading you and preparing you at this moment to meet those individuals who will play a key role in your greater development. And Knowledge is moving them as well. You have a destiny to meet each other, but destinies can be changed. The course of things can be altered. In this world, chance plays a great part in determining whether things happen or not. And in this, your decision making and the decision making of the others whom you are destined to meet can have a significant impact on the outcome. The movement of Knowledge is constantly thwarted by the ambitions, the willfulness and the stubbornness of the personal mind.

In order for you to carry out your mission, you must have great allies because God knows you cannot do it alone. However, others cannot perform your role for you. You must do that. Certain individuals

139

will help you to find your role, to experience it and to refine it over time. You have a purpose to be together, and you will attempt, however unknowingly, to try to find each other. This represents a greater attraction in life than any of the personal or romantic attractions that people feel and exert upon one another. This is something very different, very unique and very special. You will have very few of these relationships. If you are fortunate and if you prepare wisely, several of these relationships will come into being in your experience.

You are trying to get to these individuals because they hold a key to your life. They are trying to get to you because you hold a key to their lives. You cannot know your purpose alone, for your purpose can only be realized, experienced and expressed within the context of the appropriate relationships. If you try to establish these relationships with those that you love or prefer, then your purpose will not emerge, and Knowledge will be silent. You will be left with your own ideas to guide you and to protect you—a very poor guide and a very dangerous approach.

Knowledge will recognize those allies who have been sent from your Spiritual Family to assist you. This is a very different kind of recognition from the kind of recognition that people experience in their romantic engagements and different even from the experience of affinity that you might feel with a person here or there with whom you share some distant past. You are not meeting your ally because you had some previous engagement in the world. This relationship is for a greater purpose. And if this relationship can be found and recognized, accepted and properly understood, it will yield a greater reward than all of your other relationships combined.

To prepare, you must learn something about The Way of Knowledge, and you must learn to differentiate between what is known and what is wanted or believed. Until this happens and until this differentiation has been experienced sufficiently, you will not be prepared for your true allies.

Only in very rare cases will these relationships ever represent a partnership such as a husband and a wife. In most cases, these people will be companions—people who journey with you, who are part of the provision that you need and whose Knowledge contains a key to your Knowledge, and vice versa. This is a different kind of relationship. It is not here to fulfill your personal mind. It is here to engage you with your deeper mind.

Should you be fortunate to encounter one of these people, then you will feel a different kind of resonance within yourself—not the intoxicating thrill of romance and not the fascination and fantasies that accompany the glorious moments of intense attraction. You will experience a calm, a homecoming, a distant memory, something vague and wonderful but deep and penetrating. It will speak to you, and you will be able to respond.

Though you are destined to meet these people, it is possible that you will fail to find them. It is possible that they will fail to find you. You can only do your part in this regard. If you do all that you can do and you do not find them, it is because they have become lost in the world. If they do everything they can do and they do not find you, it is because you have become lost in the world. By prior agreement, you agreed that you would seek to find each other. However, the time and the place remain uncertain because how you develop in life here, what decisions you make, how much you are distracted and how many encumbrances you acquire along the way will determine if and when you can make your rendezvous.

Therefore, even though there is a destiny to these relationships, there must be a great deal of work to find them. Something greater in you must be emerging. It cannot be a distant possibility. It cannot only be a vague feeling. It cannot only arise when you are severely disappointed with others or with yourself. It must be something that is more constant and more deeply felt than this.

You were not sent into the world alone. Others were sent into the world to help you, and you were sent into the world to help them. Should you find each other, should you be ready for each other and should you be able to receive each other, then you can learn something very important about your greater purpose in life and about the nature of your destiny.

It is important to realize that in the context of these kinds of relationships there are very rarely any real leaders. Leadership roles must be assumed by certain people to carry out certain functions, yet they comprise a small minority of those who are emerging into this greater experience and awareness. Remember. You are coming here to serve and to give, to restore and to reclaim, not to dominate.

In the Greater Community, there are many remarkable truths that have been discovered—truths that are relevant to life in this world and in all worlds. One of these truths is: The Wise remain hidden. The greater you are, the more concealed you must be. The greater your power and awareness, the more careful you must be where it is revealed and with whom it is shared and the more discerning you must be in choosing the beneficiaries of your gift. This tempers all ambition. This tempers all impatience. This tempers all self-assertions that are not born of Knowledge. Knowledge only knows what is real and will not respond to anything else.

The stronger you are with Knowledge, the more you will be like Knowledge and the more difficult it will be for you to make a mistake. What are mistakes but mistakes in discernment—not knowing what something is, not knowing where you stand with it and not knowing how to relate to it? Choosing the wrong person, choosing the wrong time, choosing the wrong place, choosing the wrong moment, choosing the wrong idea—these are all problems in discernment. With discernment comes discretion—the ability to remain silent, the ability to remain concealed.

We can assure you that in the Greater Community, the Wise *do* remain hidden or they are exploited or crucified. They are misused and abused, and their gifts are lost. Only on very rare occasions are greater demonstrations made to large numbers of individuals. And these demonstrations are often final.

The Wise remain hidden—working secretly, protecting their gift, directing it towards those who are destined to receive it, and keeping it from everyone else who seeks power, privilege and other advantages.

Therefore, when you find those individuals that you are destined to meet to carry out and to substantiate your purpose, there must be great humility. They are not here for you personally. They are not fascinated with you personally. They are not in love with your images. They are bonded to something greater in you, and their affection for you and their dedication to you will outlast all other human attractions.

This is what people truly seek in their relationships. They seek to find their allies. However, what they generally find is what they are attracted to, for they are not yet developed enough to respond to and to receive greater attraction and incentive in human engagements. They are bound to the need for pleasure and to the fear of survival, and these become the criteria for their choosing. Yet, we are speaking of something very different here, something very unique and rare.

Should you meet all of your allies, it is unlikely that their number will be greater than ten. It will more likely be three or four individuals. These individuals will play a very great role in initiating, supporting and speaking for the greater purpose that has brought you into this world—a purpose that can only emerge as you gain a greater maturity as a person and as you satisfy certain desires and requirements for yourself.

Knowledge within you emerges when the conditions are right. Relationships based upon Knowledge come into being when the conditions are right. Your coming together will not likely be easy. You will have to break away from other people and many wonderful things in order to find each other. You will have to gain the freedom to do this. You will have to win this freedom. You will have to struggle for it. Although this freedom is offered to you, in order for you to reach it, to accept it and to have it, you must be free of those things that belittle it, deny it or replace it.

Destiny in life is something you should never attribute to the mundane activities in which you are engaged. People assign great purpose and value to things that are small and meaningless, temporary or expedient. They say, "I am doing this. It is for a great purpose." "I am with this person. It is for a great purpose." "I am suffering now. It is for a great purpose." "I am staying here. It is for a great purpose." "I am leaving here. It is for a great purpose." However, these are usually merely attempts to give a greater meaning to something which does not have this meaning within itself. Do not be deceived by this. Do not fall into this form of self-assurance and self-comfort.

Relationships of destiny are very rare. They do not happen every day. They are not guaranteed with every person with whom you find a great attraction, or even a great affinity. Relationships of destiny are here to serve a greater purpose. The people who become involved in them are still barely aware of this purpose and are struggling to discover it. Often they will struggle with each other, for within themselves and between each other they must find a reconciliation. They must find the basis for what is true and distinguish that from everything else.

This takes time. It is better that you do much of this work on your own before you meet each other, or you will not be able to join and participate. If you meet each other too soon, you will not be able to receive each other's gifts of verification. You will not be able to vericate for each other and confirm the greater need and greater understanding that speak of a life of destiny, a life that was anointed before you came into this world. You were assigned to each other before you came here—not to fulfill each other as people and not to satisfy each other's personal wishes, desires or needs, but to initiate, inaugurate, support and nourish a greater purpose and mission which transcend your human interests.

If you could have a vision of the Greater Community, this would be much easier for you to see. You would see relationships that possess this greater dimension and greater purpose. You would see this not only between individuals within other worlds, but between individuals living in different worlds as well. You would see relationships between individuals who have never met each other and who will never, within their own lives, have access to each other physically, but who can share what they have learned and what they have received through a greater recognition. This is remarkable and may seem incomprehensible given the normal range of experience. But true it is, and important for you.

Your Spiritual Family works in many places. You are bound to them and they are bound to you. They represent the relationships that you have reclaimed in Knowledge thus far. Some of them are in the world, and many of them are outside the world looking in, watching you. Your Spiritual Family is watching you. They represent your small working group. There are many Spiritual Families. Never think that you can assign to your Spiritual Family the person you care for, the person you love, or your brother, your sister, your mother or your father. We are speaking of something else.

If you were to find one of your allies, but they were lost in the world and could not receive you, it would be a great tragedy for you. Therefore, do not demand that they come to you now. Instead, ask that they be prepared and that you be prepared so that you can be ready for each other—ready to recognize each other, ready to take on a greater role with each other and ready to differentiate between a greater purpose and your personal interests regarding each other. These relationships will be the confirmation that the work that you have done, the work that you have consciously involved yourself in, is meaningful and necessary, even though you cannot see its outcome or fully understand its importance.

Do not look around and say, "Well, this person must be one of those people," or "That person must be one of those people because we have so much in common, and it feels so good to be together, and we have so many shared interests," or "I experience such affinity with him." Do not assign this to any person. Time and experience will reveal those individuals who have a greater purpose and mission in your life. Restrain yourself in this regard and you will avoid many foolish and costly mistakes.

You do not want to waste your life. You do not want to have to continue to unlearn things that you have taught yourself. You do not want to be disappointed again and again regarding things that you think are real and correct. Your time in life is precious. Your opportunity here is great. The more you are aware that it is great, the less you will want to waste it on any endeavor or relationship that compromises you or that leads you astray.

In meeting your ally, you might find that you are to serve them or that they are to serve you. Perhaps they are in the leadership role this time, and you are not. Perhaps it is the other way around. You will fit perfectly together if you can accept how perfectly you fit, which may not fit at all with your ideals, ambitions or notions about yourself. That is why this requires humility and sobriety. That is why it requires preparation.

Many of your hopes and ideals regarding yourself must be disappointed. Much of your reckless striving, intense desires and feverish attractions must rest quietly within you. To recognize your ally, you will need to look, listen and learn—not just in the moment but for a long time.

Many people do not want to live without definitions. They want to have everything neatly explained and explainable. They want to have everything they are doing look very orderly, be connected to their past and be understandable. This will not work in these relationships. These relationships will be mysterious. They will often be very confusing. They may even generate tremendous conflict internally and between you, depending on how ready you are to recognize each other.

What is important here is not getting to know the other person as much as it is getting to know the experience of true affinity. Yes, you will need to learn about their behavior, their idiosyncrasies, their liabilities and their difficulties. This is important. However, getting to know the experience of true affinity is getting used to having a relationship like this, which will make all of your other relationships seem very doubtful. All the other people you have committed yourself to, have attempted to give yourself to or from whom you have demanded or expected a commitment—these will be cast in doubt. What you thought you were going to do in your life, and all of your plans, schemes and goals will be cast in doubt. If you can allow this to happen, then a Greater Reality can become manifest within you. However, if you resist this or refuse it or fight against it, there will be tremendous conflict. It would be better, then, that you not meet each other at all.

In order to find each other, you will need to work within yourself and within your life to clear the way. If you are married or in a committed relationship and have all of your plans, goals and securities tied together and then you meet your ally, everything else may fall apart for you.

We will give you an example, one that you are perhaps familiar with. When Jesus found he had disciples, he needed only to call them and they joined him. This represented relationships of the great nature that we are speaking of. They did not join him because he was magnificent or because he had unusual abilities or because he was beautiful or sweet. Indeed, he was going to take them all into dangerous situations and challenge them continuously. So what enabled them to drop what they were doing and to leave their lives and follow him? It was Knowledge.

If you ask for your ally to find you and if you ask to be able to find your ally, you must be ready. This relationship will cast in doubt a great deal that you have planned for yourself and that you have established for yourself already. If you do not want to give anything up but only acquire more and more, then this relationship will be too dangerous for you. The truth will be too dangerous for you. And though you may claim a greater purpose for yourself, your real purpose will be beyond your reach.

It is so necessary for you to learn to be in a relationship of this nature, and learn it you will by learning The Greater Community Way of Knowledge. The Way of Knowledge will validate Knowledge and nothing else. It will lead you to Knowledge and nothing else. It will bring you to true recognition within yourself and nothing else. It will bring you to recognize your true allies in life and nothing else. Nothing else will be validated.

You see, people want truth, but they want many other things as well. However, truth and these other things are not that compatible with each other. As your desire for truth grows deeper and your experience of truth grows deeper, then other things become seen as either useful or useless. However, they are no longer the central focus of your life. You are no longer drawn away by love or money. You are not captivated by beauty, grandeur, glory or security. You are not seeking to escape life or to be comfortably positioned. Instead, you are seeking something that verifies who you really are, why you have come into the world and what you must do here. These relationships are a central part of this initiation.

Later, when we speak of the Unseen Ones, we will speak of a whole other realm of relationship that is related to your true allies. This will give you an even greater understanding of your purpose. As you have a life in the world, you have life in your Ancient Home. This has not been lost to you, and it is in you now within your Knowledge. You have relationships in the world, and you have relationships beyond the world. You have relationships with your Spiritual Family, and these relationships provide the context and meaning to your reason for coming into the world.

Knowledge will prepare you for these relationships. If you can find the way to Knowledge and dedicate yourself to it, then gradually all of your difficulties and dilemmas in relationship will be resolved. We can make this promise because of the nature of reality and the nature of your greater identity and purpose here. You can then choose rightly and escape the grave and seemingly hopeless suffering that afflicts so many. Then you will not be lost in the world any more. And your example, your experience and your understanding will inspire others and give them a greater possibility.

You need true companions in life, but to have them you must have a relationship with the truth within yourself, which is represented by your relationship with Knowledge. Become a student of Knowledge and this relationship will be revealed to you and then reclaimed by you. Then, your allies will be able to join you to confirm the reclamation of Knowledge, to give it meaning and scope in the world and to give definition to what you must accomplish here specifically.

————⌇⌇⌇————

Stand within your mind

and it will seem to engulf you.

Stand outside your mind

and you will be able to see through it,

direct it and use it.

————⌇⌇⌇————

CHAPTER THIRTEEN

WHAT MUST BE UNLEARNED?

—⚜—

ONSIDERING WHAT HAS BEEN SAID THUS FAR, it becomes quite apparent that you cannot learn greater things by building upon old ideas and limited concepts. An old mind cannot conceive of new things. Indeed, to learn a Greater Community Way of Knowledge and to find the greater purpose which has brought you into the world, you must not only have a new set of ideas and a greater perspective, you must actually have a greater mind. This greater mind will seem ancient but new to you at the same time.

Your mind is different from your True Being, and as such it is ultimately a vehicle for Knowledge. This is its highest function and highest service. To be a vehicle for Knowledge, the mind must be fresh and renewable. It must be able to think clearly and freely and be able to rethink or recreate its thoughts. It must be pliable and open, accessible to new experience, open to new thresholds of understanding and willing to release its own ideas in order to gain a greater perspective and a greater Wisdom at every important threshold of life. Here the mind must be renewable. To have your mind be renewed, you must realize that you have a greater foundation than the mind, and you must reclaim your relationship with this foundation, which is your relationship with Knowledge.

Without Knowledge, you will identify with your mind. You will think that your mind is who you are. You will think that your thoughts represent you, define you, govern you and determine your experience. This belief is evident everywhere. Even in your own life you can see how much you have been dominated by your thoughts, by your beliefs, by your compulsions and by your evaluations. However, Knowledge is beyond them all. You have a new footing now, a footing in Knowledge. With this, the mind can become something that can serve you rather than dominate you. The mind can become a vehicle of great service, a marvelous instrument of communication—a medium between your Ancient Home and the world in which you now live.

This is the relationship that you need with your mind. Without this, your mind will continue to reinforce its old ideas by interpreting every new experience, every new encounter and every new relationship in such a way that these ideas are validated. What a great loss this is to you, for you are denied access to people, you are denied access to new experience and you are denied access to Knowledge. Here you are frozen in the past and bound to reinforce it at all times. Without a greater authority in your life, this is what the mind will do. It will calcify and become hard and brittle. It will become impenetrable and impermeable, something that defends its point of view without any regard to reality or to changes in circumstances. This imperils you and imprisons you. This denies you and isolates you. This prevents you from having access to others and learning from them. This denies your gift and your ability to receive the gifts of others.

However, indeed, you do have a greater authority in your life. Your authority is Knowledge—the Greater Mind which you have brought with you into the world from your Ancient Home to guide you, to protect you and to prepare you for your greater service and mission here. Gain access to Knowledge and you will become free of the mind. Once you have gained sufficient freedom from the mind, then you can use the mind to serve a greater purpose. Then the mind is redeemed and renewed, its value is restored and its true efficacy and true abilities can be cultivated.

What must be unlearned is your identification with your mind. What separates you from life but your own thoughts? What dominates your attention but your own thoughts? Creating new and better thoughts might seem to open new doorways of experience, but in fact it is the relationship with your mind itself that has to be changed. Better thoughts will not release you. Better thoughts will not free you. Better thoughts will not open your life. It is true that you will need new thoughts to think, and your mind will need to open new pathways so that new experiences can come to you. But having new thoughts is not enough. You must gain an entirely new foundation within your life. Stand within your mind and it will seem to engulf you. Stand outside your mind and you will be able to see through it, direct it and use it.

Knowledge within you will enable you to do this. In fact, Knowledge will do this for you because Knowledge is who you really are. However, before you can experience your total union and identification with Knowledge, it will seem to be a distant force within your life, a force that arises and emerges only at certain times—times of great need and discord and times when you sincerely request its presence and guidance. You have a relationship with Knowledge now . You are not yet fully joined with Knowledge, so you have a relationship. A relationship is preliminary to total union.

Therefore, gain your foundation in Knowledge. Take the steps to Knowledge. Learn The Way of Knowledge. Learn to receive Knowledge, to interpret Knowledge and to apply Knowledge, and you will become ever more free of your mind and more objective about it. With this objectivity, you will be able to determine those thoughts and patterns of thought that are helpful and those that are hindrances to you. You will be able to release your thoughts and be free of them because you are no longer a servant of your mind. Your mind now is a servant of Knowledge. This is its great purpose, and this is the right relationship you need to have with your mind.

You must unlearn your identification with the mind. You must unlearn your identification with your body. Your mind and your body are vehicles of expression in life. That is the correct way to see them. As such, you will want to take very good care of them. You will want to preserve them and maintain them in a good state of health. You will be able to do this when they are no longer engulfing you and determining your identity. Then you will be able to stand outside of your mind and body and direct them. Then you will understand them and recognize their needs, their capabilities, their limits and their usefulness. This is what you must undertake, and this is the natural result of studying The Greater Community Way of Knowledge.

When people begin the study of The Greater Community Way of Knowledge, they want to use Knowledge to reinforce their thoughts. However, The Way of Knowledge teaches you to use your thoughts to reinforce Knowledge. It sets a different direction and a different goal— one towards freedom and redemption, towards empowerment, ability and self-love.

Along the way, many things will be unlearned, and this frees you from the past. What have you learned but your past? Your past represents your learning—all of your evaluations, your beliefs, your ideals, your fears, your compulsions and your patterns of behavior. However, every moment and every second that you are engaged with Knowledge frees you a little bit more from the shadow of your past and from the binding ideas and constraints of your past. Every moment with Knowledge brings you into the present and orients you towards the future. Your past cannot be a reference for the future because the past is gone, and your memory of the past and your evaluation of the past hardly represent its reality. In fact, in almost all cases, you misinterpreted the past and used it to reinforce existing ideas. Therefore, your memory of your past is more a memory of your evaluations than an accurate memory of events.

With Knowledge, you will be able to see your past in a new way, with greater objectivity and greater clarity. You will not see the past you want to see. You will see the past that existed. This will give you an evaluative tool and point of view that you would not be able to have otherwise. From this vantage point, you will be able to see the past, the present and the future in such a way that it will enable you to be in the present meaningfully and purposefully in keeping with Knowledge within you. In this way, you will be able to be true to yourself and not simply obedient to your thoughts. You will be able to honor and experience a deeper inclination and a deeper movement in your life, rather than be bound to past ideas and to those people who represent those ideas.

This is a great freedom and liberation. You need this. To prepare for the future and to have any hope of learning a Greater Community Way of Knowledge, you must be unencumbered. God's first purpose is to unburden you. This is the process of unburdening. Liberation from the past will occur as you engage with Knowledge because Knowledge is not oriented towards your past. It is not focused on what has happened to you in life thus far. It only seeks to lead you forward. As you can be led forward and find your way, then the past will become ever more distant and remote to you. The memories, the difficulties, the tragedies and the happiness will all fade. This will enable you to be more and more present in the moment, more whole within yourself and more open to others.

What must be unlearned is your relationship with your mind, but this definition is not enough. You must be free from your past sufficiently to be able to move forward in a new direction and to establish a new and greater life than the life you had known before. To do this, you cannot take everything with you. You cannot carry all of your memories like a great store of luggage. The vehicle that will take you into the present and future will not accommodate all of this. Likewise, you cannot carry all of your relationships with you—all of your past loves, all of your friendships, all of your family, everyone that you like, everyone that you dislike, all the people and your memories of them that clutter your mind and keep you emotionally frozen in the past. Knowledge will break this up and call you out of your past orientation. Knowledge will free you, and it will unburden you so that you can be available to it and open to life as it is now.

How can you value this feeling until you have tasted it? How can you see the need for it until you have seen again and again the debilitating effects of being bound to old ideas, old relationships, old interests and old activities that no longer represent you. You must see the effects of having your memory cast over you like a great shadow—darkening your skies, haunting you, hounding you and following you wherever you go. You can forgive these things because you can release them. If you cannot release them, you cannot forgive them. What is forgiveness but release? How can you release something if you are still holding onto it? The only way to release something is to go where it is not needed, where you cannot take it with you and where it has no relevance and no importance.

God frees you by giving you something important to do in life, something that takes you out of your past and enables you to establish a new life where your past pain and references have no bearing. This is what enables you to become free of the past. This is what enables you to have a new and a greater life. This is what enables you to forgive those mistakes, those tragedies and those disappointments that otherwise would follow you everywhere, haunting you and limiting you.

To be free of the past is to be free of the mind that represents the past, which is to be free of your thoughts as they are today. This allows you to have new thoughts, new experiences and to have a new beginning in life. In reality, this is what it means to be born again—to wipe the slate clean, to see things as they are and not as you have always interpreted them to be, to be open to new experiences without being conditioned against them by your past fears and disappointments. Knowledge gives you this new beginning and this great opening. This is of supreme value to you.

It will also be necessary for you to learn a Greater Community Way of Knowledge. This is necessary in order for you to be able to encounter, experience and relate to the greater purpose that you carry already which has been hidden within you all of these years. You see, you cannot hold onto everything you want and everything that has happened and hope to have anything meaningful added. When people want more, they usually want more of the past. They may say they want new things; they may say they want new opportunities. But they are really adding to an old and past emphasis in life.

Your mind must be emptied. It must be opened. How can you receive if your mind is full of a whole mass of information? The mind must be free. It is as if your house were stuffed to the ceiling with all the possessions you have ever owned—everything—and you had not thrown away anything. It is all in there, things great and small, filling your every room and hallway. And you say, "Well, I want to bring new things into my house, but there is no room. I want to create a new feeling and atmosphere in my house, but there is no space for it." Everything is cluttered, and your house becomes increasingly uncomfortable. Your experience of being in it is imprisoning, and you find yourself spending all of your time maintaining all of these possessions.

This is a good analogy for the mind. Spending all of your time servicing your old thoughts prevents you from being available to life as it is today. Life is passing you by, and you are missing it. Every moment is available to you, but you are not available to it. Life is giving you great and new opportunities, but there is no room in your mind for them.

Do not think you must simply throw away all your old ideas. Some of them may still be useful, but most of them are not. The process of becoming free from your mind is very natural. As you gain access to Knowledge, you learn about Knowledge, and every moment you spend with Knowledge enables you to recognize what must be kept and what must be discarded. Over time, you find yourself emptying out your old house. You find yourself emptying things out, getting rid of things here and there, cleaning up, making room and enjoying the newfound space, freedom and mobility within your house, within your mind.

Your mind is like the house that you live in, in the world. It is filled with whatever you put there. It is the place from which you look out into the world. It is your shelter and your protection. It is the place where your spirit generally abides. However, if your house becomes too cluttered and too uncomfortable, Knowledge will not abide there. Then,

you will find that you are living in a relic of your own past. You will feel like you are a museum keeper, someone who is taking care of old things.

The Way of Knowledge takes you out of your house and brings you back with a greater understanding. Then you will see how intolerable it is to live there and how much must be redeemed and restored. And you start throwing things away here and there, cleaning out the attics, cleaning out the basement, finding old and forgotten things here and there and getting rid of them. Then you realize that your house can be completely redone and needs to be completely redone, for it does not reflect your new experience.

This will begin a natural process of rejuvenation within your mind. Here your mind will be redeemed because it will be renewed and refreshed. It will be freed from the past because the past will have less and less influence upon you. Knowledge will also bring you into contact with new kinds of relationships—relationships that will displace the old memories that haunt you and that fill your mind with past experiences. Then your past will become less and less relevant as you proceed.

The Way of Knowledge is about the restoration and rejuvenation of the mind. This is a complete process, and it takes a great deal of time. It takes time because it works; it is natural; it follows a natural progression. Here you are not doing something artificial or mechanical to yourself. You are simply allowing your mind to renew itself and to let old thoughts die so that new thoughts can be born. This allows a natural process of death, decay and renewal to take place within your mind. Then your mind will no longer simply be a museum of old artifacts. It will become more like a garden where things are perpetually growing, bearing their fruit and giving their gifts. Like the gardener, you plow under your old beliefs and ideas so that new ones can emerge. Then your mind becomes an ever fruitful harvest of Wisdom. It keeps pace with present time. It keeps pace with new experiences. And it is able to look into the future because it is not bound by the past. You can plant new seeds of understanding here, and the soil will be fertile because it is renewed and restored.

You cannot give a new awareness to an old mind. An old mind will simply use the new awareness to reinforce its former views. An example of this can readily be seen. When people say, "Well, I don't relate to this," or "I don't experience that," what they are saying here is that it does not relate to their past. You yourself have said this on several occasions. When new things are shown to you or when new ideas are given to you, you may say, "Well, I can relate to this, but I don't relate to that." What you are saying here is "I can't fit this into my past."

This is a very important idea to understand. The Greater Community Way of Knowledge provides a whole new opportunity to develop vision and Wisdom. This will take you beyond the normal parameters of human thinking. Of course you will not be able to relate to it. It is not a part of your past. When some people hear about the Greater Community, they shake their heads and say, "I do not know what this means." Does that mean they should not learn about it? Does that mean it is not valid? What this means is that they cannot fit the Greater Community in with what they have seen, felt and learned thus far. It does not relate to their past learning. And if they try to fit it into their past learning, it becomes something about the past and not something about the present. When people look at an object, all they see is their past references about that object. They rarely see the object as it really is in the moment. They do not have young eyes. Thus, life and life's experiences, which are redeeming, renewing and educational, pass them by. If something does not fit into the past, they do not see it and they do not feel it. Then the mind does not register it. This is when the mind becomes a prison house. This is when it casts bars across your awareness and your ability to see. This is when the mind imprisons you, holds you, binds you and separates you.

You see, every new relationship is a new experience, and every old relationship can be experienced in a new way, but there must be room and the capacity for new experience. A new experience is something that is real in and of itself without any reference to the past. The less past-oriented you are, the more available you will be to these new experiences and the more you will be able to benefit from them. This is necessary for your happiness and for your well-being. It is necessary for the possibility of your having meaningful relationships with others and for your being able to learn Greater Community Knowledge and Wisdom. Greater Community Knowledge and Wisdom will take you far beyond not only your past but the past understanding of most people you will meet. It is this preparation that is so needed in the world now, for the world is feeling the great weight and the great burden of its past discord, past conflicts, past wars, past grievances and past errors. The world is so encumbered.

Occasionally someone arises and says, "I see something new. I see where we are going. I see this opportunity. I see this danger." And he or she tries to alert people around them, but people are dead to it. They do not see it, they do not feel it, they do not relate to it and they do not want it. And the person who sees is so frustrated. "I see this. It is here." But people are dead to it. Every person who has ever made a new discovery or has ever made any breakthrough in any area of life—whether in science, art, religion, politics or sociology—has faced this dead response in others, this inability to see and to know, this resistance to new experience and this reference to the past and to old evaluations.

Those who have been innovators, contributors and ground breakers in any arena have faced this. And it has been very painful. They have met with ambivalence, indifference or resistance. This is the great dilemma of humanity. This is a great liability in human awareness.

Yet into this seemingly hopeless situation, the world is emerging into the Greater Community. This will forever change human experience and will make your past as a race seem distant and remote because your past is a past without the Greater Community, and your future will be a future with the Greater Community. On a collective basis, this will confront you with new experience to such a degree that the human race itself will have an opportunity to renew its collective mind, beliefs, associations, values and ideals.

This is a long process, and the result has not yet taken place. Indeed, even at this moment people are blind to the presence of the Greater Community in the world. They cannot see it, they cannot feel it, they cannot know it and they do not want it. And if they do see it or feel it to any degree, they try to interpret it in such a way that it becomes a reminder of the things that they already feel or believe. They want to make it a wonderful thing or a terrible thing based upon their point of view about life.

How can you see with all of these restraints? How can you know anything with all of these requirements? Can you see through the prison bars of your own mind? Can you see beyond the past? Having a past reference is like walking through life backwards, always looking behind you to see where you've been. And of course you crash into things and do not know where you are going and experience all kinds of calamities, grave mistakes and stupid errors. Walking backwards, you cannot see where you are going. You stumble around, fall down and end up in places where you do not belong while always looking to see where you've been. Think of this image and you can see the great disabilities that come as a result. Realize how you are not yet able to look out on the horizon of your life and your future and say with any certainty, "This is what is coming. This is where I am going. And this is what I must do."

When people are walking backwards, they are thinking, "Where I am going to go is to get away from what I am looking at now." And they are looking backwards. Their future projections are based on their past orientation. They are not available to the moment. They cannot see what is happening now. Their minds have overtaken them. Their attention has been given to their thoughts, which are all past referenced.

The Greater Community gives you a great opportunity for liberation as a race. The gravity of its impact, the problems that it will present and the challenges it will give to humanity will either defeat you or redeem you. This is the greater problem which will unite people everywhere, for everyone will be in the same boat now. The differences between you will not matter. What difference does it make where you were born, what city you lived in, what language you speak or what religion your parents were part of? You are all now faced with a greater problem. You are all together, and you need each other.

This is the great redemption. Life is now pulling you out of the past in a very big way. The present and the future will be such a confrontation that even those who are dead to the world and to themselves will be forced to respond. And though their response may be past referenced, they will have to learn to face a new set of circumstances. Do not look at the present and the future and say, "Well, Jesus will save me," or "God will lift me out of this one for sure," or "This is not really important," or "This has always been going on. It doesn't matter." People tell themselves these kinds of things to avoid experiencing what is occurring now and to avoid being in touch with their deeper feelings and inclinations.

Knowledge will bring you into the present and prepare you for the future. It will make you alive to yourself and to the world. It will give you the eyes to see and the mind to know. Then, as you go along, you will see what you cannot take with you, what no longer fits and what is no longer important. You will see with great relief the enormous tragedies and frustrations of your former life fading away, and you will not want to renew them. You will not want to relive them. You will not want them to happen again. You will not want them to affect your decision making, color your vision or determine your behavior any longer. And more and more you will step outside your mind. Then you will be able to use your mind rather than be used by it.

Knowledge will bring about the renewal of your mind. The renewal of your mind means that your mind is refreshed, unburdened and open to the present and to the future. It is like awakening from a long and dreary sleep. You will see life anew and you will experience yourself anew. It will be a new day for you. You will be able to open your eyes to see what is in front of you and to look out on the horizon to see what is coming. The things that we have spoken of, some of which seem so foreign and so removed from your past experience, will now become ever more obvious, for you have reached the vantage point where they can be seen. Climbing a mountain is but one image to illustrate this.

To see what must be unlearned, what conflicts with your present experience and what denies, thwarts or alters your present insight, you will need the experience of a Greater Power in your life, and this Greater Power is Knowledge. With Knowledge as a growing reference point within you, you will be able to work with the mind and to understand the mind with real objectivity. Then the mind will not threaten you or haunt you. And over time you will be able to make it a useful instrument to serve a greater purpose in life. You will become more still, more observant, more patient, more tolerant and more fearless. All of this will happen because of your mind's renewal and the renewal of your relationship with Knowledge, which will become your new foundation. Knowledge will give you its qualities, its beneficence and its power. It will give you a new life.

This is God's great gift to you. You may feel, or even complain, that God has not done this or that for you in the past. What God has given you, however, is so much greater than all of your former requests. God has given you freedom, and with freedom God has given you purpose and direction. Knowledge is there to guarantee this possibility. The rest is up to you. Choose this new life. Prepare for this. Give yourself to this. Dedicate yourself to this. Then you will see all that is unnecessary in your life as you proceed, and you will find everything that is essential. Increasingly, you will want to keep what is essential, and you will want to discard what is not. Your life is precious and your time is precious. What is essential gives meaning and what is not essential takes meaning away. Then the choices become obvious, and you will have the power to make them.

——∿∿——

You will want to avoid these things

because they hold you back,

because they gamble your existence

and because they waste your life.

——∿∿——

CHAPTER FOURTEEN

WHAT MUST BE AVOIDED?

—*∿∿*—

*L*IFE OFFERS MANY DISTRACTIONS. Life will keep pulling you back to your past unless you are able to be in the moment with it. Once you have achieved a present state of mind sufficiently, then you will need to be prepared to deal with the influence of others upon you. If everyone were doing what you are doing, this would be far easier and more beneficial. However, the reality is that you will be one person among the very few who is undertaking a greater preparation to rise above the normal preoccupations, concerns and interests of people around you.

People around you will affect the mental environment for you. Because of this, you must become very selective about who to be with and what to say. Do not see this as a constraint on your freedom, for this is protecting an emerging awareness that needs protection in a world where it is not valued or honored. Life will teach you this over and over again in difficult situations where you will find yourself recoiling from other people and from situations where you don't belong or where you have committed an indiscretion. Remember, you are learning The Way of Wisdom as well as The Way of Knowledge. Wisdom has to do with how you carry Knowledge in life—how you express Knowledge, where you share it and how you hold it in regard to yourself and other people.

You will find as you proceed in The Way of Knowledge that you will value things that others do not value, see things that others do not see and know things that others do not know or will not know. What seems obvious to you will not be obvious to them. You will see both their gifts and their disabilities. They may see neither. You will have higher standards for yourself, but these standards will not be shared by other people. You will value a deeper experience of honesty, but you will not be able to communicate this freely with others. Again and again you will find out the limits that other people set before you and around you. And again and again you will feel other people's influence. You will feel yourself being pulled into idle conversation. You will feel yourself being pulled back into a state of mind that you have worked hard to emerge out of. You will feel the weight of their concerns and preoccupations, but you will not want to be encumbered by them.

This will set you apart, as it must. And at times you will feel lonely and isolated. However, you will find, even at the outset, that you will have companions. They will share their difficulties with you, and you will share your difficulties with them, for you are both experiencing difficulty being in the world.

You need to establish a new foundation for yourself out in life, as well as within yourself. Nothing is taken away from you here. This is not something that is meant to rob you of any pleasure or pursuit that you may want. It is only to assist you in following a natural process of selection and discrimination which must be cultivated as a Greater Power and awareness emerge within you. If you think that we are limiting you, then you do not understand our intent. If you think that we are holding you back, then you do not understand your real needs.

If you are responding to a greater meaning, vision and understanding, you will set yourself apart, and life will set you apart because you need to have this freedom. You cannot stay where you are and go somewhere new. And if you go somewhere new, others cannot go with you, except for a very few. As you find something that others have not discovered, you will know something that they do not know. How can you be with them in a casual way with this growing awareness within yourself? You will not want to share their compromises. You will not want to be a part of many of their activities, which only serve to avoid and deny the greater things that need to be recognized and discussed. Even at the level of personal problems, this will be the case because you will seek resolution, while others will not. You will want to face things and discuss them, while others will not. You will want to bring remedy and resolution, while others will not.

After a time, you will find yourself avoiding certain people and situations. This is correct. This is a natural reticence. It is because you are seeking to free yourself from people and situations, from conversations and endeavors that hold no merit or value for you. You can do this without condemnation of yourself or of others. You do this simply because you have somewhere else to go and something greater to know. Here you are not better than others. You are not wise while they are fools. Do not have this attitude or you will miss the whole point. This is not a contest. That emphasis is only meaningful to the personal mind, which seeks to use everything for self-assurance, self-glorification and self-protection because it is weak and vulnerable and has no foundation in life. Do not make that error, but see clearly.

Something has changed at the very core of you in a way that you cannot describe. You feel different. Your values are changing. Your priorities are changing. Your emphasis in life is changing. This steers you away from people who are not experiencing this and towards those who are. It brings you specifically towards certain individuals who share your journey. Some of them will only go a short way with you; others will travel with you for a lifetime.

You need to be with these people because they will assist and aid you. They will challenge you to go forward. They will help you when you fall back. They, too, are experiencing a great movement in their lives. They, too, are trying to sort things out. They, too, are coming to terms with their own compromises and are realizing their own denial. They, too, must find a way to change the direction, course and activity of their lives. These people will help you even if they are only with you temporarily.

You will find yourself avoiding many people and situations. In fact, after a time you will look at the general activities of most people with disinterest. Perhaps you will feel lonely and estranged. But we say, "Congratulations!" You are beginning to find your freedom. You are starting to value something that is valuable. If this sets you apart, that is fine. You need this freedom. You need this liberation. You need to be free of the bondage that other people place upon themselves and inadvertently place upon you.

Congratulations. Keep going. You will not travel alone, but you cannot take everyone with you. You will find that you cannot keep all of your friends and past acquaintances because they are part of your past, and the emphasis in those relationships is not what you are experiencing now. Allow them to depart and bless them. Do not condemn them. Do not deny them. Just let them drift away. Release them. They are going a different way than you are now. You may not know where you are going, but you know you are going somewhere because you feel the movement in your life and you see your life changing. You see that other people seem very static, and the movement of their lives seems imperceptible. However, for you things are changing rapidly now. Allow this to happen. It is coming from the very center of you. You will not understand it fully for a very long time, but you need to go forward. You cannot go back. You cannot take that loved one with you. You cannot take that one that you depend upon with you. Perhaps you cannot even take your husband or wife with you, or your children, or your parents, or your best friend. Here you must side with Knowledge. You cannot go both ways. You cannot take everything with you.

It may take a long time for you to realize and come to understand that you are being unburdened. For, indeed, there will be moments when you will feel a great loss. You will not be able to justify your actions or behavior, but you will know that you must continue. And you will know you must say good-bye to your dear friend or companion. If you try to stay together, there will be increasing discord and disassociation. It is better to recognize your diverging directions and to bless and release the other person and to not linger trying to explain or to justify your actions.

You will find as you proceed that life gives you many choices. Here you may not even be able to stay with others who are also responding to a greater calling. As you proceed, your way becomes much more specific. At the outset, you may feel like you are opening to your spiritual life, but as you proceed, your spiritual development will become far more specific in its application and direction. Those who traveled with you at the outset, who shared your journey, may have to go a different way than you. Allow this to happen. Bless them. Honor them. Do not criticize or reject them because they cannot stay with you and go where you are going. Perhaps they are going quickly; perhaps they are going slowly. They go with their disabilities as you go with yours, slowly unraveling and resolving them as they proceed.

Follow the way. Do not try to define it. Do not hold onto people. Your true companions, your allies, will never leave you, so you do not need to cling to them, shackle them or keep a rope around their neck. Let everyone else come and go. This is a natural process of definition and selection in life. Very few people have emerged beyond the general consensus of things, so the way is not that well traveled. However, others have traveled it before, others are traveling it now and others will travel it in the future. There is a way because Knowledge is in your life. There is a way because your allies are joining you. And there is a way because the Unseen Ones will guide and assist you as you need them and as you proceed in life.

Here there are certain things we can counsel you to avoid, yet you must learn how to use this guidance and this counsel as you proceed. You will not realize the full value of this counsel until you are more advanced than you are today, but that does not mean that this counsel is not meant for you at this time and will not serve you well, saving you from much misery and difficulty.

First of all, as we have said, avoid taking people with you. Tell them you are going somewhere and give them a sense of where you are going. If they cannot go, they cannot go. This does not mean that your relationship has failed; it does not mean that they are stupid or foolish, and it does not mean that you are better than they are. It simply means that you cannot go on together. You are taking a different path. Take it. Follow it. Avoid trying to bring them with you. Avoid staying behind trying to persuade them, convince them or justify your mysterious life. Bless them and release them. Recognize your diverging paths. It is fine. It is natural.

Next, avoid trying to determine where you are going. You know you are doing something important. You know you are doing something that has a spiritual foundation. You know you are doing something that is good for you even if at moments you are in grave doubt about it. You know you must go on. You know you cannot go back to where you were before. You know you want to be free. Yet beyond this, avoid trying to determine where you are going because you will not know. All you know is that you must proceed. As you advance and become more mature as a student of Knowledge, you will see the great value of this. Yet if you try to get ahead of yourself, it will cause all kinds of confusion and misinterpretations.

At the outset, the need to understand and to justify yourself is born of an old understanding which is based upon many false things. However, now you are basing your life on something true and sound, consistent and permanent, real and genuine. Trust yourself. Trust Knowledge within you. Do not keep pulling yourself aside and asking, "Am I doing the right thing? Is this the right thing?" over and over again. Do not badger yourself with this incessant questioning, for there is no answer except to proceed. Follow this and you will follow Knowledge. Hold back and you will be resorting to your old ideas once again. Do not let your fear take you away, for it will only return you to the past, to a previous belief in security which you are now working to be free of. Maximum security in this regard is a maximum security prison. You have been imprisoned, and you do not want to return.

However, if you go a little ways and stop and say, "Well, I do not want to go into something I do not understand. I do not know where I am going. What should I do? What will happen to me?" and you let your imagination take over and create all kinds of fearful and horrible images for you, then you will be in a very uncomfortable position. You will prevent yourself from going forward, but you will know that you cannot go back. Then you will be stuck right where you are.

You have not become free of the mind yet. You must break from its authority so that you can exercise *your* authority. The mind exercises authority because you do not. It is not because the mind is a tyrant or a terrible thing. The mind simply provides assurance when assurance is not provided for it. It is like an orphan child who must fend for itself until it finds a safe parent or guardian. Knowledge is your guardian. Knowledge is your Greater Self. However, until you can fully realize it is your Greater Self, it will seem like a parent or a guardian. It will seem like a guide, like a true friend. Follow Knowledge and you will return to yourself, and you will find others who are part of your mission and journey here.

Next, avoid trying to tie what you are doing to something you already believe in. If you value a certain philosophy, religion or set of ideals and you want to make sure that what you are doing is consistent with them, you will be pulling yourself backwards. Just as you cannot take people with you, you cannot take ideas with you. It is amazing that people are often far more attached to their ideas than they are even to other people. This is because they are more identified with their ideas than with anything else. Some people can walk away from a relationship, but they are so bound to their ideas, their beliefs or their assumptions that they are not free to leave them. This is what it means to wear a crown of thorns. This is when the mind is a crown of thorns. You wear it, but it torments you. It seems to give you a kingly title, but in fact it is a harness of misery. It seems to elevate you and give you stature in the world, but in fact it cuts you and hurts you, binds you and mocks you.

In order for the mind to become a halo instead of a crown of thorns, you must affirm your authority. You realize your strength by exercising your authority. In learning The Way of Knowledge, you will have to exercise your authority again and again in order to keep your mind free and open. Therefore, avoid trying to associate your old ideas and cherished ideals with what you are doing now because you cannot take them with you. They are like old relationships and old places. Do not drag them along. Let the river of life carry you. Do not cling to the rocks. Do not try to take the rocks with you. Do not try to take the scenery of your mind with you, which is the whole array of your ideas and beliefs, fears and goals.

Next, avoid falling in love. When we say falling in love, we are talking about creating a fantasy with another. Romantic love, fantasy, is the epitome of the personal mind's self-indulgence. In an attempt to validate itself and to justify its existence, it seeks union with another for this purpose. It cannot join with another; it can only use another to validate itself. This is the basis for romantic love. What you must find instead is recognition and the ability to participate with another. A beautiful face, a lovely set of eyes, a wonderful image, a charming or exotic personality, anything that attracts you and mesmerizes you, anything that holds your attention against your will, anything that keeps your mind fixated on its own ideas and prevents it from gaining access to Knowledge—these things represent a romantic approach to relationships, and these you must avoid.

Has your past not taught you this already? Do you need to be disappointed again and again in order to find out that this involvement leads nowhere? When you finally realize the real condition of the relationship, then the dream of romance is dispelled and you are left with your lack of real relationship with the other person.

People can be mesmerized by each other for years and never have any sense of who the other person is. And yet when they finally become sober, as life sobers them through its hardships and its challenges, they find that they are not really compatible with each other and that their association is shallow and temporary. Then there is great disappointment, anger and resentment.

Avoid falling in love. Seek real relationship. In real relationship you will feel tremendous affection, resonance and the desire to share your life. However, this is quite different from the falling-in-love experience that people value and hold so dear. Watch your movies and read your books all about the grandeur and the ecstasy, the danger and the uncertainty of romance. Then ask yourself if there is any real relationship there or if this is just a grand interlude, a way to escape mundane life, a way to have a wonderful dream together, a dream that seems to liberate you from all of your concerns and responsibilities. Avoid falling in love. It will take years of your life away from you. It will rob you and leave you empty and poor. You will gamble your life away falling in love, gambling on something frivolous that is without hope or promise.

Next, avoid trying to make Knowledge affirm what you want. Here you find someone you want, something you want or someplace you want to go and you go to Knowledge and you say, "Can I go? Is it okay?" If you want only approval, you will give it to yourself and you will say, "Yes, I feel this is correct. My Knowledge tells me this is correct." Yet if you go to the real allies in your life, they will look at you and shake their heads, for they will know. However, if you associate with people who do not have this capacity, oh, yes, they will assure you that it is a wonderful thing to do.

Avoid trying to make Knowledge give you what you want or support what you want. Instead, ask Knowledge, "Show me what I need to know and to do. Do not let me waste my life. Do not let me gamble with my existence." Give Knowledge this privilege, and it will support you and serve you in ever greater ways.

Next, avoid thinking that your life is going to be grand. People often think that because they are on a spiritual journey of some kind, they are going to be healers, magnificent beings, gurus, teachers, saints, pilgrims, wise men, wise women, avatars, oracles and so forth. This is all romance. Romance here is as damaging and pointless as romance in any other relationship, except that it is more difficult to unravel because it looks self-edifying.

Your role in life will be simple and hidden in almost all cases. If you are to become known, it is in a way a misfortune because the world will prey upon you, and others will use you and abuse you. They will infiltrate your life and attempt to take your gifts away from you. They will manipulate you, they will malign you, they will curse you, and they will praise you. This is reality. That is why only in rare cases will a man or woman of Knowledge become a public figure. And they will have to face the tribulation that accompanies this privilege.

The Wise remain hidden for a very good reason. And yet, when you consider this idea, you will see how much it goes against your ambition and your personal motives. After all, you may not want to give your life and devote yourself to something that will not glorify you. Even the religions of the world offer many different images of self-glorification— to become a Buddha, to become an avatar, to become Christ like, to become a shining example that everyone flocks to for inspiration, healing and beneficence. However, the reality is very different from this and needs to be different because there is no Wisdom here. Do not, then, stimulate your personal mind with these fantasies. This is not the way.

Knowledge must free you from these ambitions to the extent that they function in your mind. Everyone has them to some extent. Everyone wants to be validated, recognized, supported and appreciated, but in reality you only need to be recognized and supported by your true allies and be given the opportunity to serve others who are truly ready for your gifts and contribution. That is as great a blessing and acknowledgment as you could imagine. There will be no deception here. There will be no betrayal. There will be no usurpation or manipulation. What you give will be received and will be passed on to others. And your gift will resonate through many people and through many relationships. As the source of your gift is beyond you, your giving should not give you personal recognition. Can you claim that your purpose is your own creation? Can you claim that your gift, your skill or your role are yours alone? How can you say this when life has prepared you, guided you and made it possible for you to have a purpose, to realize your purpose, to have allies to share your purpose and to have recipients to whom you give your purpose?

Avoid self-glorification. Avoid recognition. Knowledge does not want these for you. Wisdom will restrain you. Let yourself be restrained. Knowledge will protect you, preserve you and enable you to cultivate and develop your strength and abilities without the interference and invasion of people who cannot or will not share these with you. Let life set you apart so that you may return to life with a greater ability and a greater understanding. Let Knowledge take you away from your own goals and ambitions and from your own need for self-validation and bring you back with a greater Wisdom and understanding.

Avoid talking too much. If you talk too much, you expend your energy and you disseminate your ideas mindlessly. Let Wisdom germinate within you. Do not go tell everyone about what is happening within you. Let the pressure build. Let your capacity grow. Let yourself digest the truth rather than try to pass it on to everyone. Let yourself experience the meaning and depth of the insights that come to you rather than rushing off to tell your friend, "Oh, I had this insight. It was so wonderful!"

Exercise restraint, for you will need a great deal of restraint. We cannot tell you how much restraint will save you from difficulty and tribulation. Do not let your need for self-validation overtake you here. Hold things within yourself. Let them grow. Those things that are not valuable will disappear. And those things that are valuable will slowly grow. Wisdom is slowly grown. It must grow within you, and you must be very careful with whom you share it. Your experience will demonstrate exactly what we are saying, for you will say things to certain people who cannot or will not receive them. You will share things you are excited about with people who cannot experience them. You will offer new things to people who cannot relate to them. This will throw you back upon yourself. Do not criticize others. They are not the problem. Your lack of discretion is the problem. You could not discern the appropriate place to share yourself, and you paid a price for it. This teaches you to come back to yourself and to hold within yourself the gift which is growing there.

Knowledge is very discreet with you. You should be very discreet with others. Knowledge is very discerning with you. You can learn to be discerning with others. Great things are the result of a long germination process within the individual. People are eager to share because they want self-validation. They want somebody else to tell them that they are wonderful and that they are doing the right thing. Avoid this. Avoid idle conversation. Avoid talking about spiritual ideas and great things with people who cannot receive them and with people you are not meant to communicate with.

Next, avoid gossip. Avoid discussing other people's lives. Gossip is very tempting because it makes you feel self-satisfied, and you are able to exercise your judgment in a way that seems honest and valid. But this is wasteful. It maligns other people, and you lose energy and vitality because of it. You may feel proud doing this, but happiness and real self-confirmation will be lost as a result.

Next, avoid trying to make something happen with what you know already. Your mind will keep wanting to create things, have things and justify what it is doing in order to gain security, recognition and validation. However, it may not be the time yet. When it is time, it will be time, and that will be a great challenge for you. However, until it is time, it is not the time. No matter how much you may want to put into form what you are experiencing, do not rush out and create a new organization or start a new business or make a new product. People who do that are reckless, and they will gamble their existence. And it will take a long time for them to come back to where they started, for it is often much more difficult to end something than it is to begin something. Any relationship can be started, but it can be hard to finish it—whether it is a relationship with a person, with an organization or with something you have created in the world.

Do not begin anything that does not have a greater promise. How will you know? Because Knowledge is with you. If you cannot gain access to Knowledge in this situation because you have too much desire or ambition or are too confused, then go to your ally for verication. "Is this the right thing to do?" you will ask. "I am thinking of this. I want this. This looks good to me. Should I do this?" Do not go to your friends and do not go to your casual relationships, for they may all get interested in your idea because they cannot yet respond with Knowledge. Do not take a chance on this. Go to your allies. In many situations, you will not be able to gain access to Knowledge because you are governed by your preferences or you are too afraid or too concerned for yourself. That is okay. Go to your allies. Every important decision you make should be vericated. That is a protection for you; it is a safeguard. You need this; accept it.

Avoid going into life saying, "I am going to have what I want, no matter what." That is the stupidest decision you could ever make. It is blind; it is arrogant; it is ignorant. It denies your relationships and it casts you out alone. Life is full of people doing that and, as a result, life is full of calamities. Avoid that. Let Knowledge grow slowly within you. Let change come naturally. Do not slow it down and do not speed it up. Do not say to yourself, "Well, I am doing something spiritual now. I have to become a spiritual person, a spiritual merchant or a spiritual teacher, someone who sells products and services. I want to make my living out of this." Avoid that.

Knowledge will remain silent, deaf to such proclamations. You may feel these compulsions only occasionally or you may feel them continuously, but stay with what you are doing. Don't make a change unless change is vital. And when change is vital, seek verication. Do not go it alone. No one in the world is beyond error. No one in the world is beyond temptation. No one in the world is faultless. Do not think that because you have a great and rising emotion for something that it is the right thing to do. Every failure and calamity started out with an excited interest or belief that something would be a beneficial activity or involvement. Avoid this. Keep your mind sober and open. Do not get into romance about your spirituality. You don't even know what it is yet. However, it is in you, and it is guiding and balancing your life. It is slowly freeing you from all the bonds that have held you to the past and that you now need to outgrow and to leave behind.

Next, avoid the need to understand everything. Real understanding comes later. Prior to this, people create an understanding because they want to feel self-assured. They don't want to look stupid to themselves or to other people. They want to have everything fully explained and explainable. They want to have everything justified and justifiable. They want to make everything look good and upright. They want to win approval. However, the understanding that they create here is so partial, so personally motivated and so false and unreliable that it can only break down in the face of real life. Here you do not want to create anything you will have to undo, to learn anything you will have to unlearn or to associate with anyone that you will have to disassociate from later.

Let your mind be free. Let the puzzle of your life be in little pieces. Let it come together in little groups of pieces. Do not fill it all in with your own ideas and ambitions. Others will demonstrate to you how they have done this—how their lives are fully understood and how they have a higher purpose which is fully understandable to them, when in reality, they only know a few little things, and everything else is filled in with their goals, their ideals and their ambitions. And what they have is something that is completely unreliable and not in keeping with the movement of life.

Become simple. Let your life be unexplainable. Let your life be inexplicable, for it will be inexplicable to those who cannot share it with you. You are being governed and guided by a Greater Power within you now, a Greater Power that you are coming to know through experience, a Greater Power that you are choosing by making wise decisions. Let this be. Do not claim things that are not yours to claim. Let there be big gaps in your understanding. Then you will be honest with yourself and honest with others, and you will be a refreshing presence in the world. Do not join with others in their odes to themselves, in singing their songs of self-assurance and self-validation. Remain silent and move on.

You can sing about the mountain of life or you can climb the mountain of life. If you climb the mountain of life, you don't know what's going to happen next. You only know that you have traveled it far enough to have learned something about traveling. You have learned to keep your eyes and your ears open and to not make gigantic assumptions about yourself or other people. You have learned to let your life develop, to keep going, and to build those things you know to build and to avoid those things you cannot build or should not build.

Power is concentration. If your power, your concentration, is spread out over many things, you will not have enough power for anything. Become focused on a few people, a few things and a few ideas. Don't try to collect all the spiritual information. Avoid this. Don't try to gather anything that is unnecessary. Let Knowledge move you to choose the things that you need rather than filling yourself with ideas, with books, with people, with experiences, with places to go and with things to do. In other words, don't clutter yourself with things that just have to be given up.

Next, avoid someone else's spiritual journey. Do not dabble in different religions because you will only be a dabbler. You can only know a religion if you immerse yourself within it. And if you immerse yourself in it, how can you be studying everything else? There are many people who take a very eclectic approach, who try to gather a little of this and a little of that. They have postcards from all over the spiritual universe, but they have never been anywhere. They think they understand what Christianity or Buddhism or Islam or any other religion means, but they have never immersed themselves in any of them. They have never lived them fully. They have lots of big ideas and no Wisdom. Avoid this. Avoid trying to tie in what you are doing with what someone else has done in the past or in the present. Do not make your way spiritual by saying that it is in keeping with Christianity or Buddhism or any other religion, for you don't really know. You have not yet gone far enough.

Avoid collecting spiritual ideas. They are more things to clutter up your mind. Yes, they look fascinating, interesting and inspiring, but are they necessary? The word "necessary" is important because your life *is* necessary, and you do not want to fill it up with things that are not necessary. Keep what is either practically necessary or greatly inspirational to you. Leave everything else aside. Keep your mind open and fresh. Let your library of books be small and significant. Let your conversation be simple. Use very few words. Listen more than speak. Hold your tongue when others are being foolish. Resist the temptation to correct others, to improve their situation or to dress them up to make them look better to you so that you will not have to judge them.

Immerse yourself in the journey that is opening before you. Do not try to become a part of another person's journey. Your way will then be simple and less encumbered. And if your way leads into the wilderness of life where no roads have been made, then follow it. If you seem to move away from all that is familiar and all that seems justifiable, stay with that. Trust what is in you. It is returning you to something great. It is restoring self-love and self-reliance to you. It is bringing you back into relationship with Knowledge and with the source of all Knowledge.

Avoid thinking you will be learning forever. This is not true. All avenues of learning have end points. There will come a time when you will not need to learn anything else in this world. That time is far ahead of where you are now. People think that they will be learning forever because they do not take their learning seriously. They think learning is like eating food. Well, you just keep eating more and you keep digesting and you keep eating more and more. Learning is not like eating food. It is not something you do to simply sustain yourself or to stimulate yourself. Learning is something that meets a great need in time. And this takes you somewhere. An advanced student of Knowledge is not learning what a beginning student is learning. Actually, an advanced student of Knowledge is learning new things while a beginning student is unlearning things primarily.

Avoid judging your past. Until you can see your past clearly, until it is obvious and clear to you, just keep moving forward. Like climbing the mountain, you will reach certain points where you can look out and see where you have been. However, at other points you cannot see this because you do not have the right perspective. Stay with what is necessary. Stay with what is in front of you. Give your attention to a few things and to a few ideas.

Next, avoid renouncing your worldly responsibilities. You need to build a foundation in the world in order to have a greater life. This means that you must maintain your health, your financial stability, and other things like this. Very rarely will you be asked to depart from something that seems to provide financial stability. Many people think spirituality is a wonderful place to escape to, where you leave the world and you go live another kind of existence. That is hiding out. There are times for retreat when you must seek reprieve and repose, but that is not your life. Maintain a sound foundation. Keep an accurate accounting of your life. Maintain your physical health. Then you will have a foundation upon which to build something greater. If you cannot pay your bills, you will not become a student of Knowledge because your life will be about paying your bills.

You cannot renounce the world, and do not think you have to. That is not your education. As a student of Knowledge, your position in the world will change, and you will become liberated from many of its constraints. However, you are meant to be here and to be effective here. That is why Wisdom is essential. If you were not in the world, you would not need Wisdom to be in the world. But you are in the world, and you do need Wisdom to be in here.

Avoid denying your worldly responsibilities. Just do not let them overtake you. Live simply. Keep your affairs in order so that the world will require less from you, so that you will have the time, energy and attention necessary for learning greater things. Give what you must give. Do your work, but maintain time for your development, for this is preparing the way for something greater.

Next, avoid impatience. Everyone is impatient when they begin. Everyone wants tremendous results with a minimal investment. Everyone wants a bargain from life where they have to give very little and get a great deal. Everyone wants to be comfortable and yet have all the rewards of an inspired life. Learn patience. You do not yet know what has to be unlearned and what has to be learned. You do not yet know how great the mountain is because when you are on the mountain, you can rarely see the summit. In fact, when you are on the mountain, you do not even know what it looks like as a whole. You just keep climbing. You keep going. You follow Knowledge. If Knowledge is quiet, you are quiet. If Knowledge is being still, you are being still. If Knowledge is moving, you are moving. If Knowledge does not respond, you do not respond. This is freedom of an unparalleled quality.

When you are impatient, you are exerting your personal will. You are trying to make things happen. You are impatient for the great rewards even though you have barely begun the journey. You are thinking of ways to elevate yourself to the top of the mountain. You are scheming and planning how you can get there without having to take the journey itself. These thoughts may pass through your mind infrequently or frequently. Recognize them for what they are and do not give them credibility.

Next, avoid thinking that you do not know something when in fact you do know it. Until you have really penetrated and investigated a problem or a question in life, do not say you do not know. Do not throw up your hands and say, "I don't know. How am I supposed to know?" until you have looked into it. If it is something important and requires your attention, then look into it. Perhaps you know nothing; perhaps you know a little; perhaps you know a great deal. People disclaim what they know and claim other things that are far beyond their reach, and they cannot tell the difference because they are only dealing with things at the level of ideas and not at the level of deeper experience. At the level of ideas you can have anything, be anything, do anything, want anything, assume anything or associate with anything because you are functioning at the level of imagination. You are dreaming. However, your deeper experience gives a more accurate representation of where you are, what you know and what you don't know, what you have and what you don't have.

Next, avoid making assumptions. As you advance, you will see how you make assumptions and you will become more aware of why you make them. Before that, you will simply make assumptions and be drawn into them. As you become more aware and more present to yourself in the moment, you will see your mind weaving a wonderful new idea, and you will able to stop yourself and say, "No. No, I don't think so." People are drawn to whatever looks attractive within their imagination and within the world.

Do not make assumptions. Look. Occasionally you will know something. That is enough. In the meantime, the mind will want to create and create and create and fill in all the spaces with its explanations, goals, plans and everything else. Learn to be still. You do not know this journey. You are only following it. You are learning it as you go. You may think you understand where you have just been, but you will not understand this fully until you have gotten further up the mountain and can see where you were within the context of the greater aspects of your journey. Let your mind be open and quiet. Keep it simple.

Within these things that we have mentioned, you will find other things that you will need to recognize and perhaps avoid. And you will recognize things that you need to claim. However, you will find as you proceed that your life will become simpler and simpler. You will be more focused and will have fewer things to think about. As you have fewer things to think about, and as your mind becomes more powerful and focused, your vision and experience will become more penetrating. You will be freed from being distracted by most of the things that captured your attention and your imagination before. And you will become stronger, for power is concentration, whether it is used for good or for evil.

Knowledge will make what seems insurmountable and confusing simple, day by day. It will not explain things to you; it will simply demonstrate what is true. It will not fill your mind with great explanations and cosmologies, levels of existence and being and so forth. It will empty out your mind so that you can be present, so that you can see and know and so that Knowledge and your mind can work together.

You will want to avoid these things that we have mentioned because they hold you back, because they gamble your existence and because they waste your life. Here you will learn to say "yes" or "no," instead of "good" or "bad." There is a world of difference between these two evaluations. You will say "yes" when yes is needed. You will say "no" when yes is not present. You will stay close to life and close to Knowledge. You will travel light, and your pace will quicken. You will pass by many things that would have stopped you before. And you will no longer recognize many things that drew you in previously. This represents advancement. This is what awaits you as you proceed.

As your mind becomes more focused and less distracted, you will begin to demonstrate a greater power and a greater certainty that will permeate whatever action is yours to take and whatever contribution is yours to make. And Grace will be with you, for Grace is wholehearted and comes from beyond the world.

—◦◦◦—

You have allies in the Greater Community.

They understand what you will be facing.

They have faced these things themselves.

They understand what you will

have to contend with,

for they have had to contend with

these things themselves.

—◦◦◦—

CHAPTER FIFTEEN

WHO SERVES HUMANITY?

———*ᴧᴧᴧ*———

$\mathscr{I}$N THE GREATER COMMUNITY, YOU HAVE GREAT ALLIES. They are significant but hidden. Your allies represent a very secret bond. This bond is not a political power. It is not a worldly society. It is not a power with vast armies. It is not something that can rescue you from the clutches of another alien force. You have a different kind of ally, one far more dedicated and reliable.

Your allies serve humanity because they serve the reclamation and expression of Knowledge everywhere in the Greater Community. They represent the Wise in many worlds who support a greater purpose in life. Together they share a greater Knowledge and Wisdom that can be transferred across vast distances of space and across all the boundaries of race, culture, temperament and environment. Their Wisdom is pervasive. Their skill is great. Their presence is hidden. They recognize you because they realize that you are an emerging race, emerging into a very difficult and competitive environment in the Greater Community.

They realize you are unprepared, and therefore they give to you, as they give to many other emerging worlds in this era, a greater possibility for preparation in The Greater Community Way of Knowledge. The Greater Community Way of Knowledge has been translated specifically for human beings into a form, a language and a set of concepts that are understandable to you, that are within your reach and that call upon familiar ideas and experiences. Only a Greater Intelligence could render such a preparation into the world. It is the Will of God that this be done, and the Wise who are your allies serve this unquestioningly.

Your allies in the Greater Community are alive in the physical universe. They have as their counterparts those invisible allies that you have who are called the Unseen Ones. Here, however, we shall speak of your allies within the physical universe itself, for you need to be aware that they exist and that they are aware of you. You need to be aware that they have achieved what you are now setting out to accomplish. And you need to realize that in the Greater Community you are not alone, though you will indeed feel like you are alone in the great reaches of space.

Your allies are called the Harim, which is a word meaning "those with skill" in Septoral, a commonly used language in the Greater Community. This word, though new to you, is used to illustrate both the assistance available to you and some of the realities that you will find in a greater context of life that extends far beyond the boundaries of your world and the limits of your awareness.

The Harim exist to support the reclamation of Knowledge everywhere—wherever intelligent life dwells and wherever intelligent life has originated in the physical universe. They serve as intermediaries between the invisible world where you have come from and the visible world where you live now. Great is their skill and accomplishment. Few in your world have ever achieved their state of awareness. Their mission is not simply to support and assist their own races and cultures. Instead, their role is to support Knowledge in the Greater Community. Their accomplishments make peaceful relations possible between worlds. They make higher education possible and make possible the elevation of worldly societies.

The Harim work for peace in the Greater Community, and thus their mission and their scope are enormous. They represent individuals from many worlds. Some have met each other and others have never met each other. Yet they are held together through a great network of communication that utilizes the Unseen Ones, who can go anywhere and who can deliver information from one world to another through non-physical means. This great network of communication extends to your world. It represents a marvelous accomplishment in the mental environment.

You cannot fully comprehend the magnitude of what is being presented here, but you can appreciate the fact that this great network of communication is in the world and available to humanity. Through this network of communication, a Greater Community Way of Knowledge and a preparation for the Greater Community are being given to you. Therefore, not only do you have assistance from beyond the physical universe, you have assistance from within it as well.

The Harim are not preoccupied with human development or human affairs. In their care are many worlds—worlds in various stages of emergence into the Greater Community, worlds that have matured in the Greater Community and worlds that are declining in the Greater Community. The Harim is active now in your world because of your emergence into the Greater Community. They represent Knowledge and Wisdom on a grand scale and within a far larger context, a context that makes everything that is being presented here in this Teaching universally applicable. What is true in the Greater Community must be true for your world, for your world is not different in this regard.

The Wise Ones who support your world serve as an example to show that everything we are speaking of can be demonstrated and learned regardless of the limitations and difficulties in your world. How they associate with each other and how they communicate across the great distances is a marvel and is something that you can now begin to appreciate, at least conceptually. Why are they hidden? Because they are generally not welcome in their own worlds unless their race has evolved to a high level. If their race has evolved to a high level, then it has gone into secrecy itself because the Wise remain hidden, and wise societies remain hidden for the very same reasons.

Power in the universe is recognized in both the technological and the mental arenas. There are limits to technological power, of course, though you have not reached these limits yet. The powers of the mind, the powers of a group mind and the ability to influence the mental environment, however, represent a more advanced and mature approach to the use of power in the Greater Community. The limits to physical power open greater doors to this other kind of power in the universe. Here those who are smarter can defeat those who are stronger, and those who are wiser can avoid those who are invasive.

Strength in the mental environment represents a greater development of power in the Greater Community. This is true in your world as well. Though the understanding of the mental environment is only in its beginning stages here, it potentially represents a great achievement for humanity and one that will enable you to offset the interference of other Greater Community forces in your world, whose social cohesion and technological ability far exceed your own.

The Harim recognize that nations and entire populations of any world cannot be elevated all at once. Only certain individuals can be prepared to contribute to their race in order to elevate it, strengthen it and so forth. Through their efforts and demonstrations, their own society and population at large can slowly advance. Therefore, the work is done through individuals here and there. It is not done through governments. It is not done through organized religions. It is not done through large groups. It is not done through social groups, political groups or economic groups. Instead, it is done through individuals who are prepared to assume a greater understanding and ability. Their contribution will far exceed what they could have accomplished without this preparation. What greater service can you perform for your world than to prepare it for the future in order to guarantee its future well-being and advancement? Remember, you work for the present and for the future. Human beings do not yet understand this, but this is known to be true in the Greater Community.

The Harim will not communicate to many people in the world because this is not necessary. And they cannot have direct communication on an ongoing basis. What they have learned is what you are reading today, what we are giving to you in this moment. What we are giving to you in this moment teaches what has been learned and demonstrated in the Greater Community. It represents the work of the Harim, for their example and their skill have verified what can be done in the physical universe in any particular world and what needs to be done given your world's current state and future circumstances.

Remember, the Harim do not represent a political force, a national government or any one world population. Its members dwell in secret and communicate with each other in secret. Though in some places they serve official religious or political roles, they do not represent their respective governments in their greater work. Governments by nature are concerned with order and survival. The Harim are concerned with truth and education. Therefore, their work cannot be constrained or limited by any government, either worldly or interplanetary.

The Harim's numbers are few, and their skill is only revealed to certain individuals at certain times and is rarely demonstrated publicly. They are hidden, and that is why they are able to maintain their Wisdom. Their power has been protected from the usurpation of governments, trade organizations and guilds, military powers and so forth. You cannot yet see and understand how great an achievement this is, what it means and what it can teach you about power and ambition in life. Your world now needs individuals to advance in this understanding because they can give to the world something that the world cannot give itself.

You need help from beyond the world to prepare for the Greater Community. How can you prepare yourself? You do not know what is out there. You do not know the political and economic situation as it exists even within your part of the universe. You do not know how to defend yourself, and you do not know who to defend yourself against. How will you tell who is friendly and who is not? Your visitors will be able to present any number of images or demonstrations to you. How will you know what they are doing unless you can read their intelligence? And how can you read their intelligence if you are not developed in the mental environment? How can you discern their purpose if you are not skilled in The Greater Community Way of Knowledge? How can you match a race that is thousands of years more advanced than you in technology?

The only way that you can advance, and the only way that you will be able to interpret, discern and contend with forces from the Greater Community is through the development of Knowledge. This is true because Knowledge is the only part of your mind that cannot be influenced or dominated. It is the only part of your mind that is pure. It cannot be infiltrated. It cannot be manipulated, either in the mental or in the physical environment. It is unaffected by technology. It is unaffected by the demonstrations of power. It is unaffected by the manipulations of fear. It is the only part of you that is free. Therefore, the more you associate with Knowledge and become united with Knowledge, the freer you will become, the more capable you will be in encountering new experiences and new forces in life and the more able you will be to discern your visitors' motives and activities beyond any appearance.

Perhaps you cannot yet realize the importance of this. That is because your mind is referenced in the past. The Greater Community was not relevant in your past, generally speaking, unless of course you have had Greater Community contact in this life. However, most people will have to go beyond their past referencing and what they can relate to or experience in order to entertain the greater Wisdom that is being presented here. Our words convey important messages, but most importantly they can incite a deep response in you, if you can give that response and feel it.

If you know how to prepare for the future, you will know what to do today. If you know what to do today, you will be freed from what you did yesterday. For your future will be unlike your past, very unlike your past. Your future will give you possibilities and challenges that your ancestors never dreamed of.

You have allies in the Greater Community. They understand what you will be facing. They have faced these things themselves. They understand what you will have to contend with, for they have had to contend with these things themselves. They know what the development of Knowledge means and how it must be carried out within societal life, for they have accomplished this themselves.

You will not meet these individuals. They will not jump on board a space craft and travel the long distance to your planet. They will not come and speak to the President of the United States or the United Nations or any government or group here. But they do speak to those who can be initiated into Knowledge. And they speak through means that can bridge the great gulf of time and space. They do not travel about dispensing and preaching Wisdom. Their ideas come via a different kind of a network, a network that is out of reach to even the skillful in planetary governments.

We assure you, there are many skillful individuals and groups in the Greater Community who, if you encountered them without your being strong with Knowledge, would be able to discern and control your thoughts and make you think what they want you to think. They are that powerful and effective. As you can now influence and manipulate your physical environment to a certain degree, they have learned to influence and manipulate the mental environment to an even greater degree. But they cannot influence Knowledge. In fact, they may not even be aware of Knowledge.

Perhaps you are beginning to get an image or an idea of what is being presented here. There is an effort in the Greater Community to foster good. It represents the way God works in physical existence, which is behind the scenes and through inspired individuals. God does not intervene. God does not control everything for everyone because God is wise. God knows better. God works behind the scenes through inspired individuals and through united relationships at all levels—at the level of individuals, families, groups, cities, nations and worlds.

There are greater powers at work that assist humanity and that serve humanity. They ask nothing in return except that you study The Way of Knowledge and become serious students who learn to look beyond your personal interests and fears in order to see beyond the limiting ideas of your mind. They ask that you begin to feel, to see and to ask that Knowledge reveal itself to you. They ask that you gain a greater ability, with patience and reverence for life. What can you give them in return except to receive their gifts? They do not need your wealth.

They certainly do not need your ideas. They do not need anything from the world, except for humanity to learn to live in peace with itself and to contend successfully with the Greater Community. This is a great enough challenge for an emerging world.

The Harim extend over vast regions. They are associated with each other through the Unseen Ones, who communicate with them and who deliver messages for them. The Unseen Ones represent your spiritual allies who work on behalf of worlds individually and worlds together. For now, it is important for you to consider that you are not alone in the physical universe.

In the Greater Community, there are societies that exist at every stage of evolution, and there are societies that have failed for every reason. There are societies at war. There are societies at peace. There are societies that trade. There are societies that do not trade. There are societies that belong to commercial guilds. There are societies that do not belong to commercial guilds. There are societies that travel in space. There are societies that do not travel in space. There are societies that are primitive. There are societies that have beginning technology, such as your own. And there are societies that have gone beyond the limits of technology into new kinds of education and development. There are societies that have been defeated. There are societies that have been victorious. There are societies that have gone into hiding. There are societies that search from star to star for a home. There are societies that are exclusively engaged in commerce. There are societies that are law-abiding and civil. There are societies which are not. There are societies that are physically strong, and there are societies which are not.

If you can consider these ideas, you will think of examples within your own world. Yet consider how much greater is the panorama of life in the Greater Community and how much stronger are the opposing forces there. One benefit here is that the physical universe is quite large. And though space travel is actively carried on, more actively in certain areas than in others, no one can get around that quickly. The universe is too big, and therefore societies such as yours can live in relative isolation for a very long time. There are worlds in the Greater Community that have never been discovered by other races. The universe is too vast. There are unexplored regions in the Greater Community, and there are regions that are largely inhabited. There are regions where it is safe to travel, and there are regions where it is not safe to travel. There are regions that are defended and protected, and there are regions that are not.

You live in a great municipality of life. It is as if humanity were just venturing out of the house for the first time and beginning to explore its front and back yards. You do not even know your neighborhood yet. In this neighborhood, there are big kids on the block, but you are the little tiny kid who does not know anything.

How will you prepare for life in the Greater Community? Many people think that they will simply export human culture and religion and attempt to persuade others of the superiority of their morals and ethics. However, honestly speaking, humanity at this time makes a very poor demonstration. Its great accomplishment is occurring on the individual level and on the level of small groups and associations. On the level of nations and races and cultures, your behavior is still very primitive and brutish. We are not being cruel here. We are simply giving you a Greater Community perspective.

How will you prepare for the Greater Community? You will prepare through Knowledge. Technologically you are way behind. In your social cohesion you are way behind. You are just beginning to realize the need now for world community, yet even that idea is largely rejected and is still highly unpopular. As human societies now move towards merging together and becoming more interdependent with each other, wars, struggles and ancient animosities are arising between them. However, your nations will join because they must. It is your destiny. It is your evolution. You will do it or perish. Therefore, the need is greater than the resistance.

Preparation for the Greater Community is being offered for several reasons, some of which are not so obvious. What is obvious is that you need to prepare for the Greater Community. What is not obvious is that the preparation itself will enable you to contend with the problems inherent in your own world, problems that have become severe and global in nature.

You need a Greater Community Way of Knowledge to see what you have to accomplish and to be challenged to accomplish it. You need a Greater Community Way of Knowledge in order to remain a self-determined race, or else you will fall under the control of an alien society. Your self-determination is important here, for it guarantees you a future where the greater aspects of your nature can emerge and take precedence over your more animal instincts. Such is the promise of life in your world. However, having promise does not guarantee a successful result. That is why you have allies within the world, within the Greater Community and beyond all the physical manifestations of life.

God is not preoccupied with the workings of this one world. God is not preoccupied with your success or your failure. But God has set into motion that which gives you the greatest possibility for success. When people say, "Well, my scripture says that God appeared before this man, and God appeared at the edge of the desert, and God parted the sea," they are talking about the Unseen Ones. God does not come to the world. God has never been to the world. God is everywhere. Only a tiny god could come to the world, show up, make things happen, appear before certain individuals and speak to the prophets. Only a small god could come to your house. And it is a small god. It is God's messengers, who are part of God. In the Greater Community, the understanding of God is so much greater. In the Greater Community, you don't sit and say, "Well, when is God going to come to my house? When is God going to give *me* some attention? When is God going to come and take care of *my* situation? When is God going to come and work out this problem that I am facing?" You cannot think like that in the Greater Community, for life is too big.

Go out on a clear night and look up. Your destiny is there. Your difficulties are there. Your opportunities are there. Your redemption is there. To successfully survive and advance in the Greater Community, you must become unified as a race, and you must preserve your environment, no matter what the cost. It must be done because it is your evolution and destiny. It won't happen because you want it. It will happen because it must be done.

Everything that happens in life happens because it must, not because someone wanted it to. Things that happen because someone wanted them to have no permanency. They are temporary. Yes, you can make a splash in the water, but your splash will be forgotten very quickly. Yes, you can have an impact on your physical environment, but over the span of time your mark on the world will be lost and forgotten. Yet your influence and development in Knowledge will not be forgotten, for the results of Knowledge are permanent; its results are for everyone. Even though in the course of your life you may only meet certain people and communicate to certain individuals, you are giving something into the mental and physical environment for everyone here. You are also giving something into the Greater Community. With every individual and group of individuals in the Greater Community who can receive your gift, Knowledge becomes stronger in the Greater Community. It becomes stronger with your development and your accomplishment. And it becomes weaker without it.

As you go beyond the boundaries of your world, both physically and in terms of your awareness, you enter a larger arena of life made up of greater opposing forces. Like a little child who peers out from the front door into the street and imagines what it must be like out there, you look up at the stars and you imagine what is going on out there. Everything looks so vacant and empty, so distant and so impersonal. Yet there is a great deal going on out there even though the distances are vast. And unless you go to an area where a great deal of commerce is being carried on, you will not meet many others.

The world you live in, however, is not in some remote or distant corner of the universe that no one has ever been to. In fact, your world really is not that remote at all. Few races have had occasion or the need to come here, but your world has been visited throughout its history—sometimes even very frequently, as it is now. Yet now you are being scrutinized by several different groups for different reasons. There is a great deal of planning going on about how to influence humanity, how to use humanity, how to take advantage of the world's wonderful natural resources, how to develop humanity according to the political aim of one or two other races and how to prevent humanity from falling into an enemy's camp.

Your isolation is over. The implications for this are awesome—perhaps terrible, perhaps wonderful. This gives humanity what it needs right now, which is a big collective problem. It gives you who are reading this book a sober view into your life and into your future. It calls upon a greater incentive within you to enable you to develop and to find your purpose, for you have come to serve this world at this time. It is not an accident that you came at this time and to this place. You came here to assist in some specific way the world's emergence into the Greater Community because this is the biggest thing that is happening here. This is the most consequential event in human history. This will change your thoughts, your priorities, your institutions, and eventually even your religions, for they were made for humans alone and cannot entertain the scope of the Greater Community.

In the Greater Community, God is Knowledge because God cannot be localized. God cannot be the resident of one world. God cannot give priority to one world. God is everywhere. How can you have a personal religion, like you have in the world, without God being localized? In the Greater Community, then, God is Knowledge. Knowledge is that part of God that works within the individual, initiating great relationships between individuals and setting into motion activities that contribute to the well-being of the race to which those individuals belong. Beyond this, Knowledge contributes to the well-being of all races, such as at the level of the Harim.

Do not think that this sounds too great for you to consider. You need to think of these things now. Do not return to your safe little familiar ideas and activities. Life is calling you. It is calling you to consider greater things and to call upon a Greater Power within yourself which will enable you to learn greater things and to achieve greater things. Return to your individual life, but with a greater awareness, a greater discernment and the need to understand things on a larger scale. Life is working here in spite of human goals, plans and motivations. Life is bringing humanity into the Greater Community because that is humanity's evolution.

Yet how this will be achieved and what its results will be will largely be determined by human response and response-ableness, or responsibility. You are the race that is being discovered. Therefore, you are the race that needs to be prepared. To serve you, there are races in the Greater Community who can respond to the Harim and who are influenced by them. They do not represent military forces or world governments necessarily. They are your potential allies, but they cannot become directly involved at this time.

You have the possibility for great friendships as well as great allies. Yet you have not gone far enough into the Greater Community, either mentally or physically, to see what exists there. However, you have the possibility of having great friends if you can be pure of heart and if you can focus your service not only on meeting the needs of humanity but on developing relationships with other races. These great friends come with good intentions, not to exploit you, not to control you, not to gain access to your resources, not to influence your development, not to colonize you and not to take you over. Can you have this same approach with them? Given current human behavior and understanding, the possibility does exist, but it is improbable that this will be your emphasis once you are able to travel beyond the boundaries of your world. There are Greater Community forces even in your solar system who are planning defenses against this occurring. They can keep you from venturing very far without a great deal of effort on their part.

You need Knowledge to see, to know what to do and to do what you know. You need to develop in The Greater Community Way of Knowledge. That is why this must be the primary emphasis for you. Let fear not be your motivation; let wishful thinking not be your motivation. Let Knowledge itself be your motivation. Fear will not prepare you. Wishful thinking will not prepare you. Saying everything will be wonderful or saying everything will be disastrous will not prepare you. You must prepare. Let Knowledge motivate you. Let your deeper sense of what is right and correct motivate you. Nothing is being asked of you except to receive the gift of Knowledge that is being given to your world through this Teaching.

We honor the one who has received us who has made this possible for you. However, this is a gift that must also be given by you. Do not exploit it. Do not try to use it for your personal advantage. Do not try to become a master and appoint yourself the right to interpret the Greater Community Way of Knowledge for others unless we have given you this right. To achieve this you must be very advanced, which you are not. Remember, we are the Unseen Ones, and this gift we give to serve you, to prepare you, to enable you and to direct you because God is at work in the world.

—✺—

Every student needs a Teacher.

Every traveler needs a guide.

Every explorer needs a map.

You have all of these now.

—✺—

CHAPTER SIXTEEN

WHO ARE THE
UNSEEN ONES?

———⁕⁕⁕———

*A*S YOU HAVE ALLIES WITHIN THE WORLD and within the Greater Community, you also have allies beyond the visible range of life. They are here to be a part of your education in Knowledge. No longer in the physical, they now serve those who are regaining the memory of their Ancient Home and with it the nature and direction of their greater purpose in life.

The Unseen Ones are able to operate very freely in counseling those who exist below. And yet their counsel must be wisely placed and well timed. They cannot interfere although they do offer support which enables those who are responding to them to gain a greater understanding and a greater efficacy in life. Rarely will their recipients experience them directly. Yet the Unseen Ones feed information and insights into the minds of those who can respond. In most cases, people will think that they are coming up with their own ideas. "Oh, I had this idea today. I think it is important," or "I had this feeling that I should do this." People think it is coming from them or they think it is their own intuition, when in reality it is a gift from the Unseen Ones.

The Unseen Ones, of course, do not need recognition in the world. They are not looking for students or followers. What do you have that they want except your ability to respond and to utilize what they give you for a good purpose? The Unseen Ones place their gifts carefully and well. Rarely will they speak to someone directly. Though many people hear voices that they feel have a spiritual focus, it is rare indeed that anyone will ever receive the presence and voice of an Unseen One directly.

Why is this? It is because people's focus needs to be on Knowledge and on their endeavors in the world. If you begin associating with angels, well, you will not want to associate with anything else. Who would want to do the difficult work in the world when you could pass the time with an angelic presence? Who would want to have to deal with people and all of their difficulties and all of the complexities of relationships when you could hold company with the Spirits of God? The work is in the world, and that is the focus.

In order to give receptive, responsible people the great advantages of understanding and perception, to assist them in the reclamation of Knowledge and to verify the reclamation of Knowledge itself, the Unseen Ones place their emphasis here and there. Perhaps you have heard a voice speaking in your mind or have felt a strange and sudden impulse. It could be because Knowledge within you is in communication with Knowledge in the Unseen Ones. The closer you are to Knowledge, the more you will become aware that there is a greater communication going on. Until then, you will not know where these ideas come from. You will just assume that they come from you or are a product of your intuition.

The Unseen Ones pay special attention to those who are responding. These individuals require greater care and emphasis. Those few who can advance will have a greater relationship with the Unseen Ones, whom they will rightly call Teachers. However, they will rarely experience the Teachers, and they may never know within this life who is speaking to them, helping them and guiding them. Perhaps they will simply feel that they are receiving something from the spiritual realm of life. Perhaps they will think it is the Spirit of God who is speaking to them. However they define it to themselves or explain it to others, there is a greater involvement here with the Unseen Ones.

You have counselors and guides in the world to help you learn the specific things that you have to understand here. However, learning something about spirituality, having your inner life be born, beginning the process of reclaiming Knowledge and developing an awareness of a greater purpose here all require a different kind of counsel and support. You will primarily receive assistance in this from your allies in the world, but overseeing your development will be the Unseen Ones. They will abide with you and keep track of what you are doing. Occasionally, they will counsel you directly. On very rare occasions they may let you know that they are with you. This, of course, varies from person to person and depends a great deal on the person's temperament and character as well as his or her level of development.

Take heart. You have great allies. Great things are asked of you to learn, but you have great assistance. Take heart. You are being called out of ordinary circumstances, ordinary awareness and ordinary preoccupations. Be grateful. You are being rescued from a deadly mediocrity. You are being given a real opportunity here. If you can receive this and begin to make progress as a student of Knowledge, then those forces within the world and beyond that can help you will take a greater and greater role in your life.

We have referred to the idea of the Spiritual Family several times and will speak on this now. You have come into the world from a small learning group. You are learning for yourself and for your group. You are contributing in the world for your own advancement and for the advancement of your group. Your group will evolve to join with other groups, and like rivers and streams joining together on their way to the sea, you will experience greater and greater union as you advance together.

The Unseen Ones represent the senior members of your Spiritual Family. They do not need to be in the world any more. They have learned the lessons of the world. Now they must help those who must learn the lessons of the world. They oversee your development and become actively engaged with you as you choose The Way of Knowledge, as you undertake the preparation that is meant for you and as you begin to make progress.

Your collaboration with the Unseen Ones will grow, but they cannot be your emphasis. They are greater than you and more powerful and more gracious. However, if you became aware of them, they would become the object of your devotion and attention, which is not appropriate. This would not help your studenthood, and this would not give you the right concentration or the right priorities.

The way is given to you without hero worship because you must become a man or woman of Knowledge. You will need both those more advanced than you and those less advanced than you. Those more advanced pull you along, and you pull those along who are less advanced. In this way, everyone finds proper assistance. In this way, everyone is served. In this way, everything that the Unseen Ones give into the world can resonate through human relationships and reach many people in ways that can be understood, experienced and accepted.

Whenever you or any of your ancestors ever thought that God was in the world doing something, it was the Unseen Ones—the angels of God, if you like that idea. But the idea of angels conjures up very quaint images and does not really capture the full meaning and role of the Unseen Ones. They are with you, but like the Wise everywhere, they remain hidden. They do not want to become the light of your life. If this were the case, you would seek no further. They do not want to overshadow you with their Wisdom. If they did, you would not develop your own. They do not want to become the focus of your attention. If they did, you would lose attention on those things where your attention is required. They are God's emissaries. They translate the Will of the Divine into finite existence. At every level of existence, there are translators. Ultimately, you will have the opportunity to become a translator yourself while you are in the world, translating greater Wisdom into a useful and accessible expression that others can benefit from.

There are different levels of Unseen Ones. The Unseen Ones who assist you are assisted themselves, for the chain of authority, the chain of giving, continues far, far beyond you—translating and making a greater will and purpose accessible and available to you. This is beyond your comprehension. You cannot even imagine it, and you are not required to do so.

We introduce the idea of the Unseen Ones to you so that you will know that you are not alone and that your life has great assistance. You can rely on a greater Wisdom to help you proceed, both within yourself, in your Knowledge, and beyond yourself, in the Unseen Ones and your Spiritual Family. They will enable you to find the way to strengthen yourself. However, they will not rescue you from every bad decision that you make. They will not spare you the expense of your errors. And they will not cushion every blow. But they will not punish you either. They will not reprimand you. They will only give their influence and their counsel. If you can feel this, be receptive to it and value it more than your personal wishes, then you will be their beneficiary. In this, they will be confirmed, and so will you.

Every student needs a teacher. Every traveler needs a guide. Every explorer needs a map. You have all of these now. Take heart. Now you must find the courage and the determination to proceed. Do not become fixated on the great spiritual assistance that you have. Rather, become focused on solving problems today and tomorrow and the day after. Solve a little problem today and you will be able to solve a greater one tomorrow. Start with little things. Attend to the practical matters in your life. Bring your life into greater harmony. Do not try to make everything beautiful, quiet and peaceful. This is not what we mean. What we mean is bringing things into right order.

You must translate this for yourself. People often think that spirituality is about being happy, peaceful and joyful all the time, turning life into a sort of slumber party. This is not true. Spirituality is not a form of escape. It is not a form of intoxication. It is not an aphrodisiac. It is a way to empower you by bringing you into contact with Knowledge so that you may fulfill your purpose and your mission here. Then you will be able to identify and receive those who are destined to share your purpose with you. Spirituality is to enable you to work, to enable your life to work and to enable a Greater Power to work through you. This is not a beauty school where you make yourself and everyone else look glorious and angelic. This is not a vacation from life. This is a training and a preparation. This is a study and an application. This is to make your life more full, more purposeful, more genuine and more wholesome for you and for those who will receive you and recognize you.

Even those who cannot see you and cannot recognize you will benefit as well, for there will be a greater presence of Knowledge in the world through your contribution. This brings everyone a step closer to their Ancient Home. This narrows the great gulf that separates life in the world from life beyond the physical. This brings the experience and the demonstration of God's work in the world a little bit closer because inspiration, selflessness, contribution, benefit, kindness, compassion, love, strength and self-determination are being demonstrated and added into the world. The world needs this demonstration. People are desperate for meaning. They are desperate for value. They have lost contact with their inner lives. These qualities need to be demonstrated for them and returned to them with as little religious dogma as possible, in as pure a form as possible.

This is the evidence of God's work. God does not do the work for you. God teaches you to work because you came here to work, and you need to realize your value. God gives you the power. God gives you God's messengers. God gives you allies. God gives you opportunities. And God gives you the great needs in the world, which will pull out of you and require you to give what you came here to give. If the world were sweet and wonderful, happy and carefree, you would not have any purpose in being here. You would not know what to do. You would become frustrated.

The condition of the world is ripe for contribution. You are not here to enlist people in your religion or to fortify a particular religious teaching, unless it is your specific mission to do this. Only for a few will this be the case. You will give something mysterious and wonderful in the context of relationships and in the context of helping people. Who you will help and how you will help them is something you will discover as you go along. Whom you cannot help and whom you are not to get involved with must also be learned and demonstrated to you.

You were made for something. It is waiting to be discovered. In this way, you find yourself, you validate yourself, you experience yourself and you witness yourself in action. What other way is there to find your true value? You can tell yourself you're wonderful all day long, but without the demonstration of a greater ability and quality in you, it is idle talk. This is about you giving to the world, not about you looking good to yourself.

The Unseen Ones work without recognition. The Harim in the Greater Community work without recognition. The Wise in the world work without recognition. Understand this, and you will understand how Wisdom and Knowledge can be given into situations where they are unknown and even where they are unwelcome. Here Wisdom and Knowledge can exercise their beneficence to strengthen people's inner integrity, to remind people of their greater responsibilities and to support people in being honest with themselves and in coming to terms with their deeper inclinations and sense of justice and correctness, regardless of their past political or religious persuasions.

The demonstration of God's presence and grace is given through the actions of people in relationship. The Unseen Ones demonstrate this. The Harim demonstrate this. Your allies demonstrate this. Your recipients will demonstrate this. You are giving something precious in a difficult situation. You must be hardworking and determined to do this. Do not use spirituality as a drug, as an intoxicant. Do not use it to be in bliss. Do not blind yourself with it. Use the light to find your way. Do not use it for hallucinations. The gift must be given through you in both tangible and intangible ways. Do not think you'll be a great emancipator, a great spiritual princess or prince, goddess or god. You will do simple work. You will do humble work. You will do the work that needs to be done, not the work that necessarily glorifies you. What will be honored is Knowledge within you, which will honor you. Then there will be no deception.

Here you will begin to understand how you are served and how you are supported. You will begin to understand how great individuals have helped you without overshadowing you or interfering with you. They have nurtured you and protected you, carried you away from danger and kept you going in the right direction. They have allowed you to make your own mistakes, but in such a way that you could benefit from them and not have to repeat them.

Eventually you can become like an Unseen One in the world, even while you are still living here as a person. You will give, and your gifts will work their way into the minds and hearts of people, who will not know where the gifts came from. They won't be able to find the giver. The giver is free and invisible to them. People will see things and feel things they need to see and feel. They will begin to know things that they need to know. They will remember things that they need to remember and forget things that they need to forget. They will not see where this power comes from. They will not see the source of it.

Become like an Unseen One yourself and your gifts will have the greatest impact with the least confusion and uncertainty. Humanity has been kept alive by the gracious work of many individuals within and beyond the world who remain unrecognized. And the forces of ignorance—those who are violent and fearful, hostile and resistant—will not be able to find where the good is coming from. They will not be able to stop it. They will not be able to manipulate it. It will pass through their fingers. They will not be able to clutch it. It will work in spite of their damage.

The greatest powers that are assisting you are unseen. However, they can be known, and it is your privilege to know them. The greater powers perhaps cannot be touched, but they can touch you, and you can receive their grace and utilize it appropriately, for it is you who must grow and regain your strength and authority. In this, you must be supported but not overshadowed. You must be assisted but not manipulated. You must be protected but not guarded. What great compassion this demonstrates.

As you advance, you will begin to experience these things for yourself. You will begin to be happy when you can give a gift, have it be received and have no one know where it came from. This protects and preserves you and enables the gift to have its full impact. You must be maturing as a student of Knowledge to have this experience. But its demonstration will convince you of the wisdom of the idea that the Wise remain hidden to remain wise.

—•∿∿•—

These are people who are

following something inexplicable

that they do not attempt to define or use.

Their silence is profound and inviting.

They are with the Mystery.

And the Mystery is with them.

—•∿∿•—

CHAPTER SEVENTEEN

HOW DOES REVELATION OCCUR IN HUMAN LIFE?

REVELATION IS A GIFT THAT IS GIVEN to certain individuals who will have a prominent role to play in leading others. It happens very rarely and only under very special circumstances. It is meant to initiate these individuals and to confirm their Knowledge. It occurs when time is of the essence, and they must engage with a higher purpose or lose their great opportunity altogether. Revelation is an extreme exercise to initiate something that must happen now.

These demonstrations are extremely rare, and for good reasons. They can be very frightening to the mind that is not yet ready for them. And they will most certainly be disorienting, for now you are experiencing two realities that seem to have very little to do with each other. The recipient must be ready for this, must receive it graciously and must be able to interpret its meaning and patiently exercise its Wisdom. Otherwise, it will be a traumatic event that will be misinterpreted and misunderstood.

If you could see how fragile your reality is in the world, which you would see if you were standing outside your world looking in; if you could see how easily it is upset and challenged and how weak its foundation is; if you could see how it is built upon certain assumptions that are never questioned and how it is reinforced by using past references to keep the mind stable, then you would understand how delicately the Unseen Ones must involve themselves with promising students here.

This kind of revelation is initiating. Do not demand it or expect it, for you will not know what you are demanding or expecting. People want many things, but rarely do they realize what the responsibility of having their desired experience, object or person will require. People want to have revelation because they want proof. They want to assure their personal minds that their spiritual inclinations are genuine, but this can never be proven to the personal mind. The personal mind is established in the absence of your spiritual inclinations and will generally be opposed to them until it can finally yield to them. This is not where you gain your approval. How can the personal mind, this temporary understanding, this temporary experience in the world, confirm and approve a Greater Reality that has no beginning and no end?

There is, however, a greater and more complete kind of revelation that occurs as the result of many years of dedicated studenthood in The Way of Knowledge. It is a different kind of revelation. It is not sudden and dramatic. It does not burst in upon your life. It does not intrude itself upon you. It is something you will gradually be able to feel, as the veil between physical life and life beyond the physical becomes thinner and thinner and as you experience more and more communication and are able to receive the translation of insight and information coming into your mind.

Increasingly, you will have a sense that there is a presence, an intelligence, on the other side. In fact, you will have the experience that there is a great group assisting you and cheering for you. This will ease and eventually eliminate your fear of death because you will see that your Spiritual Family is waiting there. They are there for you. You can feel them. Your eyes were not created to see such things, nor were your body's ears created to hear such things. However, your inner eyes can see and your inner ears can hear because you can feel this; you can sense it.

Communication will be coming into your mind, and you will know that it is not a product of your own thinking or imagination. This is a very subtle revelation, but its impact is enormous. It comes as the result of a great deal of preparation and advancement in exercising a greater purpose in the world. Though it may be a hope and an ideal for beginning students to have this experience in order to dispel their fears, it will rarely come here and for good reason. The emphasis in your life must first be on Knowledge and contribution. Until you are well established here, something which you yourself cannot fully determine, the presence of your Spiritual Family will remain in the background so as not to debilitate you or distract you from being able to be in the world to do your work here. The experience of your Family is so much more wonderful than the experience of trying to survive, contribute and be genuine in a harsh and difficult world.

Perhaps you think that the world is an easy and wonderful place, but it will seem barren and difficult in contrast to your Ancient Home. Contact with your Spiritual Family will renew your memories of your Ancient Home. This will make you intensely homesick and draw your attention away from the world and from all that is in the world. Should this experience happen too soon, it will be very difficult for you to generate the desire and the intention to be a participant in the world and to face the challenges which you must face. Heaven can come too soon in this regard. You may pray for it, you may want it, you may plead for it, but if it comes too soon, it will distract you. It is better that a very gradual revelation occur here. This gives you a sense of presence and an abiding experience of communication, assistance and support. Here you can maintain your focus in the world, but with the greater assurance that your Family is with you and that your destiny is assured.

Revelation is at the discretion of your Spiritual Family and the Unseen Ones who guide your Spiritual Family and represent it. Some people go for many years wanting this, urgently hoping for this, but it does not happen for them. Others have never even thought of it, and yet it occurs for them. Why is this? It has to do with a person's readiness and purpose. Some people need this experience in order to confirm their allegiance to Knowledge. For others, such an experience would be a great setback. It would frighten them, disorient them, distract them or intrigue them. Until your deeper inclinations are recognized and honored and until they become the primary experience and focus rather than having great and wonderful sensations in life, then revelation is ill advised for you and will not occur.

Revelation has to do with purpose and readiness. For some people, spirituality must be a very subtle undercurrent in their lives, something that they acknowledge but which in itself is not the central theme or focus. Intense spiritual experiences are not necessary for them and can indeed be an impediment. Yet for those whose service to the world is meant to be more of a bridge between the Divine and human life, these spiritual experiences are more likely. But again, they do not come on demand.

Expect, then, if you can advance in The Greater Community Way of Knowledge, a gradual revelation. As your eyes become clearer, as your mind becomes freer and as your experience of Knowledge becomes deeper, you will begin to feel that you have a kinship with Heaven. Your kinship will not be idealistic. It will not be philosophical. It will not be theological. It will not be ambitious. It will not be a wish. It will simply be something that is there. You won't need to talk about it. It will just be there because you are close to it. It will not intrude. It will not shock you. Instead, it will abide with you quietly and deeply. And its presence will be pervasive.

Revelation is something that must happen for certain people at certain times because they cannot delay any longer. They must become engaged now. They must take a critical next step. Others are waiting for them. Even if they do not think they are ready, they must assume their role and responsibility.

The Wisdom of Heaven determines this. You yourself cannot. Do not strive for revelation. Do not set it as part of your plans and your goals. Set out instead to become a student of Knowledge and to patiently proceed without claiming grand schemes, designs or abilities for yourself. Then you will come closer to Heaven because you will come closer to what Heaven has given you. The deeper your relationship with Knowledge, the deeper your relationship with the Divine. A relationship is not images and fantastic demonstrations. It is an abiding presence.

You have a relationship with your Spiritual Family. This can be experienced, but you must become close to your Spiritual Family. You will become close as you come closer to Knowledge within you because Knowledge and your Spiritual Family are inextricably intertwined. One will remind you of the other.

The greater your sense of purpose, the greater will be your memory of your origin. It will not be a memory of images or events, but of the experience of relationship itself. The greater your experience of purpose, the greater your experience of destiny. The more you have a sense of where you are headed and that you are only temporarily engaged in the world, the less threatened you will be by its appearances and its tragedies.

Many people claim revelatory experiences. They say angels appear to them and they receive fantastic information. They say that all kinds of dramatic events are happening regularly as part of their experience. Be very skeptical. It is possible for you to be in contact with other minds in other dimensions. It is possible for you to be in contact with minds in other worlds. It is possible for you to be in contact with other minds in this world, without knowing who you are speaking to or what their intent or motivation is. That is why students of Knowledge do not dabble in these kinds of things. That is why students of Knowledge stay close to Knowledge and close to life and do not veer off into trying to have incredible experiences. That is why students of Knowledge do not involve themselves in controversies or brag and boast about their grand experiences or their latest insight or how an angel or some other kind of divine entity has communicated to them. This is enchanting and intriguing, perhaps, but it leads nowhere and can indeed be a dangerous distraction, preventing people from meeting and facing the real needs and challenges of their lives which are calling to them even at this moment.

As you proceed, you will hear a great deal about spiritual experiences being described or discussed by others. Be discreet. Do not enter into these discussions. They are meaningless by and large. People who talk about these things do not know what they are talking about. Those who know have learned not to talk, except in rare situations to certain people. And even then, how can one describe a genuine experience? If the people you are talking to have not had this experience, they will either think you are deceiving them or they will be mesmerized by what you are saying. There is no benefit here, for suspicion and being mesmerized are not helpful in learning The Way of Knowledge. To the person who has had this experience, words are not necessary. A simple acknowledgment will do.

Conversation, speculation, argument and debate are wasteful engagements for the student of Knowledge. Seeking Divine contact, angelic experiences or prolonged bliss at the expense of your experience in the world is not the emphasis of the student of Knowledge. You have come here to learn to work, to give and to understand. You have not come here to dream, to fantasize or to find a way back to your Ancient Home. You were sent to the world at great expense and effort, but as soon as you realize that you are in the world and that you have come from somewhere else, you devise a scheme for getting out of here! You say, "I want to get out of here. This is difficult!" However, your Spiritual Family wants you to be here. They went to great effort to bring you here. They have already provided a great deal of assistance to enable you to become a functional human being so that you could learn something greater in life. Why try to escape with the work undone?

The work will reveal itself as you proceed. You do not need to say, "Well, I will decide what kind of work sounds good to me. I like doing this kind of work. That looks good. That doesn't look too hard or too dangerous or too unpleasant." You will hear much speculation about people's self-defined purposes and callings, but the student of Knowledge is wise to avoid these conversations, for they do not represent Wisdom. Your deeper experiences can only be shared with certain people in certain ways and at certain times. The vast majority of the time you will have to keep them to yourself, even around other students of Knowledge. Do not fritter away something that is sacred and meaningful. Do not reveal something that is growing and germinating within you or it will lose its vitality and potency in your life.

All this talk, talk, talk about spirituality is for self-assurance and to gain recognition, which is also for self-assurance. And what is self-assurance for but to comfort the personal mind? Do not use what is sacred for what is temporary and weak. Let the personal mind learn restraint, discretion, discernment and forbearance. If Wisdom is ever to be a reality in your life, you must learn these things. Oh, yes, you will find many people with whom you can have very interesting spiritual conversations. There will be much bragging and much self-proclamation. There will be much comparison and much criticism. Someone will say, "Well, my Teacher is very great." Others will say, "Oh, my Teacher is very great." Others will say, "I have studied five different religions." Others will say, "I have read five hundred books." Others will say, "Oh, I know all about this theology." And others will say, "Oh, yes, but this other spiritual path is much better." The student of Knowledge is wise to avoid these conversations and, when in the midst of them, to remain silent and observant.

Those who know carry the presence with them. And this presence has been able to grow because they have not been indiscreet. They have not tried to use their experience for personal gain. Instead, they have let it grow stronger and more intense within themselves. This gives them a sense of presence. You will not find this in idle dabblers or in people who are like tourists in a spiritual universe. However, you will find this in those who have had to face their own thresholds, who have had to cross their own rivers and who have had to experience and face their own doubts and fears and the wasteful consequences of their mistakes. These are people who are following something inexplicable that they do not attempt to define or use. Their silence is profound and inviting. They are with the Mystery. And the Mystery is with them. Through them a greater Knowledge, a greater comfort and a Greater Power can emerge and abide. This is the abiding revelation. Someone who is with the Mystery can share the Mystery without words, without conversation, without debate and without self-glorification. They are with the Mystery and the Mystery is with them.

This, then, is what you want to look for. This is the evidence of revelation. The skies parting and the angelic host descending are things for the story books and for mythology. Real revelation happens in the innermost part of a person. It is something you can only feel, and you will feel it in the presence of those who are close to the Mystery—those who have not squandered their gift but have let it grow, those who have learned to become still, silent and observant, those whose minds are free of the past sufficiently that they do not need to judge and evaluate every new experience and encounter that they are having, those who are strong enough with Knowledge that they do not need to use their power or the admission of their weaknesses in order to gain attention or recognition.

When you think of revelation, think of this. Do not become romantic and have illusions of grandeur. These things may attract a great deal of attention, but they cannot generate devotion, for only Knowledge can generate devotion. These things attract attachment and ambition, but they cannot lead someone to be wholehearted, for to be wholehearted is to be with Knowledge. Being without Knowledge is being willful, ambitious, cunning, clever, manipulative, shrewd and calculating. Take heed. This is the evidence that Knowledge is lacking.

Revelation grows slowly. It grows with Knowledge because with Knowledge there comes an experience and a sense of origin and destiny that the world cannot challenge. It is something that is felt and known. Details are not important. The closer you are to your purpose, the more you will have this experience. The more you are able to gain a relationship with Knowledge without abusing this privilege, the more this experience will grow for you. The freer your mind is from past-referencing, the more space there will be within you for Grace to fill. This is revelation. This is coming close to the Divine without destroying or disabling yourself as a person. This is what enables you to become a translator, a medium for a Greater Reality to express itself in the world and for great gifts to be given, even in the simplest and most mundane circumstances.

Remember, God is working behind the scenes, reclaiming the separated through Knowledge, working through inspired individuals and through meaningful relationships. God does not make a big show. God does not want people to bow down and become slaves, unwillingly, resentfully, with hostility and bitterness. This is not a worldly power we are speaking of. This is not a worldly persuasion. This is not how the personal mind works; it is something different. It is not how world governments work; it is something different. God does not threaten you. God does not tantalize you. God does not seduce you. God is present for you, and you have the opportunity to become present for God.

This relationship, however, which is so primary, can never be your sole focus, for God wants your eyes turned to the world where you have come to serve and to work. The more God abides with you as your work progresses and becomes a deeper experience and a greater commitment for you, the more God grows in your experience. Here God becomes more a context than an individual, more a greater experience of relationship than an authority. In this way, God is able to work through you without distracting you. In this way, you are able to work with God without losing your focus in the world.

How can it be that something so powerful can work through something so small and validate what is small, honor what is small and redeem what is small? This represents the great genius of Knowledge in the universe. This is God. God is great; you are small. The light works through you; it does not blind you. The presence abides with you; it does not overwhelm you. Wisdom can speak through you; it does not obliterate you. You are the emphasis; God is the source. Here your mind and your body need to become vehicles for a greater expression and purpose. To allow this to manifest in specific and mundane ways where it is intended and where it is needed—this is revelation.

Revelation, then, is a slow, growing experience of purpose, meaning and direction in life. It will emerge for you if you allow it to be present in your life and do not attempt to use it to gain advantages over other people. It will become the absolute foundation for you. Then, whatever you give in the world will be blessed with a greater experience of presence. Grace will be with you. People will experience this in your presence. Here you will give them something inexplicable that words cannot convey and that actions cannot even demonstrate. This is what will spark Knowledge within them, for their response to Grace will come from Knowledge within them and not from their personal minds. This is an initiation, and this is evidence of God's work in the world. For these people it will be a revelation, but no one will be glorified. No errors in evaluation will be made because no one will claim grandiose powers. There will be no avatars. There will be no saints. Something magical and wonderful will happen between you, something lasting and pervasive, not sudden and romantic.

If you think back on your life, perhaps you can recall one or two individuals with whom you had this experience, this abiding sense of presence. Recall how subtle it was but how unique. Recall how you felt in their presence, how there was something unusual about them—something they did not talk about, something they did not declare. There was something unusual about them. There was a presence abiding with them. Perhaps there are no words that can describe this experience, but it can be recalled because it stands out in stark contrast to every other encounter you have had, whether those encounters were pleasurable or not.

As God works behind the scenes, revelation occurs behind the scenes. This is done because it works. Then people give themselves. There is no slavery. Then people open themselves, and they claim the results. Then people honor themselves by holding sacred their Greater Source.

Revelation is part of your renewal. It will most likely be very slow and very gradual. You will not experience it every moment. In fact, there may be great gaps of time between your experiences, but these gaps of time will lessen as you advance. Instead of once every two years, perhaps it will be once every six months, and then once every three days. It does not matter because you will proceed. It does not have to happen every moment because you have learned to live without it. However, when it is with you, you graciously open yourself to it, and you know that the presence is with you because there is space in you for the presence to fill.

Will revelation happen for you? Become a student of Knowledge. Become close to Knowledge. Associate with those who are advanced in Knowledge. And associate with those who are beginning like you. Forget what you have learned before. Do not think you are advanced already. Be a beginner. Have an open mind. Do not claim advancement. How can you tell if you are advanced? One moment you might feel like you have come oh so far while the next day you might feel like you are back at the beginning. How can you tell? How can the personal mind understand these things? It can only go along. And as it goes along, it will be changed because a Greater Power will slowly emerge within you and will give a sense of security to your personal mind which it could never have received from anything else. Then your personal mind will come into service to a Greater Power within you. In this way, your body will serve your mind, and your mind will serve your spirit, which represents their right relationship. Then you will escape confusion and ambivalence—a great freedom. With this freedom, Grace will abide with you. It will be revealed to you because you will have the capacity for it and will be open to it. In silence, in quiet, the Grace of God comes to you.

—ᔕᔕ—

The evolution of the world is accelerating.

It is accelerating because of the

global population of humanity,

it is accelerating because of the

global problems of humanity

and it is accelerating because of the

presence of Greater Community forces

in the world.

—ᔕᔕ—

CHAPTER EIGHTEEN

WHAT IS HUMAN DESTINY?

—⟋∿∿⟍—

*Y*OUR DESTINY IS TO EMERGE into the Greater Community of Worlds. This is a process that will take several centuries overall, but the change within the scope of your life will be very rapid, and the challenge to human society will be immense. Let us speak on this, for this concerns you and your purpose for coming into the world.

Humanity will emerge into the Greater Community because it lives in the Greater Community. As human ascendancy has now become established on your planet, you will gain recognition in the Greater Community. You will become a force, not a great force, but a force nonetheless. You are now emerging out of your primitive cultures with great difficulty. You are seeking to associate with each other with great difficulty. Human history is like a shadow over the world, drawing people backwards, just like your personal history is a shadow over you, drawing you backwards.

Destiny is what keeps everything moving forward. Destiny is what generates the motivation to create, to establish, to explore and to fulfill. There is a destiny for you, and there is a destiny for the world. Your destiny here is to find your purpose and to find your allies, those unique individuals who are here to help you fulfill that purpose. The world's destiny is to emerge into the Greater Community. This is where it is heading. It is going in this direction no matter what human society is doing. It must go in this direction. This represents the next stage of your life in the world. It is inevitable and unalterable. That is why we speak of it in terms of destiny instead of in terms of human will and human determination.

Just as you grow from being a child to an adolescent, from an adolescent to a young adult, from a young adult to an adult and then you grow into old age, so your world has its evolutionary stages as well. There are evolutionary stages in societies. There are evolutionary stages in families. And the world has its own evolutionary process. Because humanity now spans your world, at least the surface of your world, and has gained a relative degree of control of the world with great risks, it is important now for you to know that you are entering into a new era. It is not a new age, for an age is a very long time. This is a period of transition, which will be difficult and turbulent. Its opportunities and demands will be tremendous. Its risk of failure will be substantial. It is not a time for the faint of heart or for the weak minded. It is not a time for the ambivalent or the self-indulgent. It is a time for great strength and dedication. Knowledge within you will give you this strength and determination as you become a student of Knowledge, as you advance in The Way of Knowledge and as you take the steps to Knowledge. This is because you are needed for something great in this life.

Do not compare your purpose with the purpose of your ancestors. Do not think that your purpose is the same as someone's a thousand years ago or five hundred years ago or even one hundred years ago. Your purpose is related to the needs of the world and the circumstances of the world. Ultimately, everyone's purpose serves the reclamation and the preservation of Knowledge in the world. However, what you may end up doing may seem very different from this, if only in appearance. It is the spirit with which you give, the quality of your gift and the quality of your awareness and your relationships that will keep Knowledge alive in the world. Everything else that is accomplished is to help people, to serve people, to heal people, to enable people, to strengthen people and to take care of people.

The need for Knowledge will grow dramatically. There are so many people in the world that have so little, and there are so few that have so much. The resources of the world are shrinking, and the problems of the world are growing. This is seemingly a terrible situation when you put it all together, but it is just the kind of situation that will call people into action—not just an individual here and there who is inspired, but greater numbers of people. The world will be calling them out of their self-preoccupation. The world will be calling them out of their personal interests and tragedies. The world will be demanding things of them.

This is what calls your purpose out of you. Do not think you can go off and meditate all day every day and find your purpose. You must go into the world and have it brought out of you. The world represents a relationship in which your purpose is initiated, fostered and realized. That is why seeking escape from the world or a permanent retreat from the world is counterproductive. The very tribulations in the world that you find so difficult and so unpleasant are the very things that will call out of you the greatness that you have come to give. Do not, then, condemn the world when in fact it creates the right conditions for your redemption.

The world's emergence into the Greater Community will be the greatest transition humanity has ever faced. This is understandable because humanity is a very recent race. Yes, the primitive life of your ancestors went on for a very long time, mainly because your world is such an easy world to live in compared to other worlds. However, the demands of life now are much greater, and the pace of life is much faster. That is because the evolution of the world is accelerating. It is accelerating because of the global population of humanity, it is accelerating because of the global problems of humanity and it is accelerating because of the presence of Greater Community forces in the world.

What kind of change will this great transition produce? Fundamentally, it will change how people view their place in the world and their position in the larger arena of life called the Greater Community. We introduce the idea of the Greater Community so that you can begin to think about this greater context of life and begin to understand and accept it as a governing fact of your life. It represents your destiny. It contains a greater set of influences and presents a greater set of problems, challenges and opportunities that await you. This is why your technology is racing ahead. Some of this technology was introduced from the Greater Community in order to accelerate your development. Much of it was your own creation. It is headed in a certain direction. That is why you cannot stand still, confused about yourself, involved with your thoughts, lost in your wishes or buried in your fears. Life is moving quickly. You must move too. You must become attentive and aware. You must have an open mind, an attentive mind, a watchful mind and a careful mind, but not a fearful mind.

As humanity's idea of itself changes, its social institutions and structures will change as well. Fundamentally, you will begin to see yourself as a member of your world, not simply as a member of a nation or of a group or of a religion or of a culture or of an extended family or of a political persuasion. All of these things will be overshadowed by the presence of the Greater Community, which will make them increasingly insignificant.

As this realization is passed from one generation to another, national interests will change, with a greater emphasis on interdependence with other nations and on mutual survival and well-being. Indeed, even if Greater Community forces were not present in the world, the overshadowing of your world's problems would generate this. Only it would happen much more slowly and with less likelihood of a good result because humanity would fight against itself over who gets the last of the resources, who gets the last of the benefits and who gets the greatest share and so forth.

The evolution of the world is casting a greater shadow over humanity and a greater difficulty, but a difficulty that can redeem the world and unite its population, a difficulty that can put everyone in the same boat and give everyone the same problem. Where, then, will you look for help? You may look to God, but God will point you towards one another. Therefore, you must look towards one another. "How can we work together? How can we work together to strengthen and to unify our race and to secure and to balance our world?" This won't be merely an altruistic wish. It will become a vital necessity. It will be something everyone has to think about. And those who refuse to do so will work against humanity at large and will generate conflict and discord.

This is why you must be forward thinking now and not backward thinking. You must not think about preserving the securities and the ideals that you have clung to before. You must keep pace with life in order to benefit from life and to give to life. In this way, you will not become one of life's casualties but one of its benefactors. In this way, your vital years will be given in service to the progress of the world, rather than being a hindrance to this progress.

Many people and even nations of people will struggle against the change that is coming. They will try to preserve their interests and identities to the exclusion of the world's interests and identity. This will produce great friction. However, as your world community slowly comes together, with much discord, there will be a greater feeling of consensus. World opinion will have greater and greater impact, even before a world government is established. World government is inevitable. It will happen. It will happen in order to regulate commerce. It will happen in order to prevent crime and starvation. It will happen in order to preserve the environment which different nations share. It will happen in order to regulate the quality of the larger natural resources which everyone shares, like water and air. The creation of world government will be difficult. It will be fraught with great tribulation and conflict. But it will happen because it is your destiny. If you fail in this regard, you will fail even to meet your world's needs, and this will overtake you in time. You cannot afford this, and you know it.

This is a great opportunity for people to step beyond their personal interests and to gain a greater perspective on life, and with it a greater sense of purpose. Never think that your purpose will arise from what you want for yourself. People make this mistake every day. They think, "Well, my purpose? Let's see, what do I want?" as if they were choosing from a great wish list. Purpose has to do with what the world needs from you and what you are able to give to the world, which may or may not conform to your personal goals, plans and ambitions.

The world's emergence into the Greater Community will change your understanding of religion. Here there will be great difficulty and tremendous resistance. Most religions of the world are based on an anthropocentric view of the universe. Consequently, as the presence of Greater Community forces in the world becomes more obvious and apparent, more acceptable and more generally recognized, people will either yield to a larger viewpoint and open themselves to re-evaluate their ideas and their fundamental beliefs, or they will try to reassert their religious ideas, thinking that they are in the right and that the rest of the universe somehow is in the wrong. They will think that they are blessed and guided by their religious faith, while the rest of the universe has either been spiritually denied or has been too foolish to respond. Human arrogance will demonstrate itself here in all of its destructive manifestations. You will see this, and your children will see this.

The inability of people to respond to the present and to the future because of their fixed ideas and their past referencing will create tremendous conflict. The world's emergence into the Greater Community is a great challenge in and of itself, but what will be more burdensome will be human response or lack of it. No one wants to give up his or her pleasures. No one wants to yield his or her beliefs. No one wants to sacrifice those things that seem to validate them. No one wants to close a chapter on his or her personal history. No one wants to do these things unless of course they are students of Knowledge, who will give these things up freely and set them aside in order to face life anew. However, for those who are not students of Knowledge, which will be most of the people in the world, this will be a tremendous confrontation. In fact, it will be a series of tremendous confrontations.

Destiny must move you forward, whether you are willing or not, whether you can yield or not, whether you can learn or not. The results of destiny are in your hands, but the process itself is not. Whether the world's emergence into the Greater Community has a good result for humanity or a devastating result is up to you, but your emergence will happen either way.

The challenges ahead require a new approach, a new understanding and a greater sense of identity and purpose in life. Here it will be very difficult for people to face the fact that their future will not be like the past and that they cannot use the past as a reference in determining the future. They must meet things face to face, head on. This is a great challenge, but this is what redeems people. This is what elevates a race. This is what calls upon human wisdom, ingenuity, skill, dedication and cooperation. Only a greater set of problems can do this for you now. Otherwise, without them, humanity will slowly sink under the weight of its own conflicts, its own indulgences and its own violence. Everything will deteriorate—nations, cultures, cities. Everything will deteriorate. Everyone will become poorer and more desperate.

The answer is in the heavens, in the Greater Community. Look to the heavens for inspiration. Look to the Greater Community. Heaven itself is beyond the Greater Community, but the Greater Community is where you will instinctively look for the answer. Your world needs this emergence into the Greater Community. It is not simply that it is your destiny. It also represents a great answer to a great need. However, it is not an answer that was recently given. It is an answer that was given when the world began.

The evolution of life in the world is a part of the evolution of life in the Greater Community. It cannot be apart from this. That is why your future, your destiny and the greater context for understanding yourself individually will all be found in the Greater Community. Human religion, human society and human culture are all based upon the past, and this will work against you. However, your natural inclinations for spirituality, for social cooperation and productivity, for political stability and for justice and equanimity will prepare you for the future and enable you to do whatever needs to be done in order to survive, to advance and to bring a greater order, peace and justice into the world. It will not be a perfect order, but it must be a greater order. It will not be a perfect peace, but it must be a greater peace. It will not be a perfect justice, but it must be a greater justice.

Humanity must become united, even with all of its diversity, because humanity is one race in the Greater Community. The distinctions that you make to separate yourself from others are meaningless to your visitors, except insofar as these distinctions can be exploited. They represent your weakness, not your strength.

You are emerging from tribalism in the world. The tribes now are very large, and many of them have technological power, but the mentality that governs their behavior has not yet fully changed. To work for your clan—to work for your group alone, to strike out against others or everyone—is mindless and senseless and will not work in a new world. You are, indeed, in the process of creating a new world. Old institutions will fade. Old religions will have to expand and adapt or they will die out. Old faiths will have to be given new passion or they will disappear with each new generation. Old cultural bonds will fade, as they must. You cannot live now to honor your parents or their parents. You must live to meet the requirements of life as it is now.

There will be much error. There will be grievous error. Humanity as a whole has never learned anything of a larger magnitude in a graceful way, but your adaptability is still significant. Your creative ability is still significant. Your mobility in the world is still significant. The world still has the resources to enable you to grow and to adapt to the Greater Community, in contrast to many other worlds where the resources were depleted or were never abundant to begin with. As your natural resources fade, your technology will have to advance.

Let us, then, look into your future to see how things might be. This is not a future that is way ahead of your time, but a future that you will experience and are beginning to taste even now.

First of all, everyone will become much poorer, and there will have to be more sharing. The number of people who possess great wealth will diminish compared to society at large, and there will have to be more sharing. Your natural environment will become increasingly polluted, so much so that there will be whole areas of the world where people cannot live. People will take to living indoors more and more and will even explore the possibilities of living underground. Food production will be greatly affected, and new methods will have to be established. New forms of religious expression and experience will be generated in order to be relevant to the times which you will face. National problems will spill over into other nations increasingly, requiring international intervention and cooperation to a greater degree.

Many people will starve, for there will not be enough food to go around to meet crisis situations. This will generate a national and international network of food production and distribution. You will need to get used to living with less—fewer possessions, fewer opportunities and less mobility. These are general things which we are describing. You can sense them in the world now, and you will feel them growing as time goes on.

Can you change all this? You can only adapt to changing conditions and use them to improve the condition of humanity and the condition of your mind. The present and the future will require a new mind, not an old mind. They will require a new response, not an old response. They will require human invention, rather than human indolence. They will require greater and greater adaptation and adjustment. They will challenge old forms of thinking and behavior. All of this is necessary, and it is beneficial. It is beneficial because it is necessary. And it is necessary because this is the evolution of the world. Humanity has grown too big and too powerful. It is having too great an impact on its own environment to continue without self-control, without Wisdom and without the sense of world community and world responsibility.

Destiny will utterly change your life. You have come to serve a world in transition. It will feel like a whole new age is starting, but it is simply because an old age is dying. A world in transition needs great human ingenuity and courage, which will emanate from Knowledge within you.

You are destined to gain contact with other forms of intelligent life from the Greater Community. Some will oppose you, some will abuse you, some will ignore you and some will attempt to establish a relationship with you. Each of them will offer a different kind of challenge and a different requirement. At this time, many people still think that the universe is a great, empty place. "Oh, yes, there is life out there some-where, but certainly it must be sparse, and it is all for the taking." In the future, you will go out and attempt to set your flags down in any world that you can reach, but the Greater Community will temper your ambitions and your desire for conquest. Even your need for new resources will be curtailed because you will find that the Greater Community is indeed full of activity, particularly in this region of space where you live. And you will find that the regions that you seek to claim for yourself have already been claimed.

This will require that you learn about the Greater Community and develop Wisdom and diplomacy within a larger context of life. These are skills which your race will benefit from, skills which will temper your ambition and increase your responsibility.

Not only are your visitors technologically advanced, they have greater social cohesion, or they would not have been able to reach your shores. They are coming into a world where tribal warfare is dominant, where one human being cannot recognize another, where everyone claims different allegiances and authorities. They are coming into a world where people are ruining their environment at a frightening pace. They are coming into a world where people are fearful, superstitious and self-indulgent and where there is great tragedy, suffering and human abuse.

How would this world look to you if you were a visitor coming here for the first time? Even with your human viewpoint, you can gain a perspective of how you must look to those who are visiting. Will they be compassionate towards you? Will they attempt to help you? Will they attempt to avoid you? Will they want to have a relationship with you? Can they trust you? Can you be relied upon? Are you consistent enough in order to establish relations? These are all meaningful questions for you to ask in order to gain a Greater Community perspective, even from a human point of view. Seeing yourself from a Greater Community perspective will show you what you must accomplish and what your great disabilities are at this time. This will give you a new understanding of yourself, one that is very fair and honest.

Life is requiring a greater evolution for humanity at this time. Your own life is moving quickly because life in general is moving quickly. You cannot escape this. Move to the most peaceful part of the world, and everything you do will still be affected. Do not run and hide. Prepare. Do not deny and avoid. Prepare. Do not argue against reality; do not repudiate reality. Prepare for reality. The coming of the Greater Community is the great threshold for humanity. You must prepare. The world needs a new awareness, a new approach and a new foundation for society. You must prepare.

You are now at the beginning of the transition. The generations ahead are all part of this transition. You will need to lay down the foundation for what is to come. And yet is this not what you came here to do? This *is* what you came here to do—to lay down the foundation for life to come so that future generations may flourish here and be abundant.

The preparation cannot be left only in the hands of one or two saintly or wonderful people. It must be a responsibility that is felt throughout the population. People must not look at the change ahead and say, "Well, how can I benefit? How can I keep what I have? How can I make more money?" That is mindless and destructive. What you will be facing will be too dire for that kind of approach. Everyone must feel this responsibility. Everyone must take it upon himself or herself to do something in concert with others—something productive, something constructive, something that transcends his or her own personal interests. Everyone will not do this, of course, but more people need to. You need to.

Prepare. You prepare through The Greater Community Way of Knowledge. This is the only preparation for the Greater Community. This will also prepare you to meet the world's difficulties and tribulations. It will prepare you to face and experience the dying of an old age and the difficult emergence and transition into a new life. It will enable you to go from an old mind to a new mind, from an old approach to life to a new approach to life, from an old experience of relationships to a new experience of relationships. The preparation makes this possible because it enables you to build your life on Knowledge and not on the substitutes for Knowledge.

Humanity is destined to become a part of the Greater Community. This is its evolution. This is its destiny. This is where you are headed. This is what you must contend with. And this is what you must now prepare yourself for—emotionally, psychologically, intellectually and spiritually. Do not protect your old traditions. Prepare for change. If you protect the past, you will feel that life is assaulting you, and you will fight against it. You will become violent and become an antagonist in life.

You have only three responses to reality: You can go towards it, you can go away from it or you can go against it. Go towards your future. Go towards the present. Find that strength within yourself that enables you to do this, the strength which is born of Knowledge within you. Find the desire to be in a changing world, the desire that is born of Knowledge. Let change take its course, but contribute to it for the good because your contribution is needed. You cannot be left out. If you do not contribute, you will have failed in life, and you will go home to your Spiritual Family with your gift unopened. There you will not be punished, but you will feel great regret, and your life here will be seen as unfulfilling and unfulfilled.

You are destined to learn from the Greater Community, but first you must survive in the Greater Community and contend with the Greater Community. In the Greater Community, there are races at all levels of evolution and technological skill. There are races that are dedicated to good. And there are races that are dedicated to destruction. However, because they have to contend with each other, they moderate each other. To the extent that they do have contact, they learn from each other and influence each other, physically and mentally.

If you can see yourself from outside the world looking in, you will begin to get an understanding of how they might approach you, what they might want and what they might think to be possible. We will give you a few ideas now to consider regarding the intentions of your visitors. These intentions may not hold true for all of them, but these ideas should still be a prime concern for you.

The first concern is the preservation of your natural environment. That is a prime concern because in the Greater Community natural environments such as yours are considered resources that cannot be destroyed. The need for biological regeneration elsewhere and the abundance of biological resources here make your world too valuable to be destroyed. It will not be allowed for you to destroy it. Should you proceed heedlessly, then there will be intervention, and your race will be controlled. This would be very unfortunate. It would be unfortunate because you will not have learned what you must learn. It would be unfortunate because you will have given up your authority and self-determination because you were unwilling to exercise them properly. It would be unfortunate because the opportunity to advance your race would have been missed. It would be unfortunate because your freedom would be lost. Losing all of this is a possibility. And it is largely up to you.

Your neighbors and visitors are also concerned with your aggressive behavior. It will not be allowed for you to set out on a mission of conquest, even in the local universe. You do not know what you are dealing with. It is a more mature environment out there. You are like the young adolescent, brash and full of yourself, with newfound powers and abilities but without the wisdom to know how they are to be used and without the restraint necessary to prevent you from using them against yourself or others. In this you must mature, and gaining this maturity is essential.

Contact with the Greater Community will temper your ambitions. And it will give you a different kind of perspective about life. The universe is not yours to claim. The universe is not yours to conquer. The universe is not yours to possess. It is yours to share and to learn from. You will be encountering races far more advanced than you and with very different temperaments. If you are to contend with them successfully, you must learn to contend with your own kind successfully. The differences between you and them will be great, just as the differences between you and other human beings are small. If you cannot establish harmony where the differences are small, how can you establish harmony where the differences are great?

Your destiny, then, is upon you. It is not in the distant future where you do not have to think about it. It is happening right now. You are in it. Become a contributor to it. Prepare. Gain access to Knowledge, the Knowing Mind within you, and the greater purpose which has brought you here, for this will teach you how to prepare and this will enable you to prepare. This will show you who you need to be with and where you need to be in life. The greatness of your life is needed now because of the greatness of the evolution of humanity. The greatness of your mission must become known to you because the world needs its expression and demonstration. The greatness of your contribution is needed because the needs of humanity will only grow and become more severe.

Your destiny is presented here in order to enable you to open your eyes. It is presented here more as a gift than as a warning. You know it is coming. And you now have the opportunity to prepare. And you know that you need to prepare. The preparation for the Greater Community is being given to you in The Greater Community Way of Knowledge. You have it before you at this moment. Do not judge it from your past references, but open yourself to it as a preparation for the future and as a means of gaining access to what you know now and what you can do now.

—◈—

*W*hat is pure and essential about religion

is what is translatable within it—

what can be given from one mind

to another

and from one world

to another.

—◈—

CHAPTER NINETEEN

WHAT IS RELIGION?

—⟨⟨⟩⟩—

*I*N MANY TEACHINGS IN THE WORLD IT IS THOUGHT that religion is an attempt to answer or resolve the fundamental problem of human suffering. In this sense and in this understanding, religion is a plan to enable human beings to escape their condition and attain a greater state of mind and a far better condition, either within the world or beyond, though beyond the world is usually what is emphasized.

Religion is seen as an attempt to define what human suffering is, to determine its causes and to establish an approach where these causes can be reversed or overturned in some way so that human suffering can be remedied, providing humanity a greater comfort and a greater destiny. However, let us redefine the purpose of religion so that religion can have a new meaning and a new application in your life.

In a Greater Community context, the purpose of religion is to enable Knowledge to be discovered and expressed in whatever world religion is being cultivated. Religion, then, is a means to bring about an important end. Its purpose here in this world is not to end human suffering or to resolve the human dilemma. Its purpose is not even to bridge the great and seemingly incomprehensible gulf that exists between your human mind and the mind of God. It is not an attempt to wholly unite physical life and spiritual life. In a Greater Community context, religion is the means for the discovery and application of Knowledge. Ultimately, this resolves your relationship with God and with everything else in the universe. This ends suffering. This unravels the causes of suffering and makes their existence no longer necessary. But this occurs only in an ultimate sense.

If you have the viewpoint that your world is the only inhabited world in the universe, then you will think that you must achieve the ultimate reality right away. However, you do not understand here that you will miss all of the steps in between—steps that you cannot see, steps that you do not think exist but which in reality await you. From a Greater Community perspective, the progress and evolution of life and the evolution of awareness are much greater, with many more steps and stages of development. This offers you a larger panorama in order to see what it means to live a spiritual life and what religion can mean and must mean. With this new definition of religion, many new possibilities open up. Here you are given an entirely new starting point in your understanding of what spiritual calling and spiritual reality mean while you are living in the world.

Your purpose here is not to escape the world. Your purpose here is not to leap into the ultimate reality. Your purpose here is not to completely unite your existence in the world with that ultimate reality. These things only have meaning and context in an ultimate sense, which is beyond your scope and need here. Your existence in the world is but one stage in a long process, one part of a great journey. This stage has many unique problems, yet it is part of something much greater. If you cannot appreciate this, then you will assume and expect incredible things from yourself and incredible things from your God. This will lead you to attempt to make associations and compromises and to unite things that are dissimilar in such a way that even your ability to be in the world will become impaired. Here your ability to deal with practical things will become confused and out of focus.

The world is one reality. Your Ancient Home is another reality. You cannot unite them. However, you can bring something into the world from your Ancient Home. This has meaning here. This is appropriate. The real role of religion is to provide a context, a method, a structure and the direction to enable this to happen. This will give you the encouragement, the strength, the determination and the assistance you will need to find the Greater Reality which lives within your Knowledge and to be able to express it specifically according to your nature and purpose here in life.

The purpose of religion in this context is not to answer the ultimate questions of life. These questions can only be understood and resolved as you progress through the stages of development, many of which exist far beyond the scope of your life in the world. Here it is very important to have a Greater Community perspective. With this perspective, you will be able to see what is relative and what is ultimate. You will be able to see how a pathway through this world can lead in a greater direction for a greater purpose. Here you will see that the end of your life in the world is not the end of your progress and development. Here you will see that God is not preoccupied with the world and that the world is not the ultimate test of your will and dedication. Here you will see that there is something very important for you to do here and that you do not want to have to return because you failed to realize or to carry out your greater purpose here. Then you will come to understand that the greater questions in life concern the whole universe and not simply your personal existence in the world at this time.

From a Greater Community perspective, you will see that the range of your relationships and associations far exceeds the scope of your current friendships. From a Greater Community perspective, these things become self-evident. However, from a human perspective, with an anthropocentric emphasis, these things seem incomprehensible, impossible, unattainable or avoidable.

You cannot resolve ultimate questions in a temporary reality. You cannot resolve the problem of human suffering within the context of this life alone. This is not because you need to come back into the world again and again, but because your life in the Greater Community involves a much larger process. When you leave this world and no longer need to return here, you will be a beginner in the next stage of development. That stage involves recognizing the identities of the universe. It involves participating in the Greater Community. That is why we bring Greater Community understanding, perspective and Wisdom into the world at this time. We do this not only to prepare you for your encounters with Greater Community forces but because you need a religious foundation that is far greater, more expansive and more inclusive than what you have cultivated thus far. This is not to replace your world's religions but to give them greater scope, a greater perspective and a new foundation.

You cannot see the great panorama of life from where you stand. You must go to a higher vantage point. You cannot see where you have been, where you are and where you are going and understand these things from your current position. You must attain a higher vantage point, where these things are obvious. You have no perspective at this moment to understand the greater questions of your life. You cannot even understand what Knowledge is, what higher purpose is and what true relationship is from your current position. Pose as many answers and explanations as you wish, yet you will not have the answer, and your questioning will not be resolved. The only resolution to your questioning is to take the journey because this takes you to the higher vantage point where you can look back and see where you have been within the context of what you are trying to do within the larger scheme of life. This is the only way that purpose and Knowledge can really be understood, and that is why you must advance. Without advancement, there is no real understanding. All understanding in place of advancement is only a form of false self-assurance. It has no meaning or foundation.

We bring The Greater Community Way of Knowledge to you to enable you to have this greater understanding and to recognize and climb the mountain that is yours to climb in life. Ultimate questions and ultimate answers are found along the way. You cannot understand them standing where you are now. You must make the journey. You must prepare in The Way of Knowledge and find out firsthand what Knowledge is, what it means and where it takes you.

What enables you to do this is religion. Here we must separate the word "religion" from the many associations that you may have with it. Religion is not just a church and a congregation. It is not a minister. It is not a bible. It is greater than these. We are speaking from a Greater Community perspective now. We are redefining the word "religion" for you so that it can have a new meaning and be relevant to your life, your needs and your deeper understanding.

Religion is education. Religion is experience. Religion is the means of preparation. It is not something you simply believe in or adhere to in order to gain some future salvation. It is not something that you invest in, that you sign up for or that you buy into as if you were buying lottery shares in Heaven. It is not a forgiveness or a dispensation. Religion is a means. It is a method. It is a way. It is a way to advance. It is a way to prepare. It is a way to get you up that mountain and to enable you to make the journey. Religion provides the instruction, the curriculum and the companionship that you will need to make it up the mountain and to find that vantage point where you can look out on your life and really see what it is, where you have been and where you are now.

Until you gain this greater vantage point, you can have as many definitions, theories and philosophies as you like. However, you will not know the way, and you will not know the meaning of the way. These things can only be found by making the journey itself—by entering new thresholds of understanding, by entering greater and greater rooms of experience and by gaining Wisdom. From each new threshold of experience, you will go on to take on something greater, to broaden your perspective, to continue to open your mind, to rethink your thoughts and to re-evaluate your position. This is what religion is for. This is what religion is.

The Greater Community Way of Knowledge is religion because it is a means for fulfilling your purpose here. It is a means for assisting you in climbing the great mountain of your life. It is a means for you to gain access to Knowledge and to learn what Knowledge is through proper application and understanding. In the Greater Community, this is religion. In The Way of Knowledge, there are areas of study, there are devotional experiences, there are invocations and so forth. However, the essence of The Way of Knowledge is its purpose, not its form.

The Greater Community Way of Knowledge comes from Knowledge—Knowledge of the universe, a Knowledge far more inclusive and far more expansive than anything that you can conceive of at this moment or even anything that you could experience throughout your whole life in this world. It is The Greater Community Way of Knowledge's purpose that gives its methodology true efficacy and meaning. This is religion. Here religion is a means of preparation. Religion is what points you in the right direction. Religion is what defines your true goals within your relative reality in a way that you can experience and appreciate at the deepest level of yourself.

When people hear the word religion, they think of their religious experiences—experiences of going to a church, a synagogue or a place of worship, or experiences of somebody attempting to educate them in a certain faith or faith tradition. Perhaps the word religion is associated with feelings of pain, guilt, shame or remorse. Yet to understand what we are presenting here, you must take the idea of religion and separate it from your past associations to the best of your ability. You cannot bring these past associations, this past referencing, into a new understanding.

Religion is important because you need this new understanding. Gaining this new understanding is what religion is for. This is what religious experience brings to you. You would not be reading these words and you would not be valuing them, certainly, unless you have had a religious experience. However, religious experience has nothing to do with a church or with how you were raised as a child. It has to do with gaining access to a Greater Mind within you and a greater range of experience that stands in contrast to your normal experience of the world. It establishes something that can be known rather than something you simply think, speculate about, sense or touch. It is something greater and deeper. It is something unique and meaningful, even if you cannot understand its uniqueness and its meaning as yet.

Religion in the Greater Community is not one belief system over another. It is not one allegiance to a hero or a heroine over another. It is not one theological understanding over another. In the Greater Community, religion is methods of preparation, initiation, experience and accomplishment. Sometimes ceremonies are needed for this. Sometimes no ceremonies are needed. Sometimes there are great edifices built. Usually no great edifices are built.

In the Greater Community, religion and religious education are usually carried out in a clandestine fashion because they represent a greater devotion and dedication, a greater recognition of power and a greater allegiance than can be given to any worldly power or government. That is why in highly organized and advanced societies, religion is something that is strictly controlled by the ruling powers. Therefore, in order to provide the real preparation, the religious expressions are subtle. There are rarely great edifices established in The Way of Knowledge. Rarely will you find real religion to be a part of the government of any world. Its teaching and practices are usually carried out with great care, discernment and discretion. In this, there is no great show or pageantry. There is only quiet work and preparation, quiet contribution and selfless endeavor.

Real religion gives you the greatest opportunity for self-realization. This gives you the greatest possibility to fully experience your purpose, to remember those who gave you this purpose and to experience your design and the One who designed you. You can see that religion as we are describing it here is very different from what you may have experienced in the past. And it is very different from what you see demonstrated in the world.

Because religion represents many stages in the initiation of Knowledge—the Knowledge of God, the experience of God, the experience you share with God, the Knowledge that you share with God—it goes beyond all definitions. It exceeds all historical pageantries and traditions. It is spirituality that transcends the boundaries of religion as you know it.

You see, religion and spirituality are different. Spirituality is the essence and the substance. Religion is the method and the means. In the Greater Community, because of the diversity of life, there is never just one way. The differences in nature, temperament, orientation, belief and communication in intelligent life in the Greater Community are so great that no one way could suffice for all beings. This is true in your world as well, though many people still try to make their way the only way in order to dispel their own disbelief and to give themselves false assurances. In the Greater Community, you rarely find this kind of arrogance and competition. Here religion is taken far more seriously than it is in this world. Religion in the Greater Community does not offer vast social programs. It does not promise relationships and love. It is not a means for making money. It is something that is taken very seriously, often at great risk.

Very few races which engage in space travel have religion as we are describing it. The emphasis in most advanced societies is on social cohesion. They regard with suspicion and even hostility the idea of the uniqueness of the individual, the idea of independent thinking and the idea of following a greater but mysterious power. These things are threatening to a highly developed social order. That is why The Way of Knowledge is taught in a very secret manner.

The Greater Community Way of Knowledge attracts those who have a sincere and serious approach and who are capable of applying themselves consistently. It is not for the thrill seeker. It is not a lifesaver for those who are in trouble or turmoil. It is not a temporary relief or expedient. It is not something that is used to glorify oneself or to set oneself above others. Even though all these things are evident in the world, they are not part of the real meaning of religion and of spirituality. Given all of the pageantries, traditions, edifices, beliefs and theologies that have been created and defended in the world, even up to this moment, the real experience of purpose, Knowledge and Wisdom far exceeds what these things alone can contain. A pageantry, a tradition, a theology, a ceremony or a rite of passage can only speak of something greater that far exceeds its definition and scope. Only those who cultivate Knowledge can treat these things as a means and not as an end, as a method and not as a final solution. Only those who are developing real Knowledge and a depth of understanding can realize and use religion as a means and a pathway.

The mountain of life is very great. There are different pathways. No one is quicker than the other. The question is which one is right for you. The only way you will know which one is genuinely right for you is because Knowledge will take you there. Your ambitions will not take you there. Your goals and desires will not take you there. Your quest for love or money will not take you there. Only Knowledge will take you there. There are false paths, and many of them, because of all the things that motivate people that are not Knowledge. There are many wasted endeavors and wasted lives because of all the things that motivate people which are not born of Knowledge.

Essentially, religion is The Way of Knowledge, in whatever tradition it is placed. It emphasizes real understanding. Real understanding of direction, purpose and meaning in life is born of a deeper and more profound experience, of a greater association and sense of inclusion and of yielding to a Greater Power that is active and alive in your life. You can be a Catholic, a Buddhist or a tribesman and have this experience. You could be anyone in the world and have this experience. If you continue to have this experience, open yourself to it and seek instruction and companionship, you will be following The Way of Knowledge. You will be living a religious life within a larger context of understanding. This is the meaning and value of all religions in the world. This is the essence that gives them meaning and value.

In the Greater Community, essence is more important than form because religion must be translatable from one culture to another, from one race to another and from one world to another. What is pure and essential about religion is what is translatable within it—what can be given from one mind to another and from one world to another, spanning the great differences in nature, culture, temperament, environment and so forth that exist in the Greater Community.

In Greater Community Spirituality, suffering is escaped through meaningful activity in life. However, even meaningful activity has its trials and tribulations, its failed expectations, its disappointments and its genuine losses. A genuine life in the world is not a life without suffering. But what lessens the impact of suffering, what overshadows it, what puts it in the background and what makes it relative is that a greater purpose and association are being emphasized. Most of the miseries that confound and imprison the human mind are escaped as one advances in The Way of Knowledge, but not all suffering is escaped. Life continues to be difficult and problematic. Your body has its aches and pains. Your mind has its problems and troubling thoughts, feelings and experience, but they do not dominate your attention now, and as you advance they cannot hold you back or limit your experience.

The world is a difficult learning situation. There is no easy way to be here if you are being honest with yourself. However, there is a way to be here when something meaningful is being done and being accomplished. Then when you leave, you leave with the memory of what has been done and what has been accomplished. Think of it like this: If you think of any former time in your life when you were doing something special or unique, you'll remember it by what you accomplished and what you experienced. You won't remember all the little details, all the moment-to-moment experiences, all the conversations that took place or all the activities that were carried out. What will you remember? You will remember what was done and if anything real happened in terms of your relationships with others. If something did happen or something did not happen in this regard, this alone will be the content of your memory.

This will be your memory after leaving this world. You will not remember all the moments, the hours, the days, the activities, the interests and the difficulties. You will not remember anything in your household. You will not remember what you said or what you did specifically. However, you will remember what you accomplished and what you did not accomplish, according to the greater purpose that had brought you into the world. This is what will be remembered after you leave here.

The purpose of religion, therefore, is to take you to your great accomplishment. That is why religion is important, because this accomplishment is the only thing that is important about being in the world. Everything else is just all the things that happen along the way. What is essential is what brought you here. What is essential is what will be remembered after you leave. What is essential is who you represent and what you represent through your experience, your communication and your accomplishment. Nothing else matters.

Have this greater priority in life and most of the problems that seem to beset and hinder people around you will rarely if ever be experienced by you. You will have a greater set of problems. Other people are beset with little problems, which arouse enormous reactions. Yet these little problems will only arouse in you a very small reaction because you will be reacting to something greater.

Because you live in manifest life, the sense of greatness that you experience will depend on the greatness of the problems that you are solving. If you are only dealing with little things and you are not very successful, you will feel little and unsuccessful. If you are solving greater problems that have meaning and value, you will feel greater, and you will feel that your life has meaning and value. You are what you value. You are what you do. Essentially, you are what you resolve and accomplish while you are in the world because contribution is what brought you here. You did not get kicked out of Heaven to be here. You are not in exile though you may feel like you are. You are here to do something important. You are here to engage with certain people for a certain purpose. You are here to find those people. You are here to find that purpose and to learn how to understand its meaning and its application.

Religion is what enables you to do this, religion in its pure sense. Religion is teaching, learning, giving, sharing and applying Knowledge. In its pure sense, this is what it is. We give you this new and yet ancient understanding so that you may have a new approach and new beginning. You need a new approach and a new beginning because you cannot enter new territory with an old understanding. You cannot add on something new to something old, for something new will replace what is old. New experience replaces old experience. New understanding replaces old understanding. New avenues of life take you out of old avenues of life. New relationships replace old relationships. Therefore, you cannot enter into this greater preparation and this greater mission while holding on to everything you think, believe and want or while maintaining the memories of all the little things you have done, said, felt and valued. Remember, when you leave the world, none of these things will be important to you. Your only concern will be whether you completed your mission here and whether you found the people you needed to associate with. Everything else will be forgotten.

Having the emphasis while you are here that you will have after you leave is a great gift that is being given to you now. This is a gift that will give you extraordinary power and effectiveness and one that will liberate you from so many small things that torment you. This is what lifts the crown of thorns from around your mind. This is what frees your mind. What great fame or glory can there be in the world that is not but a crown of thorns—something that gives you false majesty but that torments you and limits you, binds you and restricts you. Take the crown of thorns off your head. It does not belong on you.

The world is emerging into the Greater Community. You need to learn the ways of the Greater Community. You need to learn the religion of the Greater Community because this religion represents God's work, not only in one world, in one culture or in one language but in the entire universe. This will give greater meaning and scope to your world's religions and will give them the unifying principle they now need to have a greater application and a greater relevancy in life. Without this, the world's religions will fade away or be overwhelmed by the reality of the Greater Community. Yet the Greater Community by its very existence gives the world's religions a greater impetus and opportunity.

The Greater Community Way of Knowledge is being presented into the world to give people like you who feel an inner need and a greater association in life an opportunity to discover, to apply and to contribute Knowledge. This is your purpose. This is what you have come here to do. What you will do specifically is unique to you and to those with whom you are destined to participate. You are meant to serve the greater movement of life in your own unique way. This is religion. Yet you will need to study religion in a Greater Community context in order to have this greater understanding.

Do not, then, be afraid of religion. Do not associate it with your past. Do not associate it with all of the foolish manifestations that have been made in the world regarding it. See it anew as the means for you to regain your greater purpose in being here and with it a greater experience of destiny and companionship. Consider what you will remember from this life after you leave here, given the things that we have said. Then you will realize what is important, what is essential, what requires your attention and what your first priority must be. Then all other things will take their proper place in your life—not to be denied but to be properly oriented and properly placed.

Your attention should be on great things. This will enable you to solve small problems and keep them small. This will enable you to choose wisely in your relationships and in your career. This will enable you to choose according to Knowledge and not be dominated by what you want or are afraid of. When this is done, and done consistently, then you will be living a religious life and you will be having a religious experience. You will be living a religion that includes and yet transcends all that the world has ever known.

—◦◦◦—

Many will find their purpose

in the traditions of the world,

for there is much wisdom and value there.

However, many will not find their purpose there

because their preparation

has to do with the future specifically,

and they must learn a new way.

They must receive a new testament,

and they must prepare for a new experience.

—◦◦◦—

CHAPTER TWENTY

WHAT IS RELIGIOUS EDUCATION AND WHO IS IT FOR?

—⁓—

*R*ELIGIOUS EDUCATION IS AN ATTEMPT to build a bridge from your worldly mind to your Spiritual Mind. In whatever context, format, tradition or preparation, this is its overall intent. Therefore, religious education must be focused on Knowledge because Knowledge represents your Spiritual Mind in the world and your vital link to God and to all life everywhere. To think that religion is not concerned with Knowledge is to misinterpret and misunderstand the purpose and nature of religion. This new definition gives you a fresh and appropriate view of what religion is and what it must mean for you now.

Religious education exists in many different traditions. However, now there is a greater need. Now there is a greater context for understanding. Now there is a greater problem for humanity—a problem which can unite humanity in its approach, give focus and destiny to its efforts and bring about a greater union among its peoples. This greater context is represented by the world's emergence into the Greater

Community, which will present a set of problems and opportunities that the world's religions are not prepared to meet.

In order for you to be a person who can prepare for the future and live meaningfully in the moment, you need to become a part of what is happening in the world. You need to belong to the world while you are here. In this way, your gift will be called forth from you, and you will be able to give it appropriately and meaningfully with a greater understanding and a greater perspective.

Religious education is, therefore, fundamentally concerned with the reclamation of Knowledge. However, since there is so much religious education that is not concerned with this, we must make a very important distinction at this point. Learning traditions, methodologies and the historical context for any religious tradition are only meant to inspire you and must only be adjuncts to the real preparation itself. Unfortunately, few people are ever able to find the real preparation in their own tradition.

We do not give you a detailed historical account of The Greater Community Way of Knowledge. We do not create grand, marvelous and incomprehensible creation stories. We do not give you anyone to worship. We do not give you pageantry. We do not give you a theology that is filled with speculation and self-comforting ideas. Instead, we give you the pure approach—the means, the direction, the purpose, the content and the application. You need this now as the world is preparing to emerge into the Greater Community. All the other things that are left out of this pure approach will only hinder you, blind you, encumber you and disable you from gaining access to the true meaning and importance of your life at this time. Be grateful that you have been spared such distractions. Be grateful that you do not have to carry the weight of the world's thinking upon your shoulders. Be grateful that you do not have to bear the burden of all of the interpretation and idealism that saturate spiritual understanding and seem to conceal the real preparation and make it inaccessible and undesirable.

Religious education must teach you The Way of Knowledge. If this can be done purely, without other encumbrances, then you will have a remarkable opportunity. You have this opportunity now, not only to learn The Way of Knowledge but to learn The Greater Community Way of Knowledge, which represents the existence and activity of Knowledge within a far greater context of life. Within this greater context, the encumbrances of human pageantry, history, fantasy and idealism have no place. If you wish to retreat into the past, then return to the past. But if you do so, you will not understand who you are or why you are here now. You will not understand where you are going or what is coming for you. For you will have a future that will be unlike the past because of the world's emergence into the Greater Community. The future is never like the past anyway.

In order to learn a Greater Community Way of Knowledge, you must have a free mind. You must have a mind that can learn new things. You must have a mind that is free of past referencing. And you must have a fresh approach and a real source of inspiration. Your inspiration must now come from Knowledge itself. It cannot come from fantastic stories. It cannot come from ancient personages. It cannot come from ideals. It cannot come from supplication. It must come from Knowledge itself—that great intelligence within you which represents your true purpose and your true will in life.

So, what is religious education? If it is not an attempt to understand the past, then it must be a preparation for the future, as it should be. In reality, all religious education in the pure sense is a preparation for the future because it is preparing you to live a life that represents your true purpose and will. Yet how rare this is! You can see this very clearly, yet it is so hard to find in the world because most people are looking backwards and therefore cannot see the future approaching them. Most people are trying to make sense out of what they already believe, and as a result they cannot see what is right in front of them. So many people are guarding their ideas and their beliefs, but who can respond to the next moment when Knowledge will call upon them?

This is a Greater Community Spirituality. It is meant to take you to a greater vantage point in life. Perhaps you will go with your former tradition or some aspect of it. Perhaps you will take nothing with you.

Only what is true can accompany you up the mountain of life. What is unnecessary, or what was true before but is no longer true, you cannot take with you. You need only what is essential, and you do not want to be burdened with what is nonessential. You want your mind and your vision to be clear. Add one thing that does not belong, add one person who does not belong in your life, add one set of beliefs or requirements, preferences or associations which are not essential to you and to your purpose, and your way will be clouded and your understanding will be offset. You will lose your vision.

To prevent this from happening, we give you a new beginning, a new start. You need this because what you have learned in the past you must now leave behind at the door. To enter into this greater panorama and this greater education, you must have an open mind, a young mind, a fresh mind. Religious education deals with learning about Knowledge. Because Knowledge is completely present, it is not concerned with the past and it is not here to defend old traditions. It is here to engage you meaningfully in the moment and to prepare you for the future so that the promise of your great purpose in life may be realized and fulfilled.

The world's emergence into the Greater Community can have a tremendously liberating effect in terms of your ability to associate with life. Here you will be forced to deal with the present. And because of the great encounter with other forms of intelligent life, your associations with your memories of the past will fade. This will change your life, which is a change for the good if you can embrace it, understand it and utilize it properly.

The education in Greater Community Spirituality is mysterious because it does not call upon your past or require past referencing. Here you must learn things you do not understand, approach things you cannot relate to and study things you have never studied before. Here you cannot rely upon your former ideas, beliefs or associations. You must be vulnerable to the truth to know the truth. And you are vulnerable when you approach the truth without your former ideas and conclusions. This does not mean that you are to be open to everything, but it does mean that you are willing to learn something new and have it be demonstrated to you. If this cannot be done, then you cannot learn a Greater Community Way of Knowledge, and you cannot prepare for the Greater Community. And you will join the great majority of humanity that is involved in the past and that cannot respond meaningfully to the present and to the future.

The past has brought you to this point, to this opportunity to learn The Greater Community Way of Knowledge. It has served its purpose. This was its purpose. It has no other purpose that is lasting and meaningful. It has brought you to this point where you can receive these words. If properly understood, the past will enable you to begin life anew, with an open and a free mind.

We call upon Knowledge within you to respond. Therefore, we honor you and your intelligence. You are not asked to believe something that you cannot believe or to accept something that you cannot accept. For this to be honest and sincere, you must come to Knowledge on your own. Knowledge is the living Presence within you, the greater intelligence that you possess and that bonds you to all life. Here there is no past referencing. Here there is complete honesty. Here there is complete and true discernment. Here there is real responsibility.

Religious education is meant for any person who feels the need to understand his or her purpose and meaning in life. Any person who has begun to feel this greater and deeper need will need some form of religious education. From a Greater Community perspective, this means that they must learn The Way of Knowledge. They must learn about Knowledge. They must learn about their deeper nature and its purpose and mission in life, which are inextricably bonded to the evolution of the world.

Remember, you have been sent to serve the world in its evolution and development. You have come to participate in what is occurring at this time. Your life now and your life to come will give you the greatest opportunities and the greatest challenges to do this.

So great will be the world's emergence into the Greater Community and its impact on human awareness that the emphasis on the past, which is so pervasive in your thinking and in your current education, will become increasingly irrelevant. Here you will not be able to call upon the past to help you and to give you the strength, the insight and the skill to deal with the new experiences that you will be having. The past can only take you backwards. It cannot prepare you for the future. Only in the simplest and most mundane ways can the past prepare you for the future. To fully prepare for the Greater Community and for a new world experience, you will need something greater and wiser, more spontaneous and more complete. You already possess this within yourself.

If you are a person who needs to know the purpose and meaning of your life and who cannot be satisfied with simple pleasures or be preoccupied with normal fears, justifications and beliefs, then you must enter a religious education—a religious education in the purest sense. To learn The Way of Knowledge, which is the workings of Spirit, is to learn the nature of spirituality as it truly exists in the evolving condition of the human experience here. If you have this greater need and cannot dismiss it, rationalize it or satisfy it with the traditions that exist now and their explanations for life, then you must have a new experience and leave aside what cannot satisfy this greater calling within you.

Many will find their purpose in the traditions of the world, for there is much wisdom and value there. However, many will not find their purpose there because their preparation has to do with the future specifically, and they must learn a new way. They must receive a new testament, and they must prepare for a new experience. This represents the greatest need for humanity at this time, a need that is barely known and that is barely recognized. Anyone who can respond to this becomes a pioneer for the human race. Anyone who can respond to this becomes a great contributor to life. What keeps humanity going are those who can respond to the present and to the future. They are the ones who have advanced your race. And they are the ones who will advance your race in its current difficulties and opportunities and in the difficulties and opportunities to come.

Accept your greater need. Feel it. It contains the real meaning of your life. Though it has been a burden, a nuisance and a source of great discomfort and dissatisfaction, understand it is meant to lead you to something new. It is calling upon you. It is your calling. Though it feels like a great and pressing need that cannot be defined or explained away, it is your calling. Do not define it. Do not explain it away. Do not associate it with the past. Do not try to make it fit into the world's ideas and understanding. Give it the freedom to emerge within you. It is the inspiration, the impetus and the drive for truth. And it will take you to a truth that you have never known before and prepare you in ways that have rarely been seen within the world.

To receive a Greater Community Spirituality, there must be this great and corresponding need within yourself. You cannot do this for curiosity. You cannot do this to attempt to look superior in any way. If this is your motivation, you will not be able to learn a Greater Community Way of Knowledge. And you will deceive yourself and others, at great cost both to yourself and to your relationships. A greater need will set you apart from others who cannot or will not feel their greater need. Your task and your challenge now is to respond to this greater need within yourself and to allow it to emerge without attempting to harness it, define it or direct it. It has its own direction. It has its own purpose. It has its own will. To recognize this greater need is to honor your deeper inclinations and to reunite with yourself as you truly are and as you are truly seeking to be in life.

Perhaps you will think you are responding to something fantastic and inexplicable. This represents both the limits of your personal mind and the greatness and the importance of your deeper mind. Of course you cannot understand something great with something small. Your personal mind is small. The mind of Knowledge is great. If you think you understand it, you only limit it. If you think you can control it, you will only be fooled by it. If you think you can hold it for yourself, it will escape you.

To be a student of Knowledge, you must be open to learn. To learn, you must not determine or demand what the result will be or how the learning will take place. Open your mind, allow your greater need and purpose to emerge and you will feel a reunion within yourself. You will feel refreshed. You will feel that at last you are being recognized and acknowledged. If you can allow this to set you apart from others, without attempting to take them with you or to remain united with an old perspective or understanding, you will feel these great acknowledgments, and they will give you strength and confirmation.

Religious education is unlike the education of the world. It is not about learning facts or historical perspectives. It is not about comparing ideas. It is not about speculation. It is not about passing tests or meeting requirements. It is not about winning favor with others and gaining recognition amongst them. Religious education as it truly exists represents The Way of Knowledge. This is where you enter into the Mystery and allow a Greater Mind to emerge within you. This is where you put yourself in a position to receive so that you can learn something that you did not know before, experience something you could not experience before and see something you could not see before.

With this education, you can advance up the mountain and gain a greater vantage point in life, a greater view and a greater honesty. As you proceed, what is necessary will serve you. What is unnecessary will burden you and will have to be left aside. Then your steps will become quicker, and your burden will become lighter. And your need to associate with life that exists in the lowlands will become less and less of an encumbrance for you. This is gaining a very practical freedom, a freedom that can only be gained through an education of this nature.

Knowledge will free you and unburden you because that is its first purpose and requirement. What it will give you is something you have sought in all other things—relationship, acknowledgment, power, confidence, determination and direction in life. These things will have a real foundation now and will not fail you.

This is for anyone who feels the real need to know. This education is the answer to this need. The need calls for preparation. The need initiates you to become a real student and enables you to prepare and to support your preparation. The preparation cannot come from within you. Only the ability to prepare and the desire to prepare can come from within you. The preparation must be given to you. It represents a gift that corresponds to your deeper need. It is the answer to the question that your need expresses.

Religious education takes you into a new kind of experience—an experience of recognition and an experience of knowing things. Much of this will have nothing to do with you personally. It enables you to learn information that is useful to your purpose. In essence, it will seem more an unlearning than a learning because you will be releasing so many former ideas to create an opening in your mind and a greater capacity for learning. How can you learn if your mind is already filled with your own ideas and beliefs? How can your mind learn anything when it is protecting its current information?

Education in The Way of Knowledge deals with learning things that are essential, releasing things that are not and gaining the discernment to tell the two apart. How do you tell them apart? You tell them apart because they are so different, and you can feel the difference. The experience of Knowledge is unlike anything else in the world. Here you will develop a deeper reference point for Knowledge within yourself— not something that tantalizes your ideas or stimulates your emotions, but something that resonates with the deeper part of you that you are now able to experience and identify.

The Way of Knowledge seems very slow, but you will move with remarkable speed. You will not see your advancement except at certain points when you realize that you are at a different position on the mountain of life and that you have a different view of life around you. Then you will have a new experience of who you are, and you will have a greater sense of inner freedom. Here experience is more important than belief. Here learning is more important than the confirmation of old ideas.

Religious education must be mysterious. If you demand that everything be concrete and tangible, then you are past referencing. If you think that everything must be physical and mundane, how can you learn something mysterious and divine? The Mystery has its own demonstration, the most profound of which is the experience of Knowledge itself. But to approach the Mystery, you must enter into a realm where you do not have understanding or expertise. Here you must go in a direction that other people are not going. You must accept your departure and support it without any condemnation of others in order to carry light into the darkness, the darkness of the unknown.

The light of Knowledge will light your way. It cannot be extinguished. It can only be hidden. As it is revealed, you will not want to hide it because it will give you certainty and strength and make your life essential and meaningful. It will show you the way. When the light of Knowledge is concealed, then you will stumble about in life, trying this out, trying that out, believing in whatever seems most comfortable and self-assuring in the moment, but without any real certainty of truth and without any real efficacy in your thinking and behavior.

Religious education restores what is essential to your life. It gives you something that the world cannot give you because its source is God. The world can teach you the ways of the world. It can teach you how to survive in the world and how to prosper in the world to a certain degree. However, it cannot teach you your greater nature or purpose. It cannot teach you where you have come from and where you are going. Therefore, the more worldly a religious education becomes, the less it is able to address these greater and far more important questions. If you do not have a real sense of why you are here, then you are lost to yourself. Your only remedy, then, is to find a way to regain, to reclaim and to express this greater purpose. Here everyone is lost until they are found. And the only way they are found is to find the way that a greater purpose can be experienced directly and honestly.

The Way of Knowledge is mysterious, but it is certain. It is unfamiliar because it is new. It is new, but it is ancient. It is remarkable, but it is known. It may be shocking and challenging at certain junctures, but you can embrace it wholeheartedly because it resonates with the very essence of who you are and why you are here. It will challenge your ideas. It will force change, but only to restore you to yourself, to restore to you your essential skills, to prepare you in the world and to enable you to utilize the world for a greater education.

Here you can learn to use what the world has to offer in a new way. Instead of for survival or self-gratification, it is used for contribution. Then what the world has to offer becomes a means to serve a greater end and a greater purpose. Here you can utilize things beneficially without confusion and without complaint. Success and failure both help you now. Advantages and disadvantages both become useful. Disappointment in relationship now has a greater possibility. Here you are not being clever or cunning or manipulative. You are simply recognizing a greater purpose in everything you do, with everything you own, with every experience you have and with every person you meet. This is something natural that emerges from the very depth of you. You do not need to conjure it up. Here you are being simple and open, rather than complicated and devious.

The way is mysterious because you do not govern it. The way is mysterious because it is not dependent upon your past. The way is mysterious because it takes you beyond your former understanding. The way is mysterious, but it is known. This enables you to follow it wholeheartedly as you learn to trust it, to accept it and to learn of its ways, its direction, its meaning and its purpose. You can only be wholehearted about something that represents your Ancient Home from which you have come. You cannot be wholehearted about anything else, no matter how attached you may be to it, because to be wholehearted means to embrace something totally. This is only possible at the level of Knowledge.

Knowledge can only embrace Knowledge in the universe. It gives itself to everything else, but it is only bonded to that which represents the immortal and permanent relationships that you have in life and with life. It is towards this that your religious education will lead you. It is for this that your religious education will prepare you. If you recognize your need for this, then religious education is meant for you. And if it is meant for you, then you must recognize it, learn to accept it and find out what it means.

—◦∿◦—

In order to establish a preparation

for the Greater Community

and to bond the peoples of the world together

with a greater foundation

and a greater experience of union,

The Greater Community Way of Knowledge

is being introduced into the world.

—◦∿◦—

CHAPTER TWENTY-ONE

WHAT IS THE GREATER COMMUNITY WAY OF KNOWLEDGE?

———*༄༅*———

*I*N ORDER TO ESTABLISH A PREPARATION for the Greater Community and to bond the peoples of the world together with a greater foundation and a greater experience of union, The Greater Community Way of Knowledge is being introduced into the world. The Greater Community Way of Knowledge is being translated into human language and adapted to human nature and to the human environment. This is The Way of Knowledge that is applicable to life everywhere. It is translatable from one world to another. It represents a pure expression of religion and spirituality. It is applicable to your world and to other worlds and has a direct bearing on every aspect of your life and on all of your endeavors. It comes from the Greater Community. Therefore, it represents a larger arena of life and a larger context for application. It is being given now to prepare humanity for its destiny in the Greater Community and to enable humanity to find the strength and inner resources necessary to meet the growing problems of the world.

Because The Way of Knowledge represents translatable spirituality in the Greater Community, it is unencumbered by the traditions, history, perspective, rituals and pageantry of any world where it has been fostered and utilized. It is being presented to the human community now in a pure form—a form that can be readily accessed and learned through serious study and application, a form that can be applied both to the problems of your individual life and to the greater problems of the world itself.

What is the Greater Community Way of Knowledge? In essence it is applied spirituality. It is the application of a greater Wisdom and a greater ability that are inherent in all intelligent life. It is now being given to this world where it is needed, where it can be applied and where it has great relevance. To be effective in preparing humanity for the Greater Community, The Way of Knowledge must be presented in a pure form and must represent a translatable spirituality. It must be a spirituality that can be shared from one world to another, and it must have tremendous bearing on everything you think and everything you do.

The Greater Community Way of Knowledge can be readily used in your life. Why? Because it calls upon Knowledge within you. It prepares you for the emergence of Knowledge within you and opens the way for Knowledge within you to express itself. It is not alien or foreign to your nature because it speaks to your nature and represents your nature. It brings you to that within yourself and within other people which is the very essence and potential for Wisdom in life. It acknowledges what you have done before that has been based on Knowledge, and it calls upon Knowledge again in this moment and in the next moment—today, tomorrow and each day after. It brings you to yourself and to your purpose in life. It comes from the Greater Community because it represents your destiny. It comes from the Greater Community, which is a greater context for application and the greater context of your life.

Only a preparation from the Greater Community can prepare you for the Greater Community. Human beings left up to themselves could not prepare for a Greater Community experience and could neither adapt to a Greater Community environment nor to Greater

Community interactions. Therefore, a preparation must be given for these things. The preparation represents applied spirituality in life. It is religious in nature because it calls upon a Greater Power within you and within the universe. It recognizes the greater relationship that exists within the physical parameters of your life between you and those significant people who are meant to assist you, support you and participate with you in your greater journey in life. It represents your relationships beyond the world, both in the Greater Community and beyond physical existence itself, with your Spiritual Family.

In essence, The Greater Community Way of Knowledge could be called the way of relationship. It could be called the way of contribution. It could be called the way of discernment. It could be called the way of certainty. It could be called the way of preparation. It could be called the way of true Wisdom. All of these are applicable here. These represent different facets of this teaching and preparation. They are all part of this spiritual foundation and experience.

Encountering a translatable spirituality is a remarkable thing. The religions of your world can be translated, but in order to do this, all that is associated with them—their history and their symbolism—must be removed in order for their essence to be revealed. This is very difficult because the religions in your world are intertwined with your cultures, and their history represents the history of your cultures. You cannot easily separate them.

What is translatable in all of the world's religions is Knowledge. Knowledge represents your innate and inherent ability to recognize the truth, to respond to the truth and to represent the truth. This is not a personal truth, but a greater truth that exists within your relationships and that can be expressed across any boundary or border, any gap or differentiation. What is true here is true everywhere at the level of Knowledge.

All intelligent life in the universe possesses Knowledge. This is not to say that all forms of intelligent life are developed in Knowledge or are capable with Knowledge. However, it does mean that the potential is there. Developing this potential represents the foundation for communication, recognition and cooperation that can transcend all differences in temperament, attitude, belief or association. This is possible, and it is this possibility that we must now emphasize.

Your encounters with intelligent life from the Greater Community will be very shocking and difficult. Human beings can barely tolerate even the slightest differences amongst themselves and often use these differences as justification for alienation, for attack and for cruelty. How much greater, then, are the differences between you and other races in the Greater Community. So great are the differences there that it makes the differences between human beings seem slight and insignificant.

However, despite the great differences between humanity and other forms of intelligent life, there is something that you have in common. It is Knowledge. With Knowledge, relationship and communication are possible. Do not think, however, that all other forms of intelligent life are cultivated in Knowledge. A few are, but most are not. Because you all share a greater origin, and with it the possibility for realizing a greater purpose, Knowledge must be the foundation of any attempt to understand, discern, communicate and participate with any other form of intelligent life.

The Greater Community Way of Knowledge represents a preparation for interaction and relationship and demonstrates the possibility for this by presenting and emphasizing those things that are essential, uniform and universal in life. However, even within this universal understanding and application, The Way of Knowledge speaks to all the particulars and details of your life that require your attention. It speaks to those decisions that you must make along the way in order to find the greater purpose, direction and destiny where Knowledge itself will be the foundation of your experience.

The Greater Community Way of Knowledge is a gift to humanity. It is being given so that your preparation and your emergence into the Greater Community may have the greatest possibility for success. It is being given at this time because you are becoming a global community. Even though there is still great resistance and great conflict over this development in your world, it is happening nonetheless. The Greater Community Way of Knowledge is being presented to the world because there is the possibility that it can be learned and accepted here by those individuals who can respond to a greater understanding, perception and Wisdom in life.

The Greater Community Way of Knowledge represents the transmission of spirituality and religion in the universe. This transmission is being given to your world now. Prior to this, you did not need a Greater Community Way of Knowledge because your scope in life was limited to your interactions with each other and with your natural environment. This gave rise to the religions of the world, which have grown and have become manifest. However, now you are entering a greater panorama of life and a greater context for understanding and relationship. Here there are greater risks and greater requirements. Therefore, a new teaching must be given to humanity from the Greater Community itself. The transmission of The Greater Community Way of Knowledge is being presented now to serve this greater need. It calls upon individuals who can recognize the relevance of the future to their current experience and who can learn to see the direction of the world with new eyes and with an untainted perception.

The eminently practical aspects of learning The Greater Community Way of Knowledge, which are concerned with the particulars of everyday life, are but the smallest of its great advantages. Its greater rewards enable you to find yourself and your purpose in the world within the context of the world's evolution. This creates a greater and more permanent foundation for living here.

The Greater Community Way of Knowledge prepares one to understand the direction of the world and to contribute to the world's evolution in a positive way. At this time in history, people are responding to the world's evolution, but often in very negative and destructive ways. They are feeling the undercurrents of change, and they are experiencing the effects of change. However, many try to return to an earlier emphasis in life, something from the past that they can hold onto. Others go into disarray and break down. Others struggle and fight, declaring war on whatever they think is the most threatening aspect of the change which is permeating their lives.

Into this increasingly difficult and dissonant situation, the Greater Community Way of Knowledge is being presented. It makes it possible for you to learn everything that is being presented in this book of Greater Community Spirituality. It is the means of development, for you cannot understand Greater Community Spirituality from your current position. You cannot understand the world's emergence into the Greater Community from your current position. You cannot fully appreciate these things, for you must be prepared for them. Your mind must be expanded, your perception refined and your abilities developed and brought into a meaningful order according to your nature and greater purpose. Then you will reach a greater vantage point in life where these things, which seemed so difficult to understand and seemingly incomprehensible before, can be seen clearly and are obvious. When the truth is obvious, then you are one with the truth. If the truth is mysterious, confusing, disorienting or disillusioning, then you are outside the relationship you need to be in with truth itself.

The Greater Community Way of Knowledge is a gift from the Creator. It is not simply the offering of one race to another, one world to another, or one culture to another. It is a gift of Wisdom for your world. In order for it to find a home here, individuals must respond to it and learn it according to its teaching and its methodology. You cannot learn a Greater Community Way of Knowledge based on your own preferences and ideas. You must learn it according to its methods and develop according to its direction and process. This assures success. Tampering with it, changing it or trying to mix it with the ideas, beliefs or conclusions that you find pleasurable or familiar will only lead you into confusion.

Remember, what is being presented here is to take you to a greater vantage point in life. It is to develop greater abilities that are inherent within you, to bring out the very best within you and to minimize those aspects of your personality and your environment that hinder you and prevent you from realizing the greater truth and purpose that have brought you into the world.

The Greater Community Way of Knowledge is a teaching and a preparation. It emphasizes that religion is education, an education that must have immediate bearing on the real aspects of your life. Here you are not asked to believe but to prepare. Here you are not asked to merely follow, but to gain the ability to come into relationship with Knowledge. Here you find the truth, experience it and over time learn how to apply it in difficult situations wherever it is needed.

This represents a very different kind of education from anything you have ever attempted before. You will find certain things here that will seem familiar. You will find things that will be comforting to you. However, the education itself is something remarkably different. It is a different way of learning—a different process of learning which leads to a different result in life.

The Greater Community Way of Knowledge represents a new experience of religion and Divinity in life. Being a translatable spirituality, it can be shared and applied in a universal context, which is represented by the Greater Community. It is not a human religion for a purely human environment. It has bearing on life everywhere, and thus its truth is universal.

Though you may never in your life personally meet a visitor from the Greater Community, The Greater Community Way of Knowledge has a total bearing on the events of your life. It calls upon that which is great within you to emerge and to speak through you. It calls upon you to enter into relationship with that which is great within you. It asks you to be honest—honest at a level that you had never considered possible or even necessary before. It asks you to honor your nature, not in a superficial way or in a condescending way, but in a way that lifts you up and takes you to a greater experience of yourself and life around you.

The Greater Community Way of Knowledge represents spirituality in the Greater Community. It addresses the great need of your world at this time. The great need of your world at this time is for Knowledge and for translatable spirituality—a spirituality that bonds people together and does not set them apart, a spirituality that establishes a medium of communication between all the divergent interests, groups, cultures and nations that are currently keeping your world in strife. It honors that which is true in all the world's religions and gives them a greater context in which to grow and to adapt, in which to change and to be applied. It is not here to replace the world's religions but to elevate them. In some cases this may be possible. In other cases it may not be possible. However, the truth is that a greater foundation for religious experience and human understanding is now needed in the world, and needed desperately. It is this great need along with the evolutionary movement of the world in which you live that have brought the Greater Community Way of Knowledge to you.

The Greater Community Way of Knowledge is being transmitted through only one person. As long as this one person is capable of receiving and representing this Teaching and Tradition, it will be given through him, and he will be the medium for its expression. This is how great religious traditions have always been initiated and begun. Your history speaks of this. This holds true in the Greater Community as well. It takes one mind joined with the Mind of the universe to begin to bring a greater ability and a greater result into the world.

You are blessed, then, to receive this. You are blessed to be able to be among the first to receive a Greater Community Way of Knowledge. You receive this not fully understanding its importance, its relevance or its lasting significance for humanity. You can receive it because Knowledge within you will receive it. It is the answer to your calling. It calls you, and you have called it. And finally you have come together. You have found each other. Perhaps your first encounters will be difficult and awkward. Perhaps there is a great deal of fear, suspicion and uncertainty. Perhaps you are afraid of what it might do for you or with you. There are many bad examples of human dedication in the world that can give an incorrect understanding and a false idea about the meaning of being in relationship with a greater calling in life.

The Greater Community Way of Knowledge is not a path of belief; it is the path of inner certainty. It does not ask you to believe. Belief here is a temporary expedient to carry you from one experience of Knowledge to another. Belief here is to uphold your position that Knowledge is real, that it can be experienced and that it is of the utmost importance in your life. Here belief is an aid to your progress. However, belief can never replace Knowledge itself. If it does so, it becomes a form of subversion, a dangerous and tragic demonstration of deception and unwilling participation.

Within the Greater Community, there are races that are very advanced. They are not as common as you might think because when we speak of advancement, we speak of advancement in Knowledge and Wisdom. There are many races that are advanced technologically. And there are many races that have developed a stable social foundation. However, advancement in Knowledge and Wisdom is a greater and far different kind of advancement.

You can only learn in an environment where someone who is more advanced than you can stimulate you, challenge you, support you and give you direction. Humanity has not been able to advance itself very effectively because it has lacked the presence of a greater and more advanced intelligence. In your own life, you will learn the most being around someone else who is more competent, more determined, more capable or more understanding than you are. People of lesser ability may make you feel good about yourself temporarily, but they cannot lead you into new territory. They cannot enable you to progress. They cannot enable you to advance. They can only confirm the advancement that you have received from being with someone who was more advanced than you.

The Greater Community Way of Knowledge represents greater intelligence, understanding and ability in physical life. Therefore, it gives you a greater perspective and challenge in life. It calls you out of complacency. It calls you out of your assumptions. It gives you greater work to do and recognizes the greater nature within you that makes this work possible and necessary.

You need this challenge. Perhaps you feel that the challenges of your life are already very great, but they are not uniform. They are diffracted. With a greater context for understanding and a greater dimension to your life, your life can be brought into focus and all the aspects of your personality, which can seem so divergent from one another, can be brought into harmony. With this comes tremendous power of application. A unified mind is a powerful mind. A powerful mind can effect change in life. This, indeed, is part of the reward and the benefit of participating in a greater preparation, something you did not make up for yourself and that you do not alter to meet your past references. A greater preparation leads you out of the past and into the future. With this future orientation comes the ability to live fully in the moment, in the present.

The Greater Community Way of Knowledge represents religion in the universe. This is needed in the world now—not to become a great popular movement, not to have magnificent edifices built for it, but to become a foundation that generates a greater perception and understanding within human thinking everywhere in the world. If enough people can learn a Greater Community Way of Knowledge, they will spread this benefit wherever they go. From them it will resonate through many minds, like ripples extending out on the surface of the water. The ripple effect of Knowledge will stimulate minds everywhere. However, in order for this to happen, a sufficient number of people are needed to advance and to learn this teaching fully.

Humanity has always been advanced by a relatively small number of dedicated people. This represents development and progress in every aspect of human life. For these advancements to take place, a sufficient number of people had to be pioneers, and others had to substantiate what was pioneered. Then something greater could be established in the world. This is true in all aspects of human life, and it holds true in the Greater Community as well.

You now have the possibility of learning a Greater Community Way of Knowledge. A greater challenge and a greater reward you cannot imagine, one which you will not be able to find anywhere else in the world. Find a greater foundation in life and you will find your purpose for coming here. If you can experience this consistently, then you will remember who sent you here. This will break the seemingly incomprehensible veil that separates the world from your eternal life beyond. This will return to you the essential relationships that abide with you, support you, nourish you and carry you forward. With this strength and this understanding, a greater contribution and a greater will to give will well up within you. This is a remarkable event and represents a unique expression of a greater life within the physical world in which you live.

Receive this gift from the Greater Community. It is a gift born of your inner understanding. It is food for your own soul. It recognizes that you have greater relationships beyond the world and beyond the physical universe. In this larger context, a greater purpose and mission in life can be experienced. All that is presented in this book is made possible because the means have been provided. You do not need to be concerned with where it has come from or who has sent it specifically. What is important is that it is here, that you can respond to it and that you can benefit from it today, tomorrow and in the days to follow. The value of truth is that truth can be received, experienced, shared and given application where it is needed. In many cases, it is not necessary to understand where it comes from or where it is ultimately going.

The Greater Community Way of Knowledge is in the world because the Creator is in the world. This is not a world apart. It is not separated from the Creator, and it is not separated from the Greater Community. This is so intrinsic in life, and yet it can seem strange and new to you.

With The Greater Community Way of Knowledge, you begin to reclaim the reality of your life as it truly exists—beyond fear, beyond preference, beyond fantasy and beyond human tribulations. The Creator is in your life, and the Greater Community is in your life. These together represent the larger panorama of your life and the greater purpose that you have come to serve in your own unique way.

—ᴗᴗᴗ—

You are preparing for a greater life

and a greater experience.

It is like being on a great mission or voyage.

You will be venturing into an entirely new territory.

You will be going through a

complete revolution within yourself,

a revolution that will demonstrate

the existence of the Greater Power within you

and your relationship with it.

—ᴗᴗᴗ—

CHAPTER TWENTY-TWO

WHERE CAN KNOWLEDGE
BE FOUND?

———⟨ᴠᴠᴠ⟩———

*K*NOWLEDGE LIVES WITHIN YOU. It is the very essence of your spirituality. Knowledge represents the greater part of you that is bonded intrinsically with all life. It is within you, but only rarely will you be able to gain access to it on your own.

In the Greater Community, the idea and practice of religion vary considerably, but the essence of religion is the same. The universal reality of this essence guarantees that spirituality will live and thrive regardless of the kind of religious beliefs, attitudes or practices that are carried on in any given culture.

Knowledge lives within you. It is with you at this moment. It is a Greater Mind and a Greater Self within you. You cannot claim it as your own, for indeed you belong to it more than it belongs to you. Because you are separated from your Greater Self, it seems as if it is a remote entity, something distant, something you have to engage yourself with in a very careful way. Confusing this even further are the religious beliefs, attitudes and prior experiences which can make your return to Knowledge far more difficult than it would be otherwise.

There is so much to unlearn simply to be able to begin the journey towards Knowledge. Here old attitudes, expectations, associations, goals, beliefs and so forth can only encumber you and bog you down. Knowledge is so close, but you cannot seem to find it because you are aimed in the wrong direction. You have ideas, assumptions and expectations that can never be in keeping with the reality of a greater life.

Knowledge is found within you. However, what brings Knowledge forth is meaningful engagement with others and meaningful participation in life. Knowledge does not come on demand. You may petition it and call for it, and if your request is sincere, then it will come very close to you. However, if you have not built the bridge to it, then no matter how close it comes, you may feel its presence and you may sense it is with you, but you will still be unable to respond to it directly. Here you will be likely to tamper with its communication, altering it to meet your expectations or to fit some kind of prescribed notion or belief. It is when you are meaningfully engaged with others, in relationship with them and in relationship with life, that there is the greatest possibility for Knowledge to emerge within you.

Knowledge, therefore, is something that is difficult to find. You cannot simply reach inside yourself and pull it out. You have to go deeper within your own mind to be able to respond to it and to be able to sense its presence. Knowledge has its own mind. It emerges when it feels the time is right, for it responds to Knowledge in the universe and is intrinsically bonded and responsible to this. There is no personal Knowledge—your Knowledge and my Knowledge. There can only be your interpretation and my interpretation, or your idea and my idea. Knowledge itself, however, is consistent with all life. It bonds all life and organizes all life into a meaningful set of engagements that can bring about greater and more positive rewards, benefits and contributions for the world and for the time in which you live.

To prepare for Knowledge, you will need certain fundamental things. You will need the correct curriculum. You will need the correct instruction. You will need the correct approach and attitude. And you will need the right companions. These are the conditions that enable

Knowledge to emerge in such a way that it can be directly experienced and discerned and where there is the least possibility that its presence and message for you will be distorted or misunderstood.

It is establishing the conditions for Knowledge that enables Knowledge to emerge within you. These conditions require the basic elements that we have mentioned, and yet these conditions can be quite specific to you. For example, at any given moment some people are ready for an instructor and some are not. Some people are ready to begin formal preparation while others must prepare to be ready for the preparation itself. Some are ready to have real companionship; others are not. This readiness is determined by your capacity, by your development and by your circumstances. If the circumstances are not right, if your understanding is not right, or if you cannot take on the responsibility that Knowledge would bestow upon you, then the time cannot be now. Inevitably, however, you must have all of these elements in order to follow a way to Knowledge, to prepare for Knowledge and to enable Knowledge to emerge within you successfully.

At the outset, people think that Knowledge is small and that they are great. Even if they believe otherwise, this will still be their attitude as they approach it. Knowledge will seem distant and remote, even foreign to them. Even though Knowledge has guided them at crucial moments in their lives and has saved them from many calamities already, they are unaware of its presence and beneficence and must learn to re-experience these gradually. In the process of doing this, that which is incorrect, inappropriate or unnecessary can be recognized and set aside. Here people must give up their ideas of what Knowledge is and enter the experience itself. Often these ideas are impediments to the experience and distort people's approach and understanding.

The experience of Knowledge, if it can continue and be developed, will explain everything to you, but this takes time and patient preparation. This is where the correct curriculum and the proper instruction become very essential. Preparing for Knowledge is not an individual pursuit because its purpose is to reunite you in relationship with others, with yourself and with life. If you set out on your own, thinking that you will not need others and that you must depend completely on your own strength and initiative, you will not find Knowledge, and you will not find the way to Knowledge. Fundamentally, Knowledge is the return to relationship. It is the path out of separation. It is entering a new experience of life and a new participation with life. Here you cannot take all of your former ideas with you, and you cannot even take all of your former relationships with you.

You do not know how much Knowledge will change your life. However, you must desire it sufficiently that you are willing to take this risk. You must have at least the beginning understanding that the closer you are to Knowledge, the more certain, the more powerful and the more compassionate you will be. In other words, the more you will feel right within yourself.

People live, however, without this sense of rightness for so long that they become inured to it, and they adapt themselves to living a life of inner compromise. Here even the idea of Knowledge may seem very foreign to them, and the experience of Knowledge may be very disturbing—not because the experience is disturbing, but because it seems to threaten so many things that are assumed, believed or established.

Knowledge itself is entirely free of your creations. It is not hindered by your ideas and beliefs. The obstacles to Knowledge simply prevent you from gaining access to it. They cannot color, control, dominate or thwart Knowledge itself. However, they do prevent you from finding your way to Knowledge.

Knowledge can be found and must be found. And there is a way to Knowledge for you. Part of your involvement in finding the way will be up to you, and part will be determined by others because you will need great assistance, and you will need the right preparation.

Knowledge re-engages you in meaningful relationships. Therefore, these relationships must be possible for you. Here you cannot go off and live a solitary life, away from the world, without any contact with anyone else and believe that you can find the way to Knowledge. The Creator has sent you into the world to participate meaningfully with others and to contribute to the world. Retreat from the world is only important at certain junctures and does not represent, in most cases, a way of life. This is because Knowledge is not simply for you. The greater gifts that Knowledge will give will be bestowed upon others through you.

If your life is filled with relationships that do not represent this greater purpose and destiny, then it will be difficult for you to accept the preparation even if you find it. It will be difficult for you to accept the relationships that can really help you because they will seem to challenge and conflict with your current involvements.

Here you must realize that there is only so much you can do for yourself and that there are things that you need. You need information. You need a method of study. You need people who are more advanced than you, and you need companions. Beyond this, you need others to teach you what not to do and to show you their mistakes and your own mistakes. Indeed, you need all of life to demonstrate both the presence of Knowledge and the denial of Knowledge. There will be so many opportunities for you if you can take advantage of life's great demonstration. Eventually, you will feel grateful for everything that happens, not because everything happens for your good, but because you are able to use everything for your good. You can do this without distorting the truth, without denying pain and suffering and without putting a happy face on a difficult world. You can do this because in the reclamation of Knowledge things can become useful and serve a greater purpose even if within themselves they are not purposeful or beneficial.

The man and woman of Knowledge take what life has to offer and utilize it for a greater good. They do not distort life. They do not deny the realities or the different aspects of life. They do not call something that is bad "good" or something that is good "bad." What is important is how useful it is in serving a greater purpose. As you mature as a student of Knowledge, you will be able to gain this approach, and you will see how honest and effective it really is. Here you will be working in the world like the Creator works in the world—secretly, silently, without condemnation and with a permeating effectiveness that extends far beyond the great and stringent efforts of many people to improve life. This is not to say that your efforts will be easy but that their impact will be far more penetrating and lasting.

How do you prepare for Knowledge? To prepare for Knowledge, you must recognize a certain fundamental need within yourself. You must feel this need and separate it from other needs that may be more personal or immediate in nature. This basic need represents the yearning to discover your real purpose in life. Along with the recognition of this need must be the realization that your many attempts to fulfill this need through love, through affluence, through excitement or through stimulation have not satisfied the greater yearning of your heart. Something greater must be given to you to satisfy this—something that you cannot invent for yourself, something that you cannot piece together from all the various teachings and religious practices that you may encounter in life. Here you realize the limits of even your own independence, for in truth you need life tremendously. You need others tremendously. Realizing this, instead of becoming dependent, you will learn to become interdependent.

There are three stages of human development, which can be described in this way: dependence, independence and interdependence. Everyone begins life in a state of dependence. As an infant, you are entirely dependent upon your parents or providers for even the basic essentials of your life. As you gain more and more independence and are able to learn to care for yourself increasingly through the stages of your childhood, then you must outgrow your emotional dependence on others in order to learn to think for yourself or, in other words, to think independently. Most people in the world are struggling to attain physical and psychological independence. However, independence is only an intermediate stage; it is not the final resolution. Should you be able to break free of the bonds and the limitations that held you back before, you will come to realize that alone and on your own you can do very little. In truth, nothing can be done alone—no great realization can be found alone and no answer or resolution can be discovered or employed alone. You need greater relationships within the world and beyond the world in order to accomplish anything of real value and merit.

Therefore, along with the recognition of your inner need, you must recognize that you need greater relationships and greater assistance. This understanding represents the reality of life and not your past experience of dependence. Therefore, you must enter into this with a new understanding. Recognizing your needs and your limitations here is essential and enables you to enter into the third and greatest stage of human development, the stage of interdependence. In this stage, you are able to give yourself—your time, your energy and even your life—to an involvement with others as a conscious and dedicated act. Here real love and devotion are possible. In the earlier stages of dependence and independence, real love and devotion are not possible because they are conditioned by prevailing needs—first, the need to have others do things for you and then the need to do things for yourself. However, in the state of interdependence, you are able to give and receive in a truly meaningful way. Here devotion is possible because from a position of responsible decision making, you can give your life to something. Gaining the ability to do this represents the real value and purpose of independence. Without this, your independence will only isolate you further and further within your own mind and your own thoughts. It will become a great prison house from which the possibility of escape will seem increasingly difficult and remote.

In order to prepare for Knowledge, then, you need to feel your prevailing need to realize your greater purpose in life, a purpose you have not defined and cannot define for yourself. With this purpose, there is the recognition of the need for assistance and preparation—assistance and preparation that you cannot provide for yourself.

The Way of Knowledge will strengthen you and unite you within yourself. To a certain degree, this will separate you from others, even at the outset, because you are engaged in a path of discovery that others are not engaged in. In time, you will have less and less that you can share with them. You are preparing for a greater life and a greater experience. It is like being on a great mission or voyage. Even though physically you may not go anywhere, you will be venturing into an entirely new territory. You will be going through a complete revolution within yourself, a revolution that will demonstrate the existence of the Greater Power within you and your relationship with it.

At the outset, you will feel that you are great and that Knowledge is small. However, as you approach Knowledge, you will realize how great it is and how small you are. You will realize how small your personal mind is. And you will realize that Knowledge represents your True Self and your true existence in life. To gain this truth, you will have to build a bridge to Knowledge, as Knowledge is always building a bridge to you.

At a certain point, you will need to begin a formal preparation in The Way of Knowledge. This may change form once or several times in the course of your life. If the nature of the preparation is great enough and consistent enough with your nature, rather than with only your beliefs or attitudes, then it may serve to prepare you completely.

To prepare for the world's emergence into the Greater Community, you will need a Greater Community Way of Knowledge. To prepare to find a greater purpose, meaning and direction in the world, you will need this kind of preparation. This is what we are emphasizing in Greater Community Spirituality. Without this preparation, you will not be able to realize the many things that we have spoken of. Without true companionship and genuine instruction, even if you have the preparation, you will only be able to pass through its beginning stages. Your needs will change as you develop. As you develop, earlier needs will fade away, and other needs will come to take their place because there is a progression of levels of understanding in the development of Knowledge.

In order to find Knowledge, you must prepare for it. To prepare for it, you must ready yourself. To ready yourself, you must recognize your deeper needs and your real limitations. Recognizing your needs and limitations will enable you to begin to look for those things that will help you to progress. Here your emphasis must not be simply on gaining answers, for answers cannot satisfy your need. You already have lots of answers. You need experience and development. You need to actually make the journey in The Way of Knowledge. Unless you take the journey, you will not know what the journey is and you will not experience its destination. Without the preparation, all that we have said may seem great and wonderful, perhaps intriguing and interesting, but you will not understand its meaning, its purpose or its immense value and application in your life.

Greater Community Spirituality must be experienced to be understood. You cannot stand outside of it and understand it. You cannot look at it from a distance and know what it really means. You will know nothing about it unless you can experience it repeatedly in a growing and consistent way. This requires preparation. This is how Knowledge is learned and transferred in the universe.

Our words are only to incite a greater need, a greater understanding and a greater motivation within you. The Way of Knowledge and the reality of Knowledge can only be experienced as you progress towards them. This is a journey where you cannot lead yourself, for you do not know the way. You can only learn how to follow and how to respond. Because The Way of Knowledge reunites you with life so that you can become meaningfully engaged with life, you have only part of the answer within you. Because you are meant to be meaningfully re-engaged in life and because this engagement is represented by relationships of true value and purpose that you establish with others, you possess only a part of the answer to your great need. Your part must be matched with others, and you must be matched correctly.

It is like putting together the great puzzle of life. You have a few of the pieces, but you do not have all of them. And all of your pieces do not fit together. However, if you can match your pieces with others, then greater sections of the puzzle can be put together, beginning with the outline or perimeter and moving inward. Using this analogy, then, if you can be reunited with those who can really assist you and should you receive the preparation that is necessary, your puzzle will become joined and complete. Then the image and meaning that life presents to you can be fully realized.

At the outset you must have an appreciation of your limitations. If The Way of Knowledge were simple and easy, then everyone would learn it. But it is apparent that everyone does not learn it. In fact, it is rare that you will meet a man or woman of Knowledge in the world.

Being educated in the colleges and universities of the world does not lead to Knowledge. Being adventuresome and traveling around the world does not lead to Knowledge. Reading one book after another until your mind is absolutely full to the brim does not lead to Knowledge. These things fill your mind with thoughts, fill your life with memories and give you a great deal to think about. However, The Way of Knowledge is something else. Here you will want to lighten your burden. Here you will want to empty your mind. Here you will want to gain a greater inner freedom and will not want to spend the rest of your life defending your ideas or maintaining your memories.

This is a different kind of journey, and it is a different kind of education. It takes an instructor of real ability and experience to foster and nurture your progress here. It takes companions who can share your growing understanding and who can encourage you and receive your encouragement in return. It requires the understanding that you are entering into an area of life that extends far beyond your ideas and beliefs. Here you must be willing to proceed without knowing what you are doing and without the false certainty that you so often and so habitually give yourself. Making yourself vulnerable to life in this way enables life to reveal itself to you and enables your bond with life to become realized and strengthened. This represents a very gradual process. You will not achieve it in a week or a month or a year. It is too great for that. To think that you can have it quickly or that you can use it for yourself is to underestimate its magnitude and to overestimate your ability.

The Greater Community Way of Knowledge represents Knowledge in a far greater arena of life—an arena which has great relevance for your life and which will be the dominant context for life in the future. Everything you are doing now is for the future as well as for the moment. The future will be built upon what you do today and what you do not do today. This represents your future, the future of your children and the future of your race.

The Greater Community Way of Knowledge is being presented into the world, where it is unknown. It has no history and no background here. People are not used to it. It does not necessarily fit in with their ideas, beliefs or expectations. It does not conform to the world's current religious understanding. It comes in a naked form—without ritual and pageantry, without wealth and excess. It comes purely and simply. It is like a child in the world. It is seemingly vulnerable, and yet it represents a greater reality and a greater promise for humanity.

The Greater Community Way of Knowledge will go unrecognized by many because it does not have the trappings and allurements with which everything else seems to be laden. It is unadorned and it is pure. It is hard to understand but easy to experience and to utilize. It seems strange and remote, and yet it is so akin to your nature. It seems to come from far away, and yet it also seems to emanate from within you. It seems mysterious and incomprehensible, and yet it provides certainty with every step that is taken towards it. It seems familiar to some, and yet it is quite different. It seems different to others, and yet it is quite familiar. Its familiarity is born of a greater association and empathy within you, which you are capable of experiencing.

The Greater Community Way of Knowledge conforms to your nature and to Knowledge within you but not necessarily to your ideas, beliefs or expectations, which are all based upon the past. The Way of Knowledge speaks of the future and of your responsibility to the future. It speaks of your nature and your purpose for coming into the world. It speaks plainly and simply. It is deep and unfathomable, and yet it can be experienced fully. Like the passing of water through a great web or filter, it penetrates into the very heart of you and nourishes your growth and development here.

The Greater Community Way of Knowledge represents translatable spirituality in the universe. It calls upon Knowledge within you. It furthers Knowledge and fosters Knowledge, for Knowledge is the very root of your life and the very source of your substance, meaning, purpose and direction. It provides a way to Knowledge within you. It brings you into life and introduces you to the reality of life and the direction of life. It is both a journey into yourself and a journey into the world. Both happen together in a very special and united way. If you journey too far into yourself without understanding your responsibility or your context in the world, you will become lost in yourself. And if you journey too far into the world without building a greater association and foundation within yourself, you will become lost in the world. Therefore, relationship with yourself and relationship with the world must naturally grow together.

Knowledge is here to do something. It is not here to take you out of the world. It is not here to provide an escape. It is here to provide contribution and completion. It prepares for the future by engaging you with life now. Knowledge uses everything that you think and everything that you have made but for a greater purpose. It does not destroy your ideals. It does not destroy your relationships. It does not destroy your beliefs. It simply puts them to use. And if they cannot be put to use, they are gradually released, without condemnation or destruction. Everything then becomes useful and beneficial. The motivation for this comes from within you. Here you do not follow a hero or idolize a distant God. You do not worship a foreign individual or a foreign power. Instead, you become engaged with Knowledge, and Knowledge engages you with others. In this way, you gain your strength and authority. In this way, you learn how to give your life in the right place, for the right purpose, with the right people.

This represents the Plan of God. It represents a Greater Plan which is far beyond your ability to fully comprehend. It represents a Plan that can work through you if you can work with it. It renews you, restores you and gives you your proper authority over your thinking and behavior. And it reassociates you with the Greater Power within yourself and beyond yourself which can guide you in life and give you a greater purpose and understanding.

You begin the preparation by feeling the need. You begin the preparation by recognizing your limitations and the limitations of what you have established thus far. You begin the preparation by becoming humble and open within yourself, without assuming greater powers or extraordinary abilities for yourself. You open yourself because the need within you is propelling you forward.

This is the evidence of Knowledge within you, for Knowledge is getting ready to emerge. No longer can you be complacent with it. No longer can you deny it. No longer can you dress it up to look like some-thing else, or try to thwart it or manipulate it to give you something that you desire. Here Knowledge is moving within you, and its movement is becoming stronger. It is as if you were attempting to give birth to something—something within you that needs to come forth, that needs to present itself in the world. It is a very long pregnancy and a very long delivery. However, its reality and its emergence into the world represent your fulfillment here and the completion of your greater responsibilities to God and to your Spiritual Family.

As you begin preparation in The Way of Knowledge, you will pass through many thresholds of learning. Each is unique, and each will change your understanding to a certain degree. Here you must be flex-ible in your thinking and beliefs, for thinking and beliefs are like the eyeglasses that you wear. They either help you see or they do not. If they do not, then they are the wrong prescription for you.

You must stay with The Way of Knowledge long enough to see what this means and to be able to choose wisely. People often give up when the preparation becomes hard, confusing or disorienting. They want to return to what they believed in before because they think it gives them greater security, but they have outgrown this security already, and so they cast themselves adrift in the world.

Therefore, to learn a Greater Community Way of Knowledge, you must feel your greater need. You must realize the limitations of your current understanding. And you must not assume abilities that are not yours to assume. This openness and this honesty with yourself enable you to receive the gift that you could not receive or recognize otherwise. This is the beginning. If you have this understanding, you will be able to take the steps to Knowledge without attempting to change them, deny them, alter them or skip them. You will be able to follow a way that goes far beyond your understanding and current ability. This will take you into a new territory and experience of life.

Learning a Greater Community Way of Knowledge represents a tremendous challenge. You cannot understand it, experience it or use it from where you are now. That is why The Way of Knowledge has to take you to a greater vantage point in life. You are able to follow this not because of your ambitions, expectations or beliefs, but because Knowledge within you moves you forward.

Knowledge will take you one little step at a time. This is moving quickly. There is so much to learn, to unlearn and to re-evaluate. Gaining a Greater Community perspective and Wisdom both within a larger context of life and with specific everyday problems will require a new approach and understanding. Here you will learn what small problems are and what great problems are, what the small problems require and what the great problems require. This brings about maturity within you as you proceed. But to proceed, you must prepare and you must stay with the preparation.

It is a remarkable accomplishment to learn a Greater Community Way of Knowledge in a world that has seemed forever isolated. It is a great accomplishment to recognize the need for this and to be able to develop the understanding, the perspective and the experience necessary to allow Knowledge within you to respond to life and to issue forth its great gifts, which are meant for the world at this time.

Knowledge is like a secret cargo hidden within you. You cannot find it on your own. You cannot gain access to it on your own. You must prepare for it and prepare with others to receive it and to contribute it. What you carry within you is a great gift and a great blessing for humanity. It will be given in ways that are specific and mundane—ways that provide the necessary resources, abilities, understanding and effort to enable humanity to progress, to advance and to meet its challenge to survive and to prosper as a race according to its own destiny, a destiny which you share as long as you are here.

―⟫⟪―

You stand at the threshold of

receiving something of the greatest magnitude,

something that is needed in the world

and something that is being

transferred to the world

and translated into the world.

You are among the first

who will receive this.

Receive it well.

―⟫⟪―

CHAPTER TWENTY-THREE

HOW IS KNOWLEDGE TRANSLATED IN THE GREATER COMMUNITY?

—⟨⟨⟩⟩—

*B*ECAUSE INDIVIDUALS AND GROUPS in the Greater Community who are advancing in Knowledge often have to remain secretly hidden in their own respective worlds, Knowledge is transferred through very mysterious means. This brings into play the involvement of the Unseen Ones. Because these individuals and groups rarely have direct access to one another and cannot send messages or information over normal channels, their insights and their accomplishments must be translated and transferred through spiritual agents whom we call the Unseen Ones.

The Unseen Ones have made it possible for The Greater Community Way of Knowledge to be presented in the world. No one brought this material here by physical means. No one transmitted it through mechanical devices. It was given to the Unseen Ones and then transferred to the world that you live in. It has been translated in such a way that you and your race would be able to understand it and apply it in order for it to have the utmost meaning and relevance within your own world.

God works through mysterious means. This is what preserves the sanctity and purity of The Way of Knowledge, particularly as it is being introduced into a new world. Here it must be given in as pure a form as possible. Here the very essence of The Way of Knowledge itself is separated from everything that has been added on to it, from wherever it has been previously and from wherever it exists at this moment. This gives you the recipient, for whom this Teaching is being introduced, the greatest possibility and the greatest encouragement for success.

As the Creator works mysteriously in your world, so the Creator works mysteriously throughout the Greater Community. Knowledge is not welcome or known here in the world, and it is rarely welcome or known in the Greater Community, except by a few individuals and a few very hidden and advanced societies. Therefore, it must find a different means of travel between worlds. This accounts for its universal application. This accounts for the fact that the Creator is everywhere working to reclaim the separated through Knowledge.

The Greater Community Way of Knowledge is being translated into many worlds and has been translated into many worlds in the past. The translation involves putting its teaching and preparation into a form and a context with examples relevant to each particular world— not only to that world's language and culture but to its specific needs at the time. The introduction of The Greater Community Way of Knowledge is given when a world has reached a point where the Teaching is greatly needed and where there is a possibility that it can be received, learned and applied. This is determined by the Unseen Ones, for no individuals in any world could determine their world's readiness for The Greater Community Way of Knowledge.

It is true in the history of your world that certain individuals have been ready for a teaching such as this. However, their numbers have not been sufficient, their environmental conditions have not been conducive and their world problems have not been demanding enough to call for such a teaching to be given to your world. But because your world is now preparing to emerge into the Greater Community of Worlds, a greater process of evolution and development which is beyond the awareness of most people in the world today, and because of the evidence of growing global problems and dilemmas, this has called for a greater Wisdom to be given to the world. This also calls forth the greater Wisdom that is inherent within you and within the Knowledge that you carry even at this moment. Timing is essential here. The conditions must be right. Minds must be ready, and the environment must require such a preparation and teaching to be given.

It is the evolution of all worlds where intelligent life has been seeded that at some point they will emerge into the Greater Community. How this happens varies from world to world. However, in almost all cases it involves Greater Community forces entering into these worlds. In other words, these worlds are discovered before their races discover anyone else. This sets into motion a great process of change and evolutionary development. This calls for a greater Wisdom and a greater preparation to be given to these worlds. It is for the Unseen Ones to determine when, where and how this is to be done and how the translation is to be made. Here it is essential for at least some of the Unseen Ones involved to have had their origin in the world to which the teaching is being introduced. It is their experience, then, born of their participation over a long period of time in the world that is destined to receive such a teaching, that will enable the translation to occur.

The translation of The Greater Community Way of Knowledge into your world is made possible because the Unseen Ones who have lived in your world and are familiar with its customs, its communication, its nature and its problems are able to bring a universal teaching within the scope of human reach and need. This translation process is quite essential, for without it you would not be able to utilize this teaching and apply it, either within the context of the simple and mundane problems of your life or within the context of the greater problems that overshadow humanity's development now.

Solving problems within both of these contexts is an important emphasis because if you cannot apply Knowledge in simple and direct matters, matters within the sphere of your own activities, then you will not be able to apply it or learn it in the greater issues and challenges that you face. That is why in learning a Greater Community Way of Knowledge or in learning any teaching that leads you to Knowledge, you must start with the basic application first. If you cannot apply it to your health, to your relationships, to your financial requirements and to other survival necessities, then the possibility for you to address the greater issues of your life will be very, very limited.

Therefore, the translation of a Greater Community Way of Knowledge must be given in such a way that you can use it and apply it in solving the simple practical difficulties that you face. It must be applicable so that anyone from any culture in the world to which it is given can use it effectively. Here it must bypass local customs, rituals, religious orientations, habits, beliefs, language barriers and so forth. It must be so pure and so essential that it can be used by anyone from any part of the world to which it is given who is ready to receive it, to learn it and to apply it.

Language always has its limitations. The Greater Community Way of Knowledge is being given in the English tongue because the English language will over time become the international language of your world. It will not be the only language, but it will be the international language. And that is why this teaching is being given in this tongue. In time, it will be translated into other languages by its advanced students.

The translation process continues. It is a translation process to bring the Greater Community Way of Knowledge into your world, and it is a translation process to introduce it around your world into different cultures. The essential emphasis here is that The Way of Knowledge can be learned and applied by those who need it in whatever culture it is introduced. Regardless of the language difficulties involved, Knowledge is inherent in each person.

There is nothing in the world that can prepare you for the Greater Community. You must have a preparation from beyond the world because you do not know what you are preparing for, you do not know how to prepare and you do not understand the difficulties, challenges and opportunities that lay ahead. It is for this reason that the Creator has given you a new understanding and a new challenge in learning. To give the human race the possibility to meet its current needs and to prepare for its remarkable future in the Greater Community, a Greater Community Way of Knowledge is being given because it is needed and essential now.

At first, The Greater Community Way of Knowledge will be learned by a few individuals here and there. It will not be learned by everyone because everyone is not ready to learn it. But for those individuals who are ready and who can courageously follow its steps, The Greater Community Way of Knowledge will enable them to gain a greater understanding, perspective and ability in life. This, then, can be translated to other people through their contribution, communications, efforts, relationships and so forth.

Thus, the translation process continues through many different levels of interaction. It is translated into the world, and it is translated within the world. And through those who can study and learn it patiently and effectively, the translation of Knowledge will continue because their efforts, their actions and their demonstrations in life will provide inspiration, insight and encouragement for those with whom they come in contact. The impact of their activities will be lasting and resonating. This is the evidence of Knowledge. One act or one event can resonate through many minds who were not present at the original act or event. You have seen this in the development and continuance of the world's religions, and you will see it in the development and continuance of a Greater Community Way of Knowledge, if it can be successfully learned and initiated here.

The initiation process is entirely natural, but it can be obstructed. It can be thwarted. That is why, at this time, as the first generation of human beings attempt to learn a Greater Community Way of Knowledge and to understand Greater Community Spirituality, the possibility for failure is great. Therefore, your adherence, your study, your intention to learn, your patience, your compassion and your ability are very crucial to the possibility of a Greater Community Way of Knowledge and Theology being introduced and learned here. Perhaps you who are reading these words will be one of the pioneers in this. It is through your studenthood that greater things can be created for the future, for you are working for the future now. This represents a greater understanding and a greater reality regarding your life and your presence in the world.

Knowledge translates itself through many levels of interaction, and thus it carries its impact from person to person, from heart to heart and from mind to mind. Beyond traditions, beyond cultural distinctions and beyond all kinds of differentiation, Knowledge traverses the great gulfs that seem to separate people, cultures and nations in the world. Because Knowledge is inherent in each person, each person can respond to Knowledge as he or she learns to perceive it and to experience it.

This is the effect of inspiration. It bridges all gaps and traverses all boundaries, reaching minds here and there and everywhere. This is the power of Knowledge. This is the power of the Creator. It is not a power that you can see and touch. It is not a power that you can harness and use. It is not a power that you can display and use to dominate others. It is not a power that your world recognizes or understands. It is a pervasive power because it works at an entirely different level of life—a level of life of which you are a part, but of which you are yet barely aware.

This translation process will assure continuance for the human race. It will assure continuance for the possibility of humanity learning from its mistakes and capitalizing upon its strengths and greater abilities. This is required because of the evolution of the world and because of the problems of the world. Therefore, as a few individuals are able to learn a Greater Community Way of Knowledge, the effects of their learning and their resulting contribution will help to elevate the minds of others. This will continue to resonate through groups, cultures, tribes and nations and through families, marriages, friendships and all other kinds of relationships.

The translation of Knowledge must first be initiated. If no one in the world can learn a Greater Community Way of Knowledge, then it cannot be translated within the world in which you live. However, if a few can learn to follow Knowledge, abide with Knowledge and recognize Knowledge as the Greater Power that is with them and in them, then greater works can be done, greater examples can be made and greater demonstrations can be established. This will produce a resonating effect that will enable Knowledge to be translated from person to person in ways that are mysterious and pervasive and in ways that are lasting and meaningful.

This gives a great responsibility to those who are the first generations to learn a Greater Community Way of Knowledge. They are the pioneers, for they will establish greater parameters of understanding and the possibility for the development of greater abilities. It is incumbent upon them, then, to take their studenthood very seriously and to have the understanding that their purpose will elevate them above the mundane problems which circumscribe everyone around them. This will give them a greater power and a greater responsibility to contribute and to serve others.

It is always difficult for the first pioneers to establish new ground in any field of endeavor, whether they are pioneering new places or a new understanding. They face resistance from the world around them. They face misunderstanding. They face resentment and indifference. They even face hostility. However, they will forge the future for your race. They set a new direction, and they keep the race moving forward.

The world's emergence into the Greater Community will be occurring over the next one and a half centuries. Therefore, what you are doing now in learning a Greater Community Way of Knowledge is establishing the foundation and preparation for the future. This will give meaning to the present and will give you an understanding of why things are happening in the world and the direction in which they must go.

This growing Wisdom inside you, born of your honest studenthood, will give you the ability to counsel others, to assist others and to work in the arenas where you can have the greatest benefit and the greatest effect. This will give you the satisfaction of experiencing and expressing a greater purpose in life, a satisfaction that is unparalleled by any pleasure or any advantage that the world can bestow upon you.

Here you will become a translator as you translate a greater understanding into the normal activities of life and as you translate your greater relationship with the Unseen Ones and with your Creator into your relationships with other people.

The Will of the Creator is translated through many different levels of interaction. This represents the Greater Plan of the Creator, of which you are an intrinsic and necessary part. You are not only a recipient of the Greater Plan, you are part of its transmission—if you can become a student of its presence, its will, its purpose and its method. This is the greater opportunity that you have in life. This is the greater reward and fulfillment that is awaiting you. It is born of your Ancient Home, and it is needed now in the world in which you live.

The Unseen Ones transfer Knowledge wherever Knowledge can be received. This is a very natural process. If Knowledge cannot be received, then it is not transferred. If the promise for Knowledge to be received and translated is great, then The Way of Knowledge will be presented—a way of learning and a way of translating what has been received. In this way, the translation process will continue through those who are fortunate enough to receive it in the first place. They will be the pioneers. It is upon their courage and their establishment that the possibility for learning will increase and expand to meet new challenges and to resolve old ones.

The translation process is beyond your comprehension because it encompasses the entire scope of the universe. Yet your experience of the Divine has the possibility to expand, to grow and to become evermore magnificent and effective, evermore a form of security and a foundation for courage for you. However, do not try to understand this intellectually, for if you do, you will create an understanding that is minuscule. It will not contain or reflect the greater meaning, purpose and message that we are expressing to you at this moment.

Be thankful that a greater purpose and a Greater Power are at work in the world. It is not an alien power. It is an inherent power. It is not a foreign power. It is not a domestic power. It is great because it includes life everywhere. It is something that has always been here, and now the need for it has grown in scope. The Greater Community Way of Knowledge is an expansion of the Knowledge that humanity has attempted to learn throughout the ages.

Never think that Greater Community Spirituality is a replacement for the world's religions. It is here to give them greater scope and greater depth and understanding. However, Greater Community Spirituality will become a new foundation because it represents a greater perception and a greater experience of life. In this, it will infuse itself into the world's religious understanding. And from this, the world may grow as a whole. Not everyone can believe in the same teaching or follow the same teacher or demonstration. However, everyone can move forward together because of the great translation of truth as it truly exists in life.

The Greater Community Way of Knowledge has only been introduced through one person. If this one person can be joined by true students and true companions, then the translation process into the world can truly begin and be substantiated. It only takes one person to be a seed for something great in the world, but for this seed to grow and to develop, it requires the involvement of other people—a selfless involvement in nurturing and presenting something of great meaning and value.

This process of learning and contribution is what will restore you, redeem you and reunite you with Knowledge. Knowledge is your real life because it is your greater life. It is your immortal life as it exists in the world today. It is the example and demonstration of the Creator nurturing and upholding your development and your existence here within a myriad of changing conditions.

You stand at the threshold of receiving something of the greatest magnitude, something that is needed in the world and something that is being transferred to the world and translated into the world. You are among the first who will receive this. Receive it well. Become a student of Knowledge. Learn The Greater Community Way of Knowledge. Then, all of the Wisdom that has ever been established in the world will have a greater context and a greater possibility for expression. Then your life in the world will be discovered, realized and justified. Here you will not merely be a witness of this great process; you will be an inherent part of it. Your role will be significant. No matter how small and specific your contribution may be in life, the importance of its demonstration and development is significant and cannot be denied.

The future of the world is up to you. You can be part of the critical demonstration and contribution. That is why this is the time to rise above self-preoccupation, selfish endeavors, self-protection and so forth. This is a time to reach deeper within yourself to a deeper response within you. We are not speaking here to your fears or to your wishes. We are not speaking to your ambitions or to your goals. We are speaking to Knowledge within you, for it is Knowledge within you that must respond. It is Knowledge within you that will bring you to Knowledge in the world. It is Knowledge that has brought you to a Greater Community Way of Knowledge. It is Knowledge that has brought you to your spiritual preparation. It is Knowledge that will redeem you, restore you and give you a new foundation for life. Knowledge within you must respond to Knowledge in the universe, for Knowledge within you is interdependent with life. It relies solely upon Knowledge in the universe, which is represented by the Creator.

Do not think, however, that Knowledge within you will do everything for you. Knowledge within you will bring you to those people, those opportunities and those situations that you will need in life in order to advance and to find the true path for yourself, yet it is your ability to respond that is significant here. Your ability to respond, your response-ability, is the essential thing that must be emphasized. It is not your intellectual understanding. It is not your academic education. It is not your cleverness or your personality. It is your ability to respond to something great. And you are able to respond because of the greatness that is within you, which is Knowledge. Knowledge within you must find Knowledge in others. This is how Knowledge is restored, redeemed and kept alive in the world.

The Greater Community Way of Knowledge is being introduced so that Knowledge may be kept alive in the world as the world emerges into the Greater Community. Humanity's emergence into the Greater

Community will present problems and challenges that you have never faced before. This will call upon a greater development, a greater skill, a greater discernment and a greater desire to contribute than you have ever known before.

In the Greater Community, there are minds and cultures far more powerful than yours. There are minds and cultures which can dominate you. There are minds and cultures which can manipulate you. The strong dominate the weak in the mental environment. This would indeed be the case here except that you have Knowledge within you. Knowledge is the only part of you which cannot be dominated or controlled. This, then, establishes it as your one great advantage in life. No matter whom you are confronted with, no matter what situation you are facing, no matter what challenge or crisis you must contend with, Knowledge is the greatest resource that you have.

Knowledge will indicate what must be done, what must be learned, what must be avoided and what must be claimed. Here your intellectual understanding will have genuine direction and Wisdom behind it. Here your physical skills will have a foundation upon which to function. What you have learned in the world, which represents your intellectual and physical training, will now have a greater foundation that can be guided by Knowledge, for Knowledge is what they require in order to be truly effective and beneficial in life.

Knowledge cannot be corrupted. It cannot be influenced. It cannot be dominated by anything in the universe. It is entirely safe. It is entirely complete within you. This represents a great truth in life: The universe cannot influence the Creator, but the Creator can influence the universe. The Creator's influence is within you now, within your Knowledge. Therefore, your real safety in life, your real security, your real foundation and your real immunity from destruction, dissonance and evil are found in Knowledge. All other beliefs and foundations that you establish for yourself will not stand in the face of crisis in the world, and they will certainly not stand in the face of Greater Community intervention.

What will stand then? What will stand is the evidence of Knowledge. If you can reclaim Knowledge and develop your relationship with

Knowledge, if you can open yourself to Knowledge so that Knowledge can reveal itself to you, then you will have the greatest strength in the universe. This will counteract any danger to humanity and any danger to you. This gives you permanence and substance in life. This gives you purpose, meaning and direction.

Other races from the Greater Community whom you will encounter will be more advanced than you are in their technology and in their social cohesion. This will give them power and influence over you. However, if you can become strong with Knowledge, and if you can translate Knowledge into the world through your contribution, then you will advance your entire race and give it a greater foundation and a great ability to adapt, to survive and to succeed. This is necessary, for the Greater Community will either elevate you or destroy you as a race. This is how great its impact upon you will be.

For this reason, a greater calling for Knowledge is in the world today. That is why a Greater Community Way of Knowledge is being presented now. It is being presented so that those who will pioneer its study, development and application can begin to set the stage and build the foundation for a greater translation of Knowledge and Wisdom into the world. This is possible because the way of learning how to deal with the Greater Community and with Greater Community influences has already been established.

You have not learned this, for up until now you have not had to learn it as a race. You have never had to compete with another form of intelligent life. You have only had to compete with one another. However, now you will have to compete with other forms of intelligent life. This represents the greatest challenge that is facing you now. It is for this reason that you need to learn Greater Community Knowledge and Wisdom. This will teach you how to contend with these forces—how to discern their presence, their motives and their methods. This will enable you to respond to Knowledge rather than being manipulated or governed by external forces. This will give you freedom and permanence and will give you a power that the world cannot destroy. For the world can take your body, but it cannot take away your demonstration.

The world can take away your opportunities, but it cannot take away your Knowledge.

Knowledge is the greater power and certainty that you have sought in many other things. It is being called for now. You cannot merely wish for it; you must need it, for it is necessary. It cannot merely be a preference; it must be seen as a requirement for your life. It cannot be something you'll just try out; it must be something you'll take on, not only for your own edification and development, but for the world in which you live, for the world that you have come to serve.

The stronger you are with Knowledge, the more you become a power and a resource within the world in which you live. The stronger you are with Knowledge and the more advanced you are as a student of Knowledge, the more you will be able to contend with Greater Community forces and the great discrepancies in culture and ability that these interactions will present. The stronger you are with Knowledge, the more you will know what to do to serve the resolution of the world's chronic problems that have plagued humanity for so very long and to inspire others to greater action and greater service. The stronger you are with Knowledge, the more able you will be to contend with resistance and hostility in the world.

As the Greater Community poses a tremendous challenge to your race, it also offers a tremendous opportunity because it establishes the requirement for real social cohesion among your peoples. It requires that your nations cooperate rather than contend with each other. It requires this because all humanity is in the same situation, and greater problems overshadow it. These problems will require a greater incentive towards development and cooperation.

This is the gift of the Greater Community. With this gift comes great risk, but the opportunity that this gift presents is tremendous and must be continuously emphasized. The only thing that will bring humanity out of its incessant bickering with itself is the overshadowing by the Greater Community. The only thing that will bring humanity into a true state of cooperation is in meeting a greater and more persistent need that puts everyone in the same situation and that requires everyone to cooperate and to join forces with one another.

It has been evident in all aspects of your history that human beings are able to rise to greatness when great occasions confront them. It is these great occasions that call people into selfless activity and into cooperative endeavors with one another. You now have a great occasion of the greatest magnitude, we assure you. And it will not be momentary or intermittent. It will be continual and pressing. This gives your race the greatest impetus and the greatest requirement for development, for the resolution of conflict, for empowerment and for insight and understanding.

These are the benefits of Knowledge, yet most people in the world will receive them without ever knowing what Knowledge is or how it functions. These benefits will be made manifest in the world because a relatively small number of people have taken it upon themselves to learn a Way of Knowledge, a Greater Community Way of Knowledge. This will make possible a greater translation of Knowledge into the world, a translation from which everyone will benefit and which will give humanity a greater promise for the future and a greater ability in the present.

You will become a translator as you advance as a student of Knowledge, and the translation will happen through you naturally. It is as if a greater set of instincts were now activated and have come into play. Nothing artificial will be imposed. Only temporary restraints will be needed in order to enable you to focus your time and energy and to avoid those things that belittle you and weaken you in the process.

The Greater Community Way of Knowledge will then find a means of translation within the world. Then God can work more fully in the world behind the scenes, and everyone will benefit without knowing where the benefit came from. And everyone will be able to respond according to his or her current capabilities and capacities, however great or small they may be. This is how benefit is brought into the world. This is how humanity is furthered. This is how greater things are initiated and accomplished in life.

The translation of a Greater Community Way of Knowledge occurs between worlds and between cultures that are vastly different from
one another. This follows a great transference and translation process,
a process of such magnitude and seeming complexity that you cannot
grasp it intellectually. However, you can experience this process and you
can appreciate it, for Knowledge within you knows what it is, why it is
here and what it must do.

—◦◦◦—

To know what you must know,

to see what you must see

and to do what you must do,

you must reach a

greater vantage point in life.

To reach this,

you must take the journey,

a journey of many steps.

And the steps are in

Steps to Knowledge.

—◦◦◦—

CHAPTER TWENTY-FOUR

WHAT IS
STEPS TO KNOWLEDGE?

—◦◦◦—

*L*EARNING GREATER COMMUNITY SPIRITUALITY requires preparation of a very unique kind. This preparation must take you into the very heart of what spirituality means, and yet it must enable you to face the world realistically and practically, without denial or deception. It must be able to cultivate your strengths, while minimizing the risks of misunderstanding and misinterpretation. It must aim you high, but not so high that you cannot reach your goal. It must nurture your own inner authority, while you gain a sense of the greater authority in life that transcends your own domain. It must establish a context where all of your relationships can have a meaningful involvement and can be understood. This, then, requires a very unique approach, something that can bypass, to the greatest degree possible, your former beliefs, ideas and conditioning by the world.

To learn Greater Community Spirituality you need to learn a way to it—a way to Knowledge. Everything that we have spoken of in this book and in all of the Books of Knowledge aims you towards Knowledge itself. This is the very essence of your spirituality. This is your

True Self as you exist in physical life. This is your bond with all life and with the life that has sent you into the world to serve and to realize a greater purpose.

There must be a way to Knowledge. To follow the way, you must take the steps. You cannot leap. You cannot rush. You cannot run to Knowledge. It is too great, and there are too many things to learn and to unlearn along the way. There are too many things to evaluate and to re-evaluate. There are too many great realizations to acquire. Therefore, you must take the steps to Knowledge.

If you were climbing a great mountain, you would need to follow a path. You cannot simply rush up its embankments. And you need a preparation that will orient you to every condition that you are going to meet. You need a preparation that will prepare you for new experiences and new difficulties, and that will give you a greater perspective and the patience and reassurance that you will need to follow your way and to continue onward. You will only fail in this preparation if you do not honor yourself or if you lose sight of your greater goal.

When you are on the mountain, you can rarely see the summit. All you see are your immediate surroundings. All you feel are the changing circumstances of your journey. Rarely will you see your ultimate destination. But if you continue, you will come to know the mountain itself. You will come to learn the way by following the way up the mountain. And you will come to realize what each step means as you take each step. Holding back, judging and evaluating will never reveal anything of any meaning to you in this regard. You must make the journey, and to make the journey you must take the steps, one by one. In this way, your progress will be slow and steady. In this way, everything you learn will be deeply experienced and digested. In this way, you will not miss anything that is really essential for your development and well-being.

As you proceed, you will also learn to cultivate the necessary abilities that you will need to face life, to give to life and to understand your way in life. These abilities are patience, perseverance, compassion, discernment and discretion. These great abilities are necessary for any achievement in any field, yet to realize a greater purpose in life and to be able to experience it and apply it effectively, these greater abilities will be called upon even more, and you will need to rely upon them.

These greater abilities are necessary because you will not have great realizations every moment. You will not have wonderful experiences every moment. You will not feel confident and self-assured every moment. In fact, there may be great gaps between these experiences. Here you must rely upon your determination and perseverance. Here you must cultivate a greater perspective and understanding that transcends your immediate sensations, emotions and experiences. As in climbing a great mountain, you will have moments of great joy and moments of great difficulty. You will have moments of real certainty and moments of uncertainty. You will have the challenges of life placed in your way. And you will have important decisions to make—decisions that will affect the outcome of your journey and that will determine the consequences of your life and the lives of others.

Therefore, take the steps to Knowledge. Follow them slowly. Move consistently. Neither race ahead nor fall behind. Consistency here is important, for consistency enables you to learn at a pace that keeps you moving forward. Here you will not exceed your capabilities. Here you will not miss anything that is important. Here you will not be sluggish, idle or inconsistent. Consistency in following the steps to Knowledge, in following a preparation that you did not invent or design for yourself, will give you greater consistency in all other aspects of your life and will enable you to be one person, the same person, in all situations. Then you will no longer be a conglomeration of splinter personalities any more. You will become one person with one focus and one orientation.

Words cannot describe what an experience this is, how much strength and ability it will give you and how it will liberate you from so many debilitating distractions and allurements that only frustrate and aggravate you now. Here the real depth of your nature, the real depth and purpose of your ability and the importance of your mind and your body will become fully realized through experience. Here your mind will not need to create a great philosophy about life, for you will be living life and will be close to life. Only when you are removed from life and separated from it do you need a great deal of ideas and idealism with which to justify and direct your experience. However, when you are close to life and when your life is genuine and real, your mind is free of this great burden. A free mind is a mind that can refocus itself. It is a mind that can rethink its thoughts and can respond to the environment. It is a mind that can gain greater insight and application.

So what are the steps to Knowledge? How do they work? Where do they take you? And how can they be followed successfully? *Steps to Knowledge* is a preparation that represents the translation of The Greater Community Way of Knowledge into human experience and the human world. This translation calls upon the greater spirituality which you carry within your Knowledge.

Steps to Knowledge is given in a series of advancing programs. They are well delineated and mapped out. They give you a great freedom of experience. The main emphasis is to follow each step as it is given—without altering it in any way, by consistently applying yourself and by being determined to finish the stage that you are in. This will be a great enough challenge in and of itself because you may be tempted to change the preparation to satisfy your current ideas, to reassure yourself or to keep things in a familiar framework. However, *Steps to Knowledge* will take you beyond the familiar into new arenas, beyond where you are today into something greater for tomorrow, beyond your current abilities and understanding into a greater set of abilities and a greater understanding.

Here you must be willing to go beyond your fixed ideas and cherished beliefs. Here you will enter into a new experience where you are not sure who you are, why you are here or what you are doing. However, this uncertainty is not permanent. It represents a transition from one understanding to another. You will go through many of these transitions as your mind gains a greater and greater vantage point in life. Using the analogy of the mountain, you will not have a vantage point at every moment where you can see where you are going and where you have been. Instead, at most times you will need to focus on taking the steps in front of you and negotiating the journey itself, and you will not always have reassurance about where you stand at any given moment.

Here Knowledge is your guide. Knowledge is strong and consistent. It is pure and unaffected by the world. It gives you a greater strength, a greater motivation and a greater ability in life—so much greater that nothing can compare with it. And of its many great rewards, the greatest is the reunion within yourself, for at last you will feel like your life is real and that you are doing what you came here to do. However inexplicable your way might seem and however confusing the events of your life might be, you are taking the steps to Knowledge. You are coming closer to your inner reality. You are becoming able to engage with the world more realistically, more soberly, more effectively and more compassionately. Your compassion will be born of your experience of taking such a journey, for here you will realize what really holds people back. You will realize what freedom really means and how it must be earned and secured in life.

The steps to Knowledge are specific. They are presented to you in the program *Steps to Knowledge*. You need to only follow them and not change them. And as you learn to follow them, you will learn to follow them at their pace, which may be a faster and more consistent pace than what you are used to, but it will be a pace that you can follow. It will not be beyond your abilities although it will exceed what you have accomplished thus far.

Every bit of progress you make in following *Steps to Knowledge* will have an immediate impact on your life and circumstances. For if you develop certainty and ability in one area, then they will eventually transfer over into the other areas of your life. You do not want to live a life of contradiction. You will increasingly want your life to be a uniform expression of truth and meaning. This will enable you to translate Knowledge and Wisdom into more and more aspects of your life. As you do this, you will become stronger and stronger with Knowledge, for Knowledge will be emanating from you, not just here and there, not just in this circumstance or that circumstance, but increasingly and more completely.

Knowledge is the Great Presence that you carry within you. And as you open yourself to it and allow it to demonstrate its reality to you, you will become an expression of its life, which is your genuine life in the world. Here you give yourself to the Greater Reality within you. Here you surrender to that which is the only thing that you can surrender to and the only thing that you can devote yourself to, which is Knowledge in yourself and Knowledge in others. This is the truth that permeates all manifest life and holds true throughout the universe in all dimensions and realities. This is the truth that restores to you what you came here to give and what you came here to realize.

The way is simple but difficult. It is simple because you need only follow the steps. Here you are given a map up the mountain. And you are asked not to deviate from this map but to follow it surely and consistently. However, it is difficult because people are not used to following something without altering it to meet their past references. It is difficult because you must give yourself to your preparation, and you must trust your preparation. Both at those times when it is wonderful and at those times when it is difficult, you must approach it with the same trust and the same consistency. This generates tremendous power within you. This enables you and indeed requires you to exercise your own individual authority over your thinking and endeavors. This is necessary in order to live a real and meaningful life. And this is what will bring you to your greater calling and purpose, for this lays the foundation for this calling and purpose to arise.

As you advance and become more mature in your understanding and participation, then, and only then, will your calling slowly take shape. It will not be a definition. And it will not be something that will be revealed to you all at once. It will be something that you will find as those things that are unnecessary or lack meaning in your life fall away or are given up. What is left is what is essential. Then you are free to find your way to that which you must realize. This is the way you find it, for it cannot be found in any other way. You must not only come to the great realizations about your life; you must learn the way to them, for learning the way to them will teach you how to help others find the way to their great realizations in life. You must learn the way in order to show the way and to share the way, to strengthen those who are behind you and to recognize those who are far ahead.

Steps to Knowledge, therefore, is both easy and difficult. It is easy because it is direct. It is easy because you do not need to define the way. It is easy because it saves you from many mistakes and calamities that could only thwart your attempt and lead you into failure or disaster. However, the simple way is difficult because people are not simple. Being simple means to be trusting and to be able to discern that which warrants your trust from that which does not. Being simple means to be wholehearted and to be able to take control of your life and to manage it effectively. Being simple means to have a focused and free mind that is not burdened with unnecessary evaluations and that is not trying to carry the great weight of other people's experiences or expectations. Your mind will function at a much higher level when it is unencumbered by these things.

As this happens, your relationships will become refined and redefined, and those individuals who are your true companions will find their way to you. And you will be able to recognize them and receive them, for you will be taking the way yourself. This will show you how to discern meaning in relationships, for meaning in relationships can only be discerned by following something of a greater importance and magnitude in life.

Discernment, then, becomes not a matter of judgment and criticism but a means for recognition. Instead of good or bad, it becomes yes or no. You know what to follow and what not to follow. You know who to be with and who not to be with—all without judgment and condemnation. How simple this is and how direct and natural. How life confirming this is for you who can receive it. Yet how difficult this can seem if you are used to trying to negotiate your life, to make your own goals or to establish your own way based upon your preferences and your fears. How difficult this is when you are trying to manipulate your own mind and the minds of others.

The Greater Community Way of Knowledge will teach you to become simple and powerful. It will relieve you of being cunning and weak. The Way of Knowledge will teach you to become strong and penetrating in your abilities. It will free you from the burden of being shallow and diffracted.

The steps to Knowledge are mysterious. You will not be able to understand them until you are far ahead and can look back and see where they have taken you. Just as in climbing a great mountain, what meaning does each step have until you see where it has taken you and what it has given you?

Therefore, as you take the steps to Knowledge, do not judge them. Some you will like, and some you may not like. Some will seem familiar, and some will seem new. However, do not judge them, for you cannot understand them until you realize where they are taking you. And you cannot find where they are taking you unless you follow them. This is the way through the jungle of life. The path is narrow. It is specific. It takes you through dangerous situations. It takes you through allurements. It takes you through disassociation. It takes you through all forms of distraction. It takes you through them and beyond them. Therefore, to understand the steps to Knowledge you must see where they are taking you and you must go where they are taking you.

Steps to Knowledge and The Greater Community Way of Knowledge are something entirely new and different. Whoever you are and whatever you think you have accomplished and learned in life, you will have to start here as a beginner. Forget what you have learned and begin anew. Do this and you will learn the most that can be learned. If you do not do this, you will merely try to evaluate everything that happens and every step you take according to your past references. This will keep you in the past and prevent you from coming into the present and moving into the future. *Steps to Knowledge* frees you from the past by giving you a way out of your past and out of the world's past. For nothing from the past can lead you into the future effectively.

The Greater Community Way of Knowledge represents the present and the future. It is a preparation to live fully in the present and to prepare fully for the future so that you will have the opportunity to live in the present in the future. This is why what is easy seems difficult. To follow what is easy, you must become simple and find escape from the complexities of your life that only keep you chained to the past and to a state of ambivalence. To journey into life you must follow a different way.

Therefore, begin as a beginner. Do not assume you know a great deal, for indeed you do not know a great deal. Do not assume that you have great abilities, for within a larger context of life you do not have great abilities. Accept your condition humbly, without condemnation. In this way, you open yourself to learn what can only be learned by opening yourself. Do not judge the steps, for you cannot judge them. They are taking you out of your past. They are not a confirmation of your past.

Your past is what is behind you. The future is what is ahead for you. The present is how you experience your relationship to the past and to the future. To experience the present, you must have a correct relationship with both the past and the future or you will never be able to enter the present fully. Knowledge is in the present at every moment. It represents a completely present state of mind. It is the *only* present state of mind. The closer you are to Knowledge, the more present you are to life. And yet your present state of mind is fully united with the movement of the world and with the future of the world. It is not something you invent for yourself as a psychological exercise or as a form of escape from a world that you cannot accept or experience. That only leads to disillusionment and greater disassociation from life.

Steps to Knowledge takes you into life as it is and as it will be. It takes you into your life as it is and as it will be. It enables you to engage with others as they are and as they will be. How simple this is, yet how seemingly difficult it can seem at the outset. As you learn to take the steps to Knowledge and to follow them effectively, your burden will become lighter, for your mind will become free of that which is unnecessary for its happiness and fulfillment. Your life will become free of damaging engagements and meaningless pursuits that have never given you what you have really sought.

These things fall away naturally. They are not taken from you. You leave them aside because you cannot take them with you into a greater experience of life. They are left at the door. You give them up voluntarily. Now you are unburdened. Then the way becomes simpler and greater. With this simplicity and greatness, your experience and understanding become deeper and more penetrating. Your mind becomes more focused and consistent. Your determination becomes stronger. Your discernment of others becomes clearer and more revealing. Your ability to abide with both truth and uncertainty becomes greater and greater. Here your capacity for relationship becomes far more expanded. This enables you to engage with the great relationships with which you are meant to be engaged in this life. This builds within you a greater capacity for relationship, which will open you to your relationship with the Creator and with the Greater Community of Worlds.

It may be difficult to begin, but if you can begin, you can proceed. If you can proceed, you can progress. If you can progress, you can advance. If you can advance, then you can understand all the stages that preceded this. Then you will understand what it means to begin. Then you will understand what it means to progress and to advance.

Steps to Knowledge does not require that you worship any hero or any personality. It does not require that you accept a creation story about life that is implausible and impossible. It does not require that you believe in a pantheon of gods, images, symbols, rituals, pageants or personalities. It only brings you to the great question of what you really know. And it does not answer this question in words, but instead takes you into the experience of Knowledge itself, slowly, through many steps and stages of development. If you proceed, you will advance. If you advance, you will understand. If you understand, then you will know.

Steps to Knowledge will give you a new life—not a life that is foreign to you but a life that is home to you, not a life that is bonded to your past experiences and evaluations, but a life that is genuine in this moment and that has greater possibilities and greater relationships. This satisfies your most fundamental needs and deepest questions. It satisfies these by taking you to their fulfillment. To know what you must know, to see what you must see and to do what you must do, you must reach a greater vantage point in life. To reach this, you must take the journey, a journey of many steps. And the steps are in *Steps to Knowledge*.

We have provided the steps themselves to enable you to learn a Greater Community Way of Knowledge. They will take you to your destination, but you must follow them and be patient because there are many things for you to learn along the way, many of which you are not even aware of. And there are many things which you must acquire and strengthen along the way, things which you cannot see at the outset.

The Greater Community Way of Knowledge can be learned. It can be experienced. It can be integrated. It can be applied. And it can be lived. To make this possible, we provide the steps. Follow them, not blindly but with your eyes open. Follow them where they lead you, not with great assumptions about what they will do for you but with a present state of mind. Learn to walk the way and you will see that there are those ahead of you and those behind you. Those ahead of you will encourage you, show you the way and give you the strength and conviction that you must proceed whether you understand or not.

Steps to Knowledge will take you through those times of great transition when you are uncertain about what you are doing and who you are. It will take you beyond those points where you define yourself and your existence to a greater experience and realization. It will take you through those difficult moments when you must make difficult decisions. And it will take you into those wonderful moments when you will experience your relationship with yourself and others in an entirely new and permeating way.

Here you will realize that you are advancing and that others are advancing with you, not only in this world but in other worlds as well. For The Greater Community Way of Knowledge and *Steps to Knowledge* are being taught in many worlds—more than you can count. This represents the Greater Plan of the Creator and a greater purpose and mission in life to restore the universe to its state of pure union and simplicity.

You, then, are following an Ancient Rite of preparation, born of the Great Will of the universe. The preparation in The Greater Community Way of Knowledge is being provided for you and for your world—a way of Knowledge not only into the mystery of your life but into the greatness of the Greater Community into which your life is now emerging. This represents a greater possibility for you who are reading these words, for you are responding to a greater calling and meaning in life—a calling and meaning that you have brought with you, which reside within you and which must now be called forth from you.

—◦∿◦—

You look for Grace; you cannot find it.

You open yourself to Grace, and it appears.

You claim Grace for yourself,

and it is nowhere to be found.

You yield yourself to Grace,

and Grace gently emerges.

You speak the truth—

the truth of what you really know,

not the truth of what you want or believe—

and Grace is standing beside you.

You look at the events of your world

with compassion and deep understanding,

and Grace looks with you.

—◦∿◦—

CHAPTER TWENTY-FIVE

WHAT IS GRACE?

⸻ ⸎ ⸻

*G*RACE MUST BE A PRESENCE AND AN INTELLIGENCE that can enter into and abide in any situation, in any world, in any climate, in any condition, in any culture and in any race. It must be something that can enter silently and abide with circumstances as they are. It must be something that can enter at the invitation of a genuine and sincere request. It must be something that can abide with a man or woman of Knowledge, something that can abide with them without dominating them and exist with them and in them without manipulating them. It must abide with them in such a way that the authority of the person who is its recipient is not overshadowed or usurped. Grace must be something that can be translated from one mind to another and transferred from one world to another.

What can possibly do all of these things? A greater presence that can abide with but not overwhelm the person who is receiving it. A greater intelligence that can exist with but not dominate the lesser intelligence that is receiving it. A greater intensity and motivation in life that can gently persuade and nourish an emerging sense of real purpose, meaning and direction in the life of the person who is receiving it.

Grace must be something very powerful because it inspires individuals to do great and selfless acts. It inspires them to do things that transcend their own personal interests, limitations and concerns, and yet it in no way violates their own authority. Grace respects their own position in life while giving them a greater ability and a greater scope of awareness. Grace must be something very intelligent to give this strength without overwhelming the recipient.

Grace must be something that is not concerned with the appearance of things. It must be something that has a greater origin, meaning and ability, beyond the scope of any worldly race, culture, tribe or group. Surely this cannot be a human invention. Surely this cannot be the product of a purely human god. Surely this cannot conform to human expectations or human images. It must be something far greater and more permeating, more transcendent and yet more able to descend into the world, into any world, where it is welcomed and needed.

Grace represents the evidence of the greater relationship that you have with the Creator. Grace is not your possession. You cannot use it, harness it, manipulate it or direct it, for it represents a Greater Will and purpose in the universe.

You possess a special kind of Grace within you. This Grace is called out of you in the presence of the Grace that exists around you. It is called out of you to meet specific needs in the world. And it is called out of you to initiate, establish and strengthen the important relationships that you will need to have in order to find your greater purpose and mission here. The Grace within you is Knowledge, the Knowing Mind, the Mind that is a part of the Mind of the Creator.

The response to Grace generates Grace. It is not the source of Grace. It is part of the mechanism of Grace which enables you to receive it, desire it and welcome it into your life. You look for Grace; you cannot find it. You open yourself to Grace, and it appears. You claim Grace for yourself, and it is nowhere to be found. You yield yourself to Grace, and Grace gently emerges. You speak the truth—the truth of what you really know, not the truth of what you want or believe—and Grace is standing beside you. You reach out and genuinely touch another's heart, and Grace envelopes both of you. You look at the events of your world with compassion and deep understanding, and Grace looks with you.

You respond to a greater need in another, and somehow Grace speaks through you. It is neither within you nor beyond you exclusively. It is more that you are immersed in it, and at special moments you are able to experience this immersion, this already existing union with life.

Grace does not come and go, except in your awareness. Grace is not here at this moment and then gone the next. Grace does not go around the universe visiting individuals here and there. Grace is present everywhere, at every moment. It seems to appear because there is an opening for it and a need for it. It comes because it is genuinely desired. It abides with you, and yet how seldom you experience its presence.

Grace is with you, but it is in the background. It is in the background because it is giving you the freedom to find your way and to come to terms with your deeper inclinations and awareness in life. It is in the background as if it were twenty feet behind you. It is not really twenty feet behind you, but this may be how you will experience it. It seems to come into your consciousness as you are available to it and as the situations that you are in call for it.

Grace always emphasizes and validates your relationship with another and with the Creator. In fact, you may think of Grace as the evidence of genuine and abiding relationship. When you experience this relationship with yourself, with another or with the greater panorama of life, you will feel Grace—a sense of wholeness, completeness and inclusion, a sense of reunion and gratitude. These are all the evidence of Grace, all the evidence that a greater and more permeating relationship is being recognized, acknowledged and experienced.

Grace, then, is the evidence of God's presence in the world. However, even more important than this, it is the evidence of your intrinsic relationship with the Creator. Grace is the evidence of Knowledge within yourself because you are able to receive it and respond to it. Eventually, as you become strong with Knowledge, if you can follow the way to Knowledge and take the steps to Knowledge, then you will be able to actually dispense Grace into the world, not as a conscious act, but as something that happens spontaneously. Here Grace will emerge from you because you will be a wellspring for Grace in the world.

No matter what your activity or specific endeavor in life, you can become a demonstration of the presence of Grace. This will have a great impact on those who can receive your gifts and on those who can witness your acts. Grace ignites Knowledge in others. It stimulates others at the deepest level of their being. It brings with it a memory and a confirmation, however long forgotten, that there is a greater purpose and meaning in life. It is part of the reality that you have brought with you from your Ancient Home.

The evidence and the demonstration of Grace call some people forward while others retreat and still others fight against their own experience. However, its power and efficacy cannot be denied. It has a potency in life that is unmatched by anything else. No one who feels it can be neutral regarding it. And everyone who witnesses it must respond.

Grace is evidence of a greater union and relationship that you have with others, with the world and with your Creator, but Grace also is the potency that carries great ideas and great inspiration from one mind to another. Here it is like a conduit that enables the transmission of Knowledge to pass from one mind to another. This activates Knowledge in each person as it passes from one mind to another, like an electrical current passing through one terminal to another, carried by the power of Grace. Here your real associations with people become activated and evident.

Grace seems to come and go, a momentary experience perhaps, something that is in great contrast to the vast majority of your experiences of being in the world. But it is always there. Think of it like this: It is as if the Greater Self in you and the greater relationship that you have with others momentarily became ignited, as if the ground were illuminated one dark night by flashes of lightening, and for those moments, you realized there is so much there that you could not see before. And after the momentary flashes, you return to darkness. But Grace, for that moment, that tiny moment, has illuminated your life and has given you a greater vision of what is present in your life, what is in the background of your life and how you really stand with things around you.

These flash points are very significant because they herald the possibility of a greater union and association with life, a greater involvement and endeavor with others and a greater experience of purpose in reality. This is an experience the world cannot give you, for it must be presented to you from the Greater Intelligence and Will of the universe. This Will transcends all Greater Community societies, all groups, all races and all other powers. It is the Will of the Creator as it is manifesting itself in the changing conditions of physical life.

Welcome, then, the flash points of Wisdom. Welcome, then, the momentary demonstrations of Grace. Welcome, then, those experiences that can show you where you are, what you need to do and how you really stand with others. You can have this realization without judgment, without comparison and without condemnation of yourself or others, for Grace brings with it a confirmation, not a judgment. It brings with it a recognition of how things really are, not how you want them to be or expect them to be. Just as the lightning illuminates the ground around where you stand and shows you things you could not see in the darkness of your own personal perception, so Grace illuminates your way, giving you a greater understanding of where you are, who you are associating with and what you must do. It lights your way and it reassures you that your endeavor is not an individual one and that the world you see around you is not all that can be seen, felt and known. It shows you that the troubled interactions between people do not represent their real associations and their real possibilities together.

Grace is the evidence of the Greater Reality that permeates everything you see. However, you do not see this Greater Reality because you are dominated by the reality that you do see, and you are dominated by your thoughts about that reality. A Greater Reality becomes discovered when there is a desire for it and a preparation to reach it. It becomes discovered when there is a need for its presence and activity within the mundane appearances and activities of your life. This need, this recognition and this openness enable Grace to emerge. At first, it will emerge momentarily like great flashes of lightning. It will emerge momentarily like the sudden appearance of an angelic presence. It will emerge suddenly like a warm glow and a hazy feeling that you are not alone and that there is a real confirmation in what has just been said or done. You will feel it initially in a sudden feeling of rightness within yourself and in the sudden recognition and appreciation of another.

However, as you follow in The Way of Knowledge and as you take the steps to Knowledge, this experience will grow for you. It will grow most significantly because the seemingly great gulf between you and the Greater Reality that permeates your life and that gives your life its real meaning and purpose is being penetrated. The veil that seems to separate you from this experience and awareness is slowly being dissolved.

It is not that you will have more experiences of Grace in a momentary sense. It is that Grace will become closer and closer to you. The Greater Reality and your personal reality will come closer and closer together. As they come closer and closer together, your personal reality will change and be strengthened. It will have a greater focus and a greater emphasis on meaning and accomplishment. This is where your values and your interests gradually change in a way that is so natural and life confirming for you that over time you will not doubt that a Greater Power is at work in your life.

You will see the evidence of this Greater Power in your own changing feelings and emphasis. You will see the evidence of this in your changing relationships and their changing emphasis. You will see the evidence of this in the presence of your deeper inclinations, which will now have greater access and greater expression in your personal mind and in your conscious experience. You will see the evidence of this in what you value and what you seek. You will seek things that are permanent and that are bonded with life. You will not seek to impose your individual will but to express a Greater Will that confirms your existence and that honors the presence of all who are here with you, regardless of their difficulties or their mistakes. This will give you an emphasis on forgiveness and accomplishment, on recognition and right decisions. This will be an entirely different emphasis than what you had felt before.

Grace will be more and more with you, but in a subtle and pervasive way. Instead of flashes of lightning illuminating your life momentarily, it is as if a great dawning were occurring and the shadows of your life were gently being dissolved by the presence of a great light emerging on the horizon. Here the evidence of what is really in your life and where you really need to go slowly becomes realized.

Your decisions will either bring the experience of Grace or deny it. No matter how difficult your decisions are or how seemingly serious their consequences, when you make a decision that is in keeping with Knowledge, you will feel this presence with you. Perhaps you will feel anxiety about the anticipated or the imagined consequences, but you will feel a rightness in your life. This will give evidence that Grace is with you, for every decision that you make that is in keeping with Knowledge will acknowledge the presence of Grace in your life. Every determination that you make that is in keeping with the greater truth within you will give you a greater experience of this truth and a greater sense of its presence and activity in your life and in the world around you.

Grace is something that is emerging slowly, like a very slow dawning of the light. Here things that seemed mysterious or incomprehensible before can be recognized, felt and known. Perhaps you cannot explain them because the experience is beyond words, but that is not so important now because you realize that an explanation can never illuminate the life of another.

It is only the presence of Grace and the activity of Knowledge that can give others a greater experience and perception of their lives and a greater determination within themselves. Here you come to understand that Grace is the evidence of the Creator's presence in the world—a presence that works behind the scenes and that does not overshadow, dominate or manipulate those who are here. This presence gently reassures people and calls upon Knowledge within each of them to enable them to respond and to learn the way of relationship, which is The Way of Knowledge.

There is Grace in your life, and to enable you to experience it and eventually to express it and generate it, you are presented with a preparation in The Greater Community Way of Knowledge. Follow this preparation. Receive it, for this is the gift and the means that will bring you to a greater understanding and experience of your purpose and to the greater purpose in life of which you are a part.

The answer to your prayers is a means of preparation. If you were sunk in a hole in the ground and could not climb out, the answer to your prayer would be a ladder sent down to enable you to find your way out. Being in the world is like being in a deep, dark hole in the ground. All you see is the darkness and the confinement of that which entraps you. The answer to your prayer for freedom, for resolution, for peace, for strength and for accomplishment is a ladder sent down to you—a ladder which you must climb, a ladder which will lift you out of your seemingly hopeless circumstances into a greater experience of where you have been, where you can go and what can be done.

Grace brings with it the means for experiencing it. It is not something you simply beg for and is given to you in little tiny increments. Grace is given to you because the preparation for it is given to you. You must find your way to it. It is with you, but you are not with it. This demonstrates the great dilemma of your life and the most serious problem of your life—that Knowledge is with you, but you are not with Knowledge. Grace is with you, but you are not with Grace. Real relationship is with you, but you are not with real relationship.

Where can you possibly be if you are not being with what really is? Where can you possibly be if you are not being with the Greater Reality that is the foundation, meaning and context of your life? The only place that you can be is in your thoughts. And your thoughts weave themselves around your awareness until they are all that you can see. They govern your perception, and they govern your behavior. They determine your goals and aspirations. Your thoughts represent the hole in the ground and the walls around you that block your vision, that contain your experience and that limit your freedom and your ability to be in meaningful relationships.

To be lifted out of this situation requires preparation, and it requires you to follow this preparation because you yourself must climb out. In this, you will regain your strength, your determination, your perseverance and your true will born of Knowledge. Here you learn the way of escape, not from the world, but from the contradiction of being dominated by your own personal mind.

Grace reminds you that this is possible. Grace enables your escape to take place, and Grace encourages you to proceed. The door to your prison cell is open. You can push it open at any time. You can walk out into the light of day. For this to happen, however, you must be willing to have a different experience of yourself and a different determination within you. You must be open and desiring of a greater life—a life that is not in keeping with your past and that will bring you out of the confinement of living within your personal mind. As a result of this escape, even your personal mind will be refreshed, renewed and restored, for your personal mind's greater purpose is to serve Knowledge. Your personal mind, like your personal body, is a temporary vehicle in life. Its greatest service, its greatest union and its greatest security are born of its service to a Greater Power—the Greater Power that assures your reality, your mission, your origin and your destiny.

This Greater Power is with you now. Knowledge is with you now. Grace is with you now. The Creator is with you now. The relationships that you will truly need in life exist now. You must find your way to them, and they will find their way to you. Find the way to Knowledge, and Knowledge will be able to emerge into your mind. Find your way to Grace, and Grace will have a place to abide with you—not just momentarily but permanently, as it is meant to.

The experience that we are speaking of can only be realized as you open yourself to it and as you become truly honest about your deeper inclinations. Here we must give a greater definition of honesty: Honesty is not only knowing what you feel; honesty is feeling what you know. Here your personal mind and the deeper mind that is your true nature touch each other, and there is Grace. Here there is sobriety about life. There is quiet awareness. And there are deeper feelings and motivations.

As you touch Knowledge—your Greater Self and your greater association with life—then Grace will be experienced. Knowledge takes you to Grace again and again, not as a momentary experience, not as a highlight of a long and dreary life and not only as a flash of lightning, but as an abiding reality and experience within yourself. You can find a way to Knowledge because a way has been given. You can take the steps to Knowledge because the steps have been given. This is the work of Grace, for Grace would be incomplete if it did not give you the means for its total realization and experience. The Creator would be leaving you out in the cold of life if a way to the Creator were not given to you.

The evidence of Grace is expressed in those wonderful and reassuring moments when a greater truth is experienced and a greater association and relationship with life is felt. However, the evidence of Grace is more completely substantiated by your realization that you have a great need to fulfill your purpose and mission here and that this need is more powerful and more urgent than anything else that you feel or recognize.

This great need calls for and readies you to prepare. It gives you a new direction and a new impetus. It calls God to you, and it calls you to God. It calls you to those significant people that you will need in your life, and it calls them to you. It is as if a great switch had been thrown and all of a sudden a whole new set of factors come into play. Subtle will be your experience of them at first, but you will know within yourself that something has changed. You turned a corner somewhere. You crossed an invisible line. Something happened to you somewhere back there. Now you feel a little bit different. There is something growing and emerging within you, a deeper experience from a part of you that you can barely recognize and certainly cannot define.

Your great need and the great need of the universe have just recognized each other. As a result of this recognition, a greater purpose is stimulated—a purpose that you will have to carry like a great pregnancy and that you will have to labor with to a certain degree in order to bring it forth into the world. It will change your ideas, and it will alter your experience, but only to bring them into a greater resonance and a greater relationship with the purpose that you carry, the mission that you serve and the life to which you are intrinsically and forever bonded. Then you will come to know Grace not only as a momentary experience, but as an activity in your life. And your understanding of this will grow and expand as you are able to proceed.

Here Grace will be something that you can identify, even during those moments when you cannot feel it directly, because you will know it is there. This will not require belief as much as it will require acceptance. Here you will not be trying to believe in something you cannot experience. Instead, you will be trying to accept something that you know is in your life. And you will know it is in your life because you will have experienced it increasingly and because you will have seen the evidence of its work within you and around you. This is the silent, subtle activity of the Creator reclaiming the separated through Knowledge. It is renewing you and others by the activation of a greater awareness and a greater purpose that has brought you into the world—a purpose in keeping with the evolution of life, a purpose that is yours to find and to discover.

The real confirmation of Grace will come as you are able to realize that there has been a greater intervention and support in your life to enable you to meet a greater need and a greater desire. This will renew your awareness that you are in relationship with something very significant here. Then Grace will not merely be a momentary and dramatic experience, but instead will become the living foundation of your life.

—⁘—

Jesus is now an Unseen One,

not only in this world

but in the worlds whose races

humanity is destined to encounter.

Though others will claim to represent him,

he will not reappear,

for his mission is done in this regard.

His work now is with the Unseen Ones.

—⁘—

CHAPTER TWENTY-SIX

WHO IS JESUS?

—⟪ⵗⵗⵗ⟫—

*J*ESUS REPRESENTS A MAJOR FIGURE IN THE EVOLUTION of the world, an initiator—one of the principle initiators of a great period that is now coming to a close in the world. Let us talk about Jesus within the context of the evolution of the world, for this will give you a greater understanding of his role and of the great results that have been demonstrated by his life and by the translation of Knowledge that he helped generate.

Jesus was sent into the world by his Spiritual Family to be one of the individuals who would inaugurate a new era in human development and evolution. We call this the era of civilization. The purpose of this era was to slowly take humanity from its tribal identity and tribal isolation towards an international and interracial involvement. This international and interracial involvement has been cataclysmic and very difficult, but it has led to humanity's becoming established in the world—not only in its tribal states, but in its larger states representing many races and cultures, ideas and beliefs.

Christianity and all the other major religions have fostered a bridge between cultures and between races. These are not simply religions of one tribe or one group. They are religions for all of humanity. This is not to say that everyone can adhere to them, follow them or receive them, but they bridge the normal boundaries that seem to separate people and cast them apart. The religion of forgiveness, the religion of reunion with the Divine, the religion of human development, the religion of compassion—all of these tremendous movements in the evolution of religion in the world were fostered by the establishment of the world's religions, which have brought the world to its present state.

Perhaps you might think that the world is in a terrible state now and that not much has been done to bring humanity to a greater union. However, if you could understand how life was in your world twenty-five hundred years ago, you would see how very far you have come. You would see how much your races have intermingled and how much they have found a new basis and foundation for sharing their ideas and their deeper yearnings and inclinations.

As we have said repeatedly, religion must serve the world in its current state of evolution. The world's major religions have all evolved the race towards a greater interaction between different peoples. This is especially true of Christianity, which has spanned your globe and now connects people who may otherwise have no association with one another. Now they have a common faith. Now they have common rituals and common observances. This is a remarkable accomplishment in a world that is still deeply mired in tribal identities.

The teaching of compassion, forgiveness, and devotion and the example of Jesus all serve to unite people across these great and difficult gaps of separation. Jesus' accomplishment, then, was to help usher in the age of civilization. Civilization in this age is distinct from earlier civilizations which were primarily tribal civilizations. In your current age, civilizations involve not only one tribe and one language, one group or one family, but bridge far beyond these boundaries. And though humanity has quarreled and struggled with itself through all of these transitions and developments, a greater foundation nonetheless has been established for human experience beyond tribal custom and identity.

At the time that Christianity was introduced, it was revolutionary. Its emphasis was to spread its message amongst nations and amongst different peoples. It was not only meant for one group or one locale.

It was not only meant for one tribe or one nation. Its emphasis was to bridge the gaps between different cultures and different nations, to bond people together through a higher association in life and to create a greater foundation for recognition, communication and cooperation. Humanity has been struggling with this challenge ever since, but much progress has been made.

Jesus set into motion a direct relationship with the Divine through the intermediary of the Holy Spirit, which in Greater Community understanding would be defined as Knowledge itself. This relationship emphasized the Divine reality within each person and the possibility for personal revelation and spiritual development. Humanity has been struggling with this ever since, yet it is a remarkable achievement that Christianity is present in the world and that it is accepted by millions of people in different countries, from different cultures and backgrounds. This is a religion for international civilization, as is true of many of the other religious movements that were initiated in the world and that have advanced into a more modern age.

To understand Jesus's contribution, we must look back and see what has occurred. Wisdom indeed can be gained in hindsight here. Life before Jesus and life after Jesus are different. There has been a remarkable change. This change took centuries to take full effect, but it did take full effect. In many instances, the spread of Christianity was destructive and immoral. However, it was following an evolutionary track. It had to happen. Just as the world is now preparing to emerge into the Greater Community, nations in centuries past were destined to interact with each other, to confront each other, to dominate each other and to spread their cultures around the world. This has happened to a very large degree.

Now we have world religions rather than simply tribal religions. Given the evolutionary process of cultural and social development in the world, and given the progress and evolution of religious and spiritual understanding, you can see that this has been a great step forward. Religion must always keep pace with the evolution of the race which it is intended to serve. Its ability to do this or its inability to do this will determine how beneficial it will be and how great a service it will render.

You are now at a new threshold, an even greater threshold than your race faced over two millennia ago. Your emergence into the Greater Community will be the greatest challenge and the greatest opportunity your race has ever experienced. This great threshold will be faced by everyone, not simply by one group, one nation or one culture. This has the possibility for genuinely uniting the world. This also has the possibility for separating the races of the world into a final self-destruction.

To enable humanity to advance and to adapt to this greater set of circumstances in the Greater Community and to all the attending problems and opportunities that they will offer, religion must evolve. Though Jesus has established a foundation here, even Christianity must now evolve to meet a whole new set of circumstances.

Resistance to Greater Community awareness in the world today is primarily centered in the world's religions. These are religions for man. They are human religions with a human god and a human emphasis. They do not account for life in the Greater Community. Yet the reality of life in the Greater Community will challenge their precepts and will challenge the institutions that have been built upon these precepts. Therefore, it is likely in the years to come that the greatest resistance to the acceptance and realization of Greater Community life will come from the world's religious leaders and the defenders of their respective faiths.

However, religion must keep pace with the evolution of the world, and that is why The Greater Community Way of Knowledge is being presented into the world at this time. It has come at just the right time. It gives you a head start in preparation, but even with a head start, time is short because Greater Community forces are in the world today. Their influence over humanity and their impact on your environment are growing. You must be prepared not only to accept their presence, but to encounter them and to deal with their impact on you, both physically and mentally. This requires a new foundation for religious experience. The world's religions will need this if they are to survive in the next era of human development and evolution.

Religions have life spans. This is true throughout the Greater Community. Religions have life spans because they serve eras of development. Then they are either replaced or they change and expand in order to adapt. If they cannot adapt, they will be replaced because the reality of life will make their teaching and their emphasis less and less relevant and meaningful.

In the Greater Community, religions are initiated, they reach a maturity and then they enter old age where they die off. Out of their old age a new impetus, a new meaning and a new message can be given to restore and to renew the race's spiritual vitality and to give this vitality an immediate relevancy to life as it is expanding and developing.

Jesus set into motion a great era of development, an era that would serve and challenge people all around the world. His was not the only example, but he was a primary figure. Though he has been idolized and deified, though he has been condemned and scorned, and though he has been used by groups, organizations, tribes and governments for their own purposes, his example still remains—the recognition of one person by another across all boundaries of culture, race, economic position, language and orientation. His example provided a greater foundation for relationship, a greater foundation for recognition and a greater possibility for mutual development and achievement. This has been necessary for the development of international societies. This has also been necessary for the development and advancement of your race into a technological age.

Now you are at a new beginning. Now you have a greater challenge. Jesus knew that his time and place were crucial. He knew that he would have to play a very visible role in initiating a process that would extend far beyond his own life and awareness. He knew that the effect of his presence would cause violence, warfare and great tribulation, not only for his followers but for other generations of people to come. However, even he could not see at that time the full extent and impact of his contribution. He could not see how it would be used and how it would be misused and misappropriated in the years and centuries to come.

However, he demonstrated a great truth—that a person's purpose, however great or small, however visible or invisible to the eyes of others, must be in accordance with the needs and evolution of the world. Here religion serves whole eras of human development. This is understood from a Greater Community perspective, a perspective which you now have an opportunity to learn and to utilize.

In the history of nations more advanced and longer established than yours, and in the experience of civilizations which have destroyed themselves through indulgence, manipulation or ignorance, it is evident everywhere as a universal principle that religions are born, they change and they die. In other words, they have a life. Their life extends far beyond the lives of the individuals who founded them, for their service is meant to be correlated to the greater evolution and development of the world in which they were introduced.

At this time in your world, certain religious traditions will die. Others will be renewed and reborn and given new emphasis and development. An old Christianity cannot meet a new set of circumstances. It must be a new Christianity, a Christianity that is renewing itself continuously—just as within the life and scope of a person's experience, an old orientation cannot meet a new problem, an old belief cannot meet a new set of circumstances and an old identity cannot interact with a new identity. This is why humanity must be prepared for the Greater Community. This is why its religious traditions must evolve into this greater arena and participation in life. They must do this without a past reference, for the past is gone and life has changed.

Those principles that are universal and timeless must find new expression now. They cannot be held as the vestiges of antiquity. They must find a new expression because that which is permanent must find expression in changing circumstances. The expressions will change. The traditions of expression will change. And the emphasis of expression will change.

What Jesus set into motion has universal application, but only in its purest sense. What has been made of his teaching will not be able to survive in a Greater Community context to any great degree. His emphasis on devotion, on forgiveness, on tolerance and on spiritual identity has permanent value. Here we must distinguish between the founder of a faith and the establishment of the religion that is built upon that faith.

Christianity is a religion for humanity with a human god and a human emphasis. It cannot account for life in the Greater Community. In order for this to happen, its theology will have to change and expand. Its idea of the Divine will have to change and expand. Its notion of God's involvement in the world will have to grow enormously. Its teachings will have to be separated from the folklore of the past. Its theology and application will have to change and to adapt. If it cannot do this, it will die. No matter how virulent its defenders will be and no matter how strong its seeming resurgence, it will be overtaken by the reality of a changing world.

In your own life, in order to meet life anew, you must have a new and open mind. Your mind must be renewing itself and refreshing itself. As you enter new stages of development as a person, what worked before at an earlier time may no longer be useful or applicable. You need new eyes to meet new experiences. You need a new faith, not an old faith. You need a new religious experience, not an old religious experience. You must look forward now and not backward.

Many traditions and many long-standing associations and ideas will fall away given the enormity of human problems and the greater challenge that will be presented increasingly as humanity becomes aware of the Greater Community reality and its impact upon individual and national life here in the world.

The Greater Community Way of Knowledge is not only a preparation for the Greater Community; it is a new foundation for religious understanding and experience. It is a foundation that will enable the world's religions to advance into a new life with a new relevancy. And yet some of the world's religions will not be able to advance, for they are already old and burdened and encrusted with the past. A Greater Community reality will be too much for them. Which religions will survive and which will not will be up to the people who participate within them. This will depend upon their ability to adapt and their ability to renew their faith and their experience. Yet the fundamental change will be profound.

You must not exercise human arrogance regarding the Greater Community. If you believe that humanity is a blessed race and that the rest of the Greater Community is made up of barbarians who have not received God's endowments, then you will be making a critical and fatal mistake. This will deny your ability to learn, to evolve, to adapt and to meet the greater challenges that lay ahead. Humanity is not a blessed race. It is not unique. It is not the centerpiece of creation. It is not God's favorite child. God's work is everywhere. All genuine religious traditions in the Greater Community are initiated through Knowledge and establish a means and a methodology for individuals to experience a greater purpose and meaning in life within the circumstances in which they live.

A theology of the universe is necessary now, not simply a theology of human psychology and human sociology. You need this to unify your race and to bridge the remaining gaps that exist between you so that you can find your common ground. The real common ground in life is Knowledge itself. In this, everyone has something fundamental that is in common. It is not tied to the past, and it is not governed by personal ambition, greed or enmity. It is time now for a Way of Knowledge, not for a way where there are heroes and heroines and idols of worship. This is not the time for fantastic stories or mythology. This is a time for real demonstration, real faith and real experience.

Humanity is growing in its intellectual scope and understanding. Its religions have not kept pace with this by and large. You cannot have a religion of escape from the world now because the world is emerging into the Greater Community, and you have come to serve the world in its emergence and all that its emergence will mean and require. This is not a time to believe in heaven and hell. This is a time to come into the world to contribute and to participate. This is not a time to believe that God will judge and condemn and cast unbelievers into the infernal flames of hell. This is a time to realize that the challenge of development faces everyone. Those who can respond and who can prepare accordingly will be the great beneficiaries and the great contributors to their race, and they will experience a satisfaction that those who are unable to do this will not find no matter what their status or position in life.

Where is Jesus today? Because of his great demonstration and because of the many misinterpretations of his demonstration and the tremendous idolization that has occurred regarding him, he is now an Unseen One in the world. He is an Unseen One not only in this world but in the worlds whose races humanity is destined to encounter. He will not reappear in the world. Though others will claim to represent him, he will not reappear, for his mission is done in this regard. His work now is with the Unseen Ones.

Here you must expand your ideas considerably, for there are many Unseen Ones in the universe. There is not one who is paramount amongst them. For when you graduate from this life, you are a beginner in the next stage of life. You do not simply return to Heaven to spend eternity in repose. You enter another stage of service and activity, learning and preparation.

Jesus is in the world. Take comfort. However, he will not come again in the flesh. Who will come again in the flesh claiming his name will be someone from the Greater Community. Beware. If you can become strong with Knowledge, you will know and will not be deceived. Yet, if you fervently want to believe and are governed by the weakness of belief, then you can be persuaded. A Greater Community presence can perform seeming miracles for you. They can do things that seem magical and inexplicable, and many people will fall down in belief and adoration because of this. The world is not yet prepared for the Greater Community. And there is not enough discernment amongst your people to distinguish Greater Community demonstrations from the reality of God's demonstration.

Jesus is in the world reinforcing Knowledge. Jesus is in other worlds as well, for your destiny lies in your interaction with other worlds now. The possibility for success here must be reinforced by the Unseen Ones, who speak to those who can respond with Knowledge. This is possible because The Greater Community Way of Knowledge is being taught here and elsewhere, as we have said.

Jesus is revered amongst your people because of his example and demonstration, but even more than this, he set into motion a process of spiritual initiation, growth and development that continues to this day and which has promise for the future. The theology that has been built upon his demonstration, however, cannot survive. His demonstration will survive because it is the demonstration of Knowledge, and it calls upon Knowledge in those who can bear witness to it. This is not faith in a set of beliefs, faith in a set of traditions or faith in a church hierarchy. This is faith in the direct transmission of Knowledge from one mind to another. In this, Jesus has great potency, and that is why he is still in the world.

You are entering a new era now. It is not the era of international civilizations. It is an era requiring a united world civilization. This is a far greater challenge and one that will take a great deal of time and probably much struggle to accomplish. What will give it necessity and impetus is the world's emergence into the Greater Community. No matter how much you may distrust your neighbor, no matter how much you may feel you are better than others, no matter how superior you may feel your culture's values, customs and ethics are over another's—this will all be equalized and minimized by the overshadowing of the Greater Community presence in the world.

This represents the possibility for redemption that the Greater Community offers you. It requires change. It requires cooperation. It requires acceptance. It requires setting aside old disputes and squabbles. It requires that you adopt a world identity, not just a national identity. It requires a greater association amongst people and a greater respect and tolerance. These are required because the world is emerging into the Greater Community. Jesus will be part of this emergence, but he must watch the great changes that are occurring in life. And he must give his counsel without interfering now. For he made his presentation, and now he has a greater and loftier service to perform.

The emphasis must now be on Knowledge because this is the essence of your spirituality, and this will give you a new direction in life. The emphasis must no longer be on beliefs, ideas, principles, images and creation stories. If you can move with life, life will move you. If you can keep pace with life, your spirituality will have a new vitality and possibility for expression.

Then you will understand Jesus—not only because you can appreciate his past demonstration and the beneficence that he encouraged and has engendered in the world. You will understand that he came into life at a unique time to render a unique service. His life was exceptional because he did not remain hidden. And he paid the price for not remaining hidden. However, his demonstration had to be very visible so that it would be remembered. Though much fantasy has been woven around his life, and though his life has been manipulated and used according to secular interests all around the world, his demonstration of compassion, tolerance and shared identity persists to this day and has great bearing for the future.

Here you must distinguish between religion and spirituality. The purpose of religion is to enable spirituality to be experienced, to be applied and to be fully utilized. When religion ceases to be able to do this and becomes an entity in and of itself, then it begins to usurp its essential and primary purpose. Here it must be changed. And change it will.

You may think of Jesus as either a man with a Divine purpose or as a Divine being with a human purpose. However you might think of Jesus, you think of him within the context of your world and within the context of human involvements and interaction. We are now challenging you to think of him as a figure in the Greater Community. He is not an extraterrestrial from outer space. He was a man who realized Knowledge and contributed Knowledge in his time and helped to set into motion, through the efforts of many other people, a greater emphasis in life and a means for re-experiencing this emphasis through a tradition of devotion, dedication and service.

Now you must think of him as an Unseen One in the Greater Community. Here you have the challenge of broadening your understanding, opening your mind and setting aside those ideas, concepts, beliefs and preferences which cannot fit into a greater reality. For Jesus to be real for you now and to be real in the future, you must have this approach. His reality and his role are consistent with everything we have said, but for you to keep pace with this, you must develop in The Way of Knowledge. You must find the foundation that will carry your spirituality into the future and give it eminent presence and ability there. Otherwise, Jesus will be a historical figure that will seem increasingly removed from life. You will identify him with an earlier time and with a passing age. And he will seem to be lost with everything that was associated with him, which will fade from view over the decades and centuries to come.

Look forward. Look over the horizon. See what is coming. What is past is past and was relevant to the past. In order for spirituality and for religion to have meaning, purpose and value now and in the future, they must be renewed and be able to respond to the greater movement of the world and to the changing needs of humanity.

Religion is like a prescription for you to see. You outgrow old prescriptions, and then you have to have your eyes re-examined. You get a new prescription which enables you to see clearly in the present. The old prescription is no longer able to do that. Think of religion in this way. Think of it as an intermediary. Think of it as a changeable structure. Think of it as a prescription for seeing, knowing and acting—honestly, truthfully and beneficially. Here you will not become attached to the form but will bond with the essence. And the essence will transcend the form, rejuvenate the form and renew it. It will give form new meaning and relevancy in your life and within the world which you have come to serve.

Your idea of Jesus must be seen in a greater context. Your idea of God must be seen in a greater context. This must be a Jesus of the Greater Community. This must be a God of the Greater Community. And there must be a spirituality of the Greater Community and a theology of the Greater Community. Do not be concerned that you may seem to be the only one thinking these things, for you are pioneering. Pioneers must go where others are not willing to go, must realize what others cannot or will not realize and must share what others cannot or will not share.

This is your challenge, and this is your great opportunity for contribution. Meet this reality and this challenge, and you will come to know Jesus because you will be facing what he faced, yet in a much smaller way, perhaps. You will know Jesus because you will share his experience. If you can do this, you will know that he is in the world today and that he will play a beneficial part in the world's emergence into the Greater Community.

—◦◦◦—

As God works in the world,

unacknowledged and unrecognized,

everyone benefits.

Such will be the case in the future,

for the Creator will take you

into the Greater Community.

The Creator will enable you to learn

Greater Community Spirituality

and will provide you the methods

of practice and study to enable you

to have a greater religious experience

and to learn its essential application

in the changing circumstances of your life.

—◦◦◦—

CHAPTER TWENTY-SEVEN

WHAT IS THE EVOLUTION OF RELIGION IN THE WORLD?

※

*R*ELIGION EVOLVES BECAUSE IT IS MEANT TO SERVE evolving worlds. Evolution is a process of change. It is a process of renewal and rejuvenation and also a process of adaptation and application. In order for religion to be meaningful in any world, it must serve that world through its various stages of development. Religion itself goes through stages of development. It has phases of growth and phases of decay. However, it has the possibility for regeneration if it can adapt itself to new circumstances and to greater ideas. In this, each religion must be flexible. The theologies and philosophies upon which each religion is built must be adaptable and responsive to a growing panorama of life and to a changing set of circumstances that represent the evolution of a race.

Let us begin by talking about the evolution of intelligent life in the world, and then we shall speak about the evolution of religion. Intelligent life was seeded in your world. This was a gift from the Greater

Community. It was a gift of greater intelligence so that your ancestors could accelerate their development within a relatively short period of time. This gave birth to the modern human race as you know it now. Intelligence was seeded in a few places and then it dispersed throughout the world.

Most of human history in the world has been one of tribal existence, where very small groups of people lived in isolation with minimal contact between cultures. This system was able to work for a long time. However, with the development of greater intellectual abilities and the development of agriculture and social organization, local human communities grew in size and began to compete with each other increasingly.

This follows a natural pattern. From this pattern, one can see what happens in all worlds where greater intelligence has either migrated or has been introduced into the native species. Cultures start out small and isolated and then grow from there. According to the natural pattern of development, greater and greater establishments are made, with greater and greater contact between groups within a given world. This leads to tribal states. Tribal states intermingle, have conflict and influence one another. This leads to greater establishments and eventually to international societies, which is where the human race is now.

The human race is at a terminal point, the terminal end of the cycle of the development of international societies. This is where tribes and groups have grown so great, have overlapped so much and are having such an impact upon the environment that they must learn new ways of cooperation. They must join forces. They must grow into a new stage of development, which is represented by a one-world community. It is this stage upon which humanity is now embarking. Regardless of the strife and difficulty that still exist between tribes, cultures, groups and nations, this is the direction of human evolution. This is the course it must follow, for better or for worse.

Races that have evolved within their own worlds reach the establishment of international communities and then become a one-world community. The development of a one-world community coincides with interaction with the Greater Community. Here having a one-world community becomes a necessity for survival and development. In worlds where intelligent life has migrated from another world, a one-world community occurs much sooner because often there is only one establishment which gains the dominant position within that world.

However, in a world such as yours, which has gone through a very long and protracted period of tribal social development and which has accelerated in recent centuries into large tribal and then international societies, you have now reached the great threshold where the world must become one community. Perhaps at this moment it seems incomprehensible that this could be brought about given the current state of the world and people's current attitudes regarding cooperation. However, we are speaking of evolution and not the wishes and will of the people. For even greater than the wishes and the will of the people in any world are their destiny and their relationship with life on a larger scale—both within physical reality and within spiritual reality.

Life is moving. It is going somewhere. It is developing and cultivating itself. Think of it like this: In your development as a human being, you go through stages of growth. You begin as an infant, you become a young child, you grow into adolescence and to young adulthood, and then to adulthood, middle age and old age. Each stage is different and requires different skills and a different understanding. Each builds upon the stage before it, but each is different and unique within itself.

All human beings go through these stages regardless of their attitudes, preferences or beliefs. This represents the evolution of their own individual life in the world. This evolution will happen, no matter what may be believed and no matter what the prevailing attitudes may be. You will go through the stages of life as an individual. This is also true with nations and even with entire races. They will go through stages of development as well.

From a Greater Community perspective, humanity at this point is in a very early stage of adolescence. Humanity is beginning to realize its power, but it does not have the responsibility, the understanding of life, or any accountability beyond itself to gain a real foundation for using its newfound abilities in a constructive way. From a Greater Community perspective, then, humanity is reckless and aggressive. It is violent and inconsistent. It does not understand itself, its environment or the nature of its real responsibilities and relationships. However, humanity is moving towards adulthood as a race. This adulthood places it within a larger community, gives it purpose and accountability there and engenders within it greater responsibilities and a greater concern for others.

Just as the individual grows from adolescence into adulthood, your race must grow from its current adolescence into its adulthood. It must learn to use its newfound powers and abilities effectively and constructively, not only for immediate gain but for its future well-being as well. This greater sense and perspective regarding the future and the results of your current actions upon the future represents maturity, both within yourself as an individual and within the thinking of your entire race. You are gaining this very slowly, and it is needed with great emphasis now in order to preserve your environment and to promote real social development according to the stage of life in which you are currently living. Humanity is developing into a one-world community and is also emerging into the Greater Community of Worlds. Together, this represents the greater context for individual and collective development. This is the context that you have come from beyond the world to serve.

Religion plays a fundamental role here, but it too must evolve. The religion of a millennium ago cannot be effective in the modern world without changing and adapting. Again we must emphasize the distinction between spirituality and religion. Think of it like this: Spirituality is the spark. It is the essence of religious experience. Religious institutions, traditions and so forth are established in order to provide a vehicle or a mechanism for people to have religious experience. This is their pure and fundamental goal. In reality, though, once religions are established, they have other goals and purposes as well—survival, the acquisition of power and competition for attention. However, from a greater perspective, the purpose of religion is essentially to create a method and a means for people to have religious experience and for this to be possible within a cultural and societal context.

The Creator is bringing essence into the world continuously, but as soon as it emerges, it slowly hardens and calcifies into form. However, the essence is being introduced constantly. Think of it like this: It is like bringing fresh water into a frozen environment. As soon as the water merges with the environment, it begins to freeze and become immobile. The more that form is associated with religion, the more religion will be bound by form and the more inflexible it will be. That is why in the Greater Community religion must minimize form and all of its pageantry so that the essence may be constantly emphasized. This provides the greatest possibility for religious experience to be rendered, both to the participants in that tradition and to their world at large.

Essence is being sent into your world now to an even greater degree because of the stage of evolution that you are in. This has brought The Greater Community Way of Knowledge into the world. It represents a new foundation for religious understanding. This foundation is presented with a minimum of structure and ritual. The structure and ritual that it does contain has to do with its methods of preparation and with very simple forms of devotional practice. These are both necessary and helpful and are quite adaptable to changing circumstances. The preparation in The Greater Community Way of Knowledge can be practiced anywhere under any circumstances, and it will be as relevant three hundred years from now as it is today.

The evolution of religion requires adaptability—adapting methods of practice and vehicles of expression for greater religious experience—in order for religion to survive and to have a place in the world. This meets the greater needs of people and serves humanity at large by fortifying the ideas of peace, cooperation, understanding and tolerance. Without this presence and without this constant emphasis, humanity would lead itself towards destruction very rapidly. Selfish pursuits, quests for power and domination, the competition for resources and the isolation of different tribes and groups would lead to an increasing state of destruction and chaos. To temper this and to give humanity greater promise and the possibility of new life and renewal, the Creator is bringing the essence of spirituality into the world constantly and is reinforcing both the old traditions and the new expressions of spirituality that hold promise for humanity, for the present and for the future.

Therefore, the emphasis here is on renewing religion—giving it new life and impetus. Religious experience transcends all theological boundaries and then returns to life to give new structure and meaning to religion and new opportunities for religious experience to be shared and translated to others. It is as if the world were a garden that is constantly being watered. It is constantly drying out, and it is constantly being watered. Even those who have developed within the context of the world's religions must break new ground. They too must come back to what is essential. And they too must fortify those practices and traditions that enable them to translate their experience to others. However, this must be done with a clear understanding of the difference between the means and the essence of religion itself.

A Greater Community Theology is necessary now because you need to experience and to practice a translatable spirituality—not a spirituality that is bound to one culture or another, that is bound to one philosophy or another, or that is bound to one temperament or another, but something that can be translated to people everywhere. It must be something that is very essential, very useful and very relevant to the evolution and development of your world at this time and as it will be in the coming centuries.

Remember, you are preparing for the future, not only for yourself but for others in your race. Like all creatures in nature, you give so that others may have the opportunity to live. This is a truth that is rarely understood and rarely experienced in the human family at this time. People seem to live for themselves alone, or only for those whom they regard around them, but in essence they live for future generations because they pave the way for the future. And the legacy that they leave for future generations will be the substance of what they gave and what they did not give, what they established and what they did not establish.

Religion, then, is a growing and evolving understanding and experience. And its methodologies and instruction must grow and adapt
as well. Spirituality must be relevant within the context of life in which
it is experienced and expressed. With this understanding, you can see
more clearly how religion has evolved within the world. The religion of
a tribe whose radius of experience is perhaps only a few miles will have
a different religious emphasis and a different theology from a religion
that has to be practiced and understood within the context of an entire
world. The differences here are great.

Consider the difference between religion within a tribal context,
where religious imagery and practices are relevant to the immediate environment, and the emphasis of a world religion, whose practices and
application must be adapted to many very different environments and
to many different people who do not regularly interact with each other
or who may have no access to each other at all. A world religion must
account for events within the whole world, and it must be adaptable to
change that exists within the whole world—change that is much more
rapid, difficult and tumultuous than the kind of change that a tribal
society is likely to experience if it is living in isolation.

When you consider the differences here, then you can begin to
appreciate the difference between a world religion and a religion of the
Greater Community. However, there are some very important things
that distinguish this example from the one that we have just given. Most
essential is the understanding that humanity is but one more evolving
race in the Greater Community. It is not the centerpiece of God's creation. It is not a privileged race or a race that is more blessed than others.
Humanity has certain advantages and certain liabilities. It has certain
strengths and certain weaknesses and flaws. However, it is not greater,
more important, more significant or more emphasized than other developing races in the Greater Community.

The move away from an anthropocentric viewpoint to a universal understanding is so great that it will change your values, your thinking and your emphasis in life. The difference between an isolated tribal
society and a world society is primarily one of magnitude. In both, the

emphasis is still on human experience, human expression and human aspirations. However, when you are living in a Greater Community context that extends far beyond human awareness, then your understanding of spirituality enters a much greater panorama. Here the idea of God becomes very different. Here the understanding of how God functions in the world and how God influences, blesses and enables individuals within the human family and within other families as well becomes far greater and more genuine to the true nature and comprehensiveness of life.

To be able to prepare for the Greater Community and to learn Greater Community Spirituality within a relatively short period of time represent a tremendous advancement for humanity. This is a great challenge. It is as if your evolution were being fast-forwarded. You do not have centuries to develop this understanding because the evolution of the world is moving quickly now, and you are behind in your preparation. It took until recent years for The Greater Community Way of Knowledge to be introduced because there has not been a sufficient global understanding. There has not been a sufficient realization of the need for truth. There has not been the impetus for change and development. And until recently, there has not been the ability to adapt.

Humanity has only recently emerged from its tribal societies. In fact, tribal societies are still very common in the world. You have just stepped into a modern age. Think of the difference of your life now and of life only one hundred years ago—a very small segment of time. You will see that you have freshly arrived on new shores. This has changed your attitude, your understanding, your emphasis, your goals and your aspirations. This has given you greater opportunities for education, self-expression and creativity, but it has also given you greater problems and difficulties to solve and an ever-increasing interaction with other people of different temperaments, cultures, races, languages and so forth.

In the world at this time, cultures are melting into each other, even as they resist and fight each other. No matter how much they attempt to separate themselves from their neighbors in the future, they will be forced together and fused together by a growing sense of interdependence and a growing need for cooperation in order to meet the problems that are shared by everyone.

Introduce into this situation the growing presence of the Greater Community, and you will see that humanity is rapidly approaching a great threshold. The impact of this threshold will be primarily experienced at the level of human understanding and in the breakdown of old traditions and ideas. This will happen rapidly from one generation to the next. Every decade, new ideas will be proposed, and new ideas will be accepted. What seems outrageous today, twenty years from now will seem like common knowledge. If the idea of the Greater Community seems revolutionary or difficult to comprehend, twenty years from now it will be on everyone's mind. That is how fast things are progressing. And that is why your ability to respond to the present, to respond to Knowledge within yourself, and to face life directly with a greater ability and a greater understanding are so essential in order for you to lead a fulfilling life and to contribute something meaningful for the future.

The evolution of life represents an expanding context for life. For example, the isolated tribal culture may remain static in its development for a very long time, but once it encounters other societies and grows beyond its initial boundaries, it will have to change and to adapt. This will change its emphasis, its culture and its religious expression to a very great degree. Its boundaries and its scope have expanded.

This expansion is the essence of evolution. It is not only expanding consciousness and awareness, it is an expanding involvement with others. Here greater influences are introduced, greater conflicts are generated and greater solutions are required. If you read human history, you will see how evident this is and how human societies which were once isolated have encountered each other, have grown into each other, have impacted each other, have conflicted with each other and have had to find a common ground of experience and tolerance with each other. This is still occurring, and there are many failures to instruct you.

Now think about the world's emergence into the Greater Community and about the impact of foreign races upon the human race, and you will see how much greater the scope and impact of this will be and how much greater the effect of its change. This will change your religions more than anything else, for no longer can you have a religion simply for humanity. This would be tribal within a Greater Community context. No longer can you have only a human god preoccupied with human affairs, for that would be tribal in the Greater Community.

In reality, the Creator is no more concerned with human beings than with any other beings. The work of the Divine in the world has always had this approach and this emphasis. Therefore, gaining a Greater Community perspective and learning a Greater Community Theology will bring you closer to the real nature and mind of the Creator. Here you will be able to understand more completely how the Creator has worked in the world in the past and how the Creator works in the world in the present moment. And the idea of Knowledge, which is so fundamental to understanding and learning Greater Community Spirituality, will become something that you can embrace.

At first, you must develop an intellectual capacity for Knowledge and an openness to its reality. Then you can find the way to it by taking the steps to Knowledge and by learning The Way of Knowledge. This will give you a foundation that will enable you to adapt to new situations as they occur. This will enable your mind to change, to renew itself and to regenerate its power in the ever-increasing presence of new experiences, new sensations and new difficulties.

Only the man and woman of Knowledge will have this great adaptive capability. In essence, they will be bringing spirituality into the world constantly, without the great burden of past traditions, interpretations or ecclesiastical studies or practices. They will not be carrying the past with them, like a great weight upon their shoulders. They will be able to step into the future, and what they bring into the future will be immediate and necessary. This will give the greatest possibility for success.

The greater the development of Knowledge in the world today, the greater will be the possibility for humanity's successful emergence into the Greater Community. This will assure your independence as a race in the Greater Community. This will assure your ability to learn from the Greater Community and to defend yourself against it when that becomes necessary. The Greater Community offers tremendous lessons regarding every aspect of life. Its successes and its failures will be available for you to learn, if you are able to learn them and if you can have a mind that is renewed and not bound to past associations. This requires a remarkable development in a human being—a development that has only been seen in the past within rare and gifted individuals. Now it must be fostered in many people, not only because of the wonderful rewards that it can engender for the race as a whole, but because it is needed. That is why The Greater Community Way of Knowledge is being brought into the world.

You will not be able to understand the Greater Community from an anthropocentric viewpoint. You will not be able to adapt to the Greater Community with this attitude and this belief as your foundation. With an anthropocentric viewpoint, you make yourself vulnerable to deception and manipulation. You weaken your great abilities of insight. You limit your skills. You close your eyes to what must be seen, and you disable yourself from doing what must be done.

You need a new foundation now, a foundation that you, as an evolving modern race, are capable of developing. The world has already shown you again and again that you have to expand your attitude, your understanding and the scope of your own perception. Your failures to do this in the past have led to difficulty, destruction and downfall. It is "adapt and survive" in the Greater Community, as it is in your own world. As you learn to enter into a Greater Community context and learn the ways of the Greater Community, you will have to adapt to survive. Once you survive, you can advance. However, in order to advance, you need to learn about the circumstances and the intelligences within this greater context. You will also need to learn what spirituality means within this greater context. And more than ever you will need to rely upon a Greater Power in life to enable you, to motivate you and to give you greater insight, greater depth and greater ability.

As God works in the world, unacknowledged and unrecognized, everyone benefits. Such will be the case in the future, for the Creator will take you into the Greater Community. The Creator will enable you to learn Greater Community Spirituality and will provide you the methods of practice and study to enable you to have a greater religious experience and to learn its essential application in the changing circumstances of your life.

Therefore, look forward not backward. Bring forward what can be brought forward, and leave behind what cannot be brought forward. In this way, you will build upon the Wisdom that your race has established already, but you will not be limited by it. You will be able to add to it, expand its application and develop your ability to understand its reality in your life.

The essence of spirituality, which lives within Knowledge within you, cannot be governed or dominated by you. You are meant to become its recipient. Once you can receive it, you can give it. And if you can give it, then you can transmit it and demonstrate it.

It is time now to look forward. It is time now to look with greater eyes, beyond all the desires and fears that hold you within your own mind. It is time to look beyond your ideas—not with hope and not with fear, not with ambition and not with expectation—in order to see what is occurring now and what will occur next.

The great waves of change in life build, and you can feel them building. They do not crash upon the shore without building up. They can be seen on the horizon once you learn to read the ways of the world. Learning The Way of Knowledge will teach you to read the ways of the world because Knowledge within you understands this. As you read the waves that crash upon the shore, you will see how they build, how they crash and which ones are coming next. You can see this by looking into the world, without projecting your hopes or your fears, without interpreting things positively or negatively, but simply by looking, seeing and understanding.

Look out on the horizon of your life. See what is coming, for waves of change are building there. And even though they might seem tremendous to you, if you can develop, you will have the capability to meet them. If you have this capability, you will be able to share it with others. If you can share it with others, it will be translated into the world.

Wisdom is handed down from person to person through a network as ancient as time. This is how the Creator gives the gift to the weakest person, for it has been handed down. If you look for it, you will find it, for it is there. If you look out onto the horizon of your life, you will see the waves building there. Look without fear. Look without hope. Look openly. Look clearly. Knowledge within you is prepared to deal with the changing circumstances of your life and with the great challenges that lie ahead. Thus, as you learn to reclaim your relationship with Knowledge, you reclaim your ability to interact with life as it is and as it will be. Without this, life will overwhelm you, and you will seek to escape it. Without this, life will threaten your current possessions and understanding, and you will resist it and seek to thwart it. There is no happiness and no satisfaction, no contribution and no meaning in resisting or avoiding life.

You have come into the world at this time to serve a world in transition. You were designed to meet the great problems and to utilize the great opportunities. You were designed to learn a Greater Community Way of Knowledge because you have come into the world at this time. You are meant to learn about a greater panorama of life. You are meant to see beyond the immediate circumstances of your life and to look beyond all of the assumptions which seem to assure you that the future will be like the present in order to see a greater expansion of human experience and the greater need for human development and contribution. This demonstrates the advancement and evolution of religion and the advancement and evolution of your race, for they are intertwined and cannot be separated.

The Creator has created a Plan that works. It works because it is relevant to the present and to the future. Your life is about the present and the future though your mind is oriented in the past. You have come here to serve the present and the future even though your ideas are rooted in the past. To receive Knowledge, to experience Knowledge, to follow Knowledge and to follow the steps to Knowledge will free you from the constraints of your past. This will enable your mind with all of its great strength and possibility to focus on what must be done now and to gain a greater perception and understanding of what will come and how to prepare for it.

If you can hear these words, you will understand their great meaning and bearing on your life, for you are not apart from the evolution of the world. The assumptions that you rely upon and the establishments of society that you rely upon for your safety, security and continuance will be challenged and will change. The ground will move beneath your feet again and again. Walk lightly. Keep your eyes open. Greater Wisdom within you can teach you how to negotiate the changing circumstances of your life—not only how to negotiate them but how to contribute to them so that this great period of transition into the Greater Community and towards a one-world society may be accomplished with minimal stress, danger and destruction.

The greatest promise for humanity lies ahead. The greatest challenges and risks for humanity lie ahead. These are imminent. They are not far in the future. Like waves that are soon to crash, they are building. These waves have come from far away. They represent the currents of life, both within your world and within the Greater Community. The deeper currents that exist in Knowledge within you are related to these greater currents of life.

The Creator loves the world and loves the universe and is united with them even though they are not united with the Creator. This greater understanding, which extends so far beyond your current thinking, lives with you today—within you in your Knowledge and between you in your relationships.

The greatest gift that can be given to you is Knowledge—a perfect guiding Wisdom within you, a bond and a timeless foundation that you have now. It is intelligent and can guide you through changing circumstances with a Wisdom, a certainty, a determination and a sense of direction that you alone could never create. The greatest gifts will be realized in meeting the greatest challenges. The greatest possibilities will emerge in facing the greatest change. The greatest demonstration of Grace, purpose, meaning and direction will be discovered as you meet a greater challenge and a greater opportunity in life.

Greater Community Spirituality represents the evolution of religion in the world. It represents the evolution of your race and your intrinsic relationship with the Greater Community. It represents your relationship with your Creator and with all in the physical universe who serve the Creator in many, many capacities. It demonstrates an essential and translatable spirituality that you can learn, that you can utilize and that you can give to others. It represents a gift, not only from your Creator, but from the Wise Ones in the Greater Community who seek to restore and to preserve Knowledge as a living force in physical existence. Their achievements and their contribution are reflected in a Greater Community Theology and in a Greater Community Way of Knowledge. Their methods of learning and their achievements in this regard are demonstrated in *Steps to Knowledge* in its adaptation into human life.

You are blessed, then, by those who walk ahead of you, by those who are more advanced. You are blessed by changing circumstances, which will bring you into a greater panorama and experience of life. And you are blessed because you are free to release your past and to only carry forward that which is essential and necessary for you to live in the moment and to prepare for the future. If you can live in the moment and prepare for the future, your life will be fulfilled and your journey here will be justified.

ABOUT THE AUTHOR

———⟨⟨⟨⟩⟩⟩———

*M*ARSHALL VIAN SUMMERS has been a teacher and pioneer in the field of inner guidance and spiritual direction since 1975. He is the founder of The Society for The Greater Community Way of Knowledge, a religious non-profit organization. In 1982 he underwent a life-changing spiritual contact experience which set the stage for the revelation of a new teaching called The Greater Community Way of Knowledge. In the ensuing years, he studied and applied this teaching in his own life. During this time, along with the help of a small group of dedicated students, he prepared these writings to be given as a gift to the world. Now, for the first time, this teaching and the mysterious tradition that it represents are being presented in the four books *Greater Community Spirituality, Steps to Knowledge* and *Wisdom from the Greater Community: Volumes I & II*. The revelation continues. . . .

About the Society

———ᘒᘒᘒ———

HERE IS AN URGENT NEED FOR KNOWLEDGE, Wisdom and contribution in the world today. Our world is emerging into the Greater Community and we are not prepared.

The Society for The Greater Community Way of Knowledge has an important mission to fulfill. The Society's mission is to present and teach The Greater Community Way of Knowledge so that people everywhere can begin to awaken to the presence of Knowledge within their lives and to prepare for our future in a Greater Community of intelligent life. The Society is endeavoring to fulfill this mission by providing the materials, the instruction and the environment necessary for learning and living The Greater Community Way of Knowledge.

The Society was founded in 1992 as a religious non-profit organization. It publishes the books of the New Knowledge Library, offers the Greater Community Contemplative Services and provides special educational programs on The Way of Knowledge and Greater Community Spirituality by its founder MV Summers.

As a religious non-profit organization, The Society is supported primarily through tithes and contributions. There are two ways that you can assist in bringing The Greater Community Way of Knowledge into the world. The first is to become a Friend of The Society. The Friends

365

of The Society is a formal program of giving in support of The Society's mission. Your financial support will make possible the ongoing publication of all the Sacred Books of Knowledge, many of which are currently awaiting funds for publication. In addition, your contributions enable The Society to present its message worldwide and to offer the programs and services which make learning and living The Greater Community Way of Knowledge possible.

The second way you can participate is to share this great Teaching with others. The Books of Knowledge are finding their way around the world through the power of relationships, where people are sharing their discovery of The Way of Knowledge. You can make a difference by reaching those who need Knowledge and Wisdom now and who feel the need to prepare. Encourage them to read these books.

FURTHER STUDY

———༄༅———

$\mathcal{T}$HERE IS A WAY TO STUDY AND PRACTICE what has
been presented in this book. The Greater Community Way of Knowledge
is the translation and application of Greater Community Spirituality for
this world. Preparation in The Way of Knowledge is presented in the
three texts, *Steps to Knowledge* and *Wisdom from the Greater Community:
Volumes I & II*, which together comprise the foundation level of study
in the Steps to Knowledge Program. Offered in a self-study format, the
Steps Program provides the perspective, the insight and the method of
preparation necessary to begin to prepare for the Greater Community
and to learn and to live Greater Community Spirituality.

The Sacred Books of the New Knowledge Library are published by
The Society for The Greater Community Way of Knowledge. To order
copies of *Steps to Knowledge* and *Wisdom from the Greater Community:
Volumes I & II*, use the order form at the back of this book, visit our
website or request the books at your favorite bookstore. To learn more
about The Society's publications, educational programs and contemplative services, please contact The Society for The Greater Community
Way of Knowledge, P.O. Box 1724, Boulder, CO 80306-1724; (303) 938-
8401; E-mail: society@greatercommunity.org; www.newmessage.org.

Steps to Knowledge

The Greater Community Book of Practices

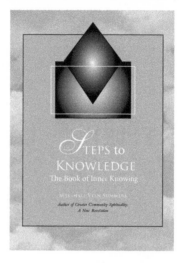

You came into the world with the Knowledge of who you are,
who you must meet and what you must accomplish.
It is time to find this Knowledge and begin to live it.

STEPS TO KNOWLEDGE takes you on the great journey of discovering Knowledge, the Knowing Mind within you, and with it the greater purpose that has brought you into the world.

STEPS TO KNOWLEDGE provides the lessons and practices necessary for learning and living The Way of Knowledge. Presented in a self-study format, it contains 365 daily "steps" that mysteriously open the mind to revelation where purpose, meaning and direction in life become apparent.

STEPS TO KNOWLEDGE is not based upon any existing world religion or philosophy. It presents a new understanding of your purpose and destiny as you discover your place within a Greater Community of intelligent life.

ISBN 978-1-884238-27-7

Step 15

I SHALL LISTEN TO MY EXPERIENCE TODAY.

*T*ODAY I WILL LISTEN TO MY EXPERIENCE to find out the content of my mind."

REALIZE THAT THE TRUE CONTENT OF YOUR MIND is buried beneath all that you have added since the day you were born. This true content wishes to express itself in the context of your current life and current situation. To discern this you must listen carefully and in time realize the difference between the true content of your mind and its messages for you and all the other impulses and wishes that you feel. To separate thoughts from Knowledge is one of the great accomplishments which you will have an opportunity to learn in this course.

THE ONE PRACTICE TODAY WILL BE DEVOTED to inner listening. This will require that you listen without judgment of yourself, even if the content of your thoughts is disturbing. Even if the content of your thoughts is disagreeable, you must listen without judgment to allow your mind to open. You are listening for something deeper than the mind, but you must go through the mind to get there.

PRACTICE 15: *One practice period.*

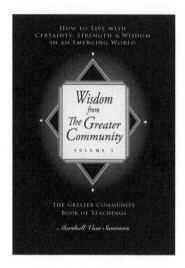

WISDOM FROM THE GREATER COMMUNITY: VOLUME I

How to Live with Certainty, Strength & Wisdom in an Emerging World

The companion text to *Steps to Knowledge*, *Wisdom from the Greater Community: Volume I* is a wise and compassionate guide for discovering the power of relationship and inner certainty in everyday life. *Wisdom I* speaks to that persistent feeling that there is something important for you to do in life. Its 35 chapters provide the Greater Community perspective on topics ranging from "Marriage" and "Achieving Peace" to "Provoking Change" and "World Evolution." *Wisdom I* cuts through the uncertainty and confusion of our time to enable you to find and to follow what you have always known.

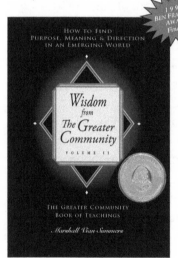

WISDOM FROM THE GREATER COMMUNITY: VOLUME II

How to Live with Purpose, Meaning & Direction in an Emerging World

Continuing the journey begun in *Wisdom: Volume I*, *Wisdom from the Greater Community: Volume II* concentrates on the needs of a world in transition as the greater context for finding your contribution and resolving personal dilemmas. It introduces the larger arena of intelligent life called the Greater Community and provides the insights and perspective necessary to prepare for a future that will be unlike anything that we have ever known. In 34 chapters ranging from "Discernment" and "Solving Problems" to "Environments" and "Visitors' Perceptions of Humanity," *Wisdom II* opens the way to living a greater life at this important turning point in history.

Wisdom
from
The Greater Community:
Volume I

ISBN 978-1-884238-28-4

Wisdom
from
The Greater Community:
Volume II

ISBN 978-1-884238-29-1

*P*LEASE REQUEST *Greater Community Spirituality, Steps to Knowledge* or *Wisdom from the Greater Community: Volumes I & II* at your local bookstore, or you may order directly from **New Knowledge Library** at 800-938-3891 or by using the order form below.

O R D E R   F O R M

_____ **Greater Community Spirituality:** @ $17.95 each............................ _____

_____ **Steps to Knowledge** @ $25 each.. _____

_____ **Wisdom from the Greater Community: Volume I** @ $25 each..... _____

_____ **Wisdom from the Greater Community: Volume II** @ $25 each ... _____

Shipping and handling: 1-3 books $4.; each additional book $1..... _____

Colorado residents add local tax .... _____

(Your tax-deductible contribution is greatly appreciated) .... $_____

T O T A L .... $_____

Referred by: _____

———*∿∿*———

☐ My check is enclosed. Please make checks payable to: **New Knowledge Library**

☐ Please charge my: ☐ Mastercard ☐ Visa

Account number _____ Exp.month/year _____

Cardholder signature _____ Date _____

(PLEASE PRINT)

CARDHOLDER NAME: _____

SHIP TO: _____

STREET ADDRESS (*Do not use PO Box*)_____

CITY/STATE/ZIP _____

EVENING PHONE NO._____

MC/VISA ONLY: FAX YOUR ORDER (303) 938-1214
Outside Denver/Boulder area call (800) 938-3891
Visit us on the Internet: www.newmessage.org

New Knowledge Library
P.O. Box 1724, Boulder, CO 80306-1724 · (303) 938-8401